IRISH RAILWAYS

A New History

Map of the Irish railway network in 1947.

IRISH RAILWAYS

A New History

TOM FERRIS ∾

Gill & Macmillan

Gill & Macmillan Ltd
Hume Avenue, Park West, Dublin 12
with associated companies throughout the world
www.gillmacmillan.ie

© Tom Ferris 2008
978 07171 4291 0

Index compiled by Cover to Cover
Typography design by Make Communication
Print origination by O'K Graphic Design, Dublin
Printed and bound in Great Britain by MPG Books Ltd,
Bodmin, Cornwall

This book is typeset in 12/14.5 pt Minion

The paper used in this book comes from the wood pulp
of managed forests. For every tree felled, at least one
tree is planted, thereby renewing natural resources.

A CIP catalogue record for this book is available from
the British Library.

5 4 3 2 1

CONTENTS

INTRODUCTION

The origins of this book came about in a conversation with a former colleague and one of my oldest friends in publishing, Fergal Tobin, the publishing director of Gill & Macmillan, who, perceiving that there was a need for a new history of Ireland's railways aimed at the interested general reader, was unwise enough to ask me to attempt to provide this.

Much has been written and published in the last twenty years on the subject of the railways of Ireland and I have had the pleasure of making some contribution to this process. However, many railway books are aimed at what I would call the 'true believers'. This is a term coined not by me but by another good friend in the world of books, David Hall, whose family has been running one of the best independent bookshops in Ireland for many decades, close to the former junction of the Great Northern and Sligo, Leitrim & Northern Counties railways in Enniskillen. True believers—David and I can clearly be placed in that category—are those who have an almost obsessive interest in all things on rails, and this manifests itself in many forms. We may appear slightly deranged as we discuss in great detail locomotives or railways which disappeared many decades ago, but we are really a good-natured and harmless bunch, though it may be unwise to approach us if we are beside a railway line lest you inadvertently stray into our viewfinders. However, beyond the true believers there is a much wider constituency which has a more balanced interest in railways. I have a completely unscientific theory, but one based on many conversations over the years, that about one in three families in Ireland has some sort of railway connection in their family history. This may be due to the fact that a job on the railway offered steady if not well-paid employment in the century which followed the Great Famine, when the only economic option for millions was emigration. A regular job for the bread-winner encouraged those families to stay and perhaps they had enough money to spare to allow their children to remain in education and gradually move up the social and economic scale. Just to add some substance to this, when Córas Iompair Éireann (CIÉ) was formed in 1945, it was the largest employer in the Irish Free State with over 21,000 staff, and as late as the mid-1950s a report into the operation of CIÉ's railways calculated that six people were employed for every mile of railway open in the Republic.

Apart from whatever socio-economic benefits the railway may have brought to individuals, there are many who have an interest in railways for a variety of other reasons. Few would deny that a steam locomotive in full flight is one of the most stirring of man's inventions. While our romantic view of the age of steam has often conveniently left out the soot, ash, occasional lineside fires and all the heavy and dirty work required to keep a steam engine on the road, for many people a long journey by rail is the most relaxing and congenial means of travel today, if everything goes according to plan, which in fairness to the operators it usually does. Besides the inherent pleasure of a railway journey, the train is the most eco-friendly of beasts and even those who have to endure a commute in a crowded DART or a railcar twice a day will know that the alternative—the endless traffic jams on the approach to our cities—is even more unattractive.

There is also the historical perspective. The building of the railways called for the raising and spending of huge capital sums previously unheard of, and to keep the formation relatively level and free of steep gradients, they were carried across the country on bridges and embankments and in cuttings, leaving a great imprint on the Irish landscape. They established uniform clock time across the country and led to a degree of social mobility, though this was a double-edged sword as they also facilitated migration and emigration. The railway age brought a demand for specialist engineering skills and led to the development of a workforce accomplished in these areas. This skilled workforce was not just to be found at the great railway workshops such as those at Inchicore or Dundalk, but in smaller concentrations around the country in unlikely places like Manorhamilton or Ballinamore, where independent local railways established workshops which had to be able to undertake a great range of tasks from rebuilding worn out steam locomotives to making and repairing wagons and carriages. The railways allowed national newspapers to be distributed across the country, improved postal services and turned many sleepy coastal villages into seaside resorts. As we will see, towards the end of the nineteenth century the railway was seen as a means of economic regeneration, and much government money was poured into them as part of a political and economic agenda. They were also caught up in the violent struggles of the post-1916 period and many were terminally damaged by the political settlement of the 1920s.

Many more learned authors than this one have struggled with the vagaries of the spelling of Irish placenames. To remove myself from this minefield I have simply used the form adopted by the railway companies. I have used placenames appropriate for the period being discussed. Thus Queenstown only becomes Cobh after the formation of the Free State. Monetary values follow the same procedure. The term 'pound' means £ sterling up to 1979; after that, in relation to the Irish Republic, it becomes IR£; and towards the end of our story the Euro enters the picture.

The railway age in Ireland is now over 170 years old, and to cover such a diverse subject over that time frame in the space available inevitably means that much of the narrative has had to be compressed and lots of detail left out. However, I hope that what follows will offer an accurate account of how the railway network grew from very modest beginnings to reach into, if not every corner of Ireland, at least every county, at its peak. An initial eighty years of expansion was followed by an almost equally long period of decline until the position of what remained of the network stabilised. Today the railways are again expanding, though for very different reasons from those which drove their growth in the nineteenth century, but once again they are beginning to occupy a significant role in the social and economic life of the country. Our story will take us from Baltimore to Belfast and from Carndonagh to Kenmare, with an occasional diversion to the deserts of North Africa and the battlefields of the Crimean War. It is a tale of both triumph and tragedy, monumental incompetence and stunning achievement. The guard has the green flag in his hand and the whistle at his lips. We are ready to depart.

| A FALTERING START

It is difficult, if not downright impossible, to determine where and when something resembling a railway was first employed by *Homo sapiens*. Woodcuts emanating from Germany in the late Middle Ages certainly show what appear to be trucks running on wooden planks or rails being used to bring minerals out of mineshafts. Similar primitive railways were in use in connection with mining activity in England by the sixteenth century. Given the close if often fraught relationship between the two islands off the west coast of Europe, it would not have been surprising if something similar had appeared in Ireland at around the same time, the only caveat to this theory being the dearth of workable mineral deposits in the country, something which we will return to later in this book. Despite this, the pre-history of railways in Ireland, as elsewhere in Europe and certainly in Britain, was linked to mining.

Perhaps the first documented railway or tramroad to operate in Ireland dated from around 1740 and was located at Ballycastle on the north Antrim coast. Hugh Boyd, a local landowner and entrepreneur, determined to exploit coal deposits found close to the town. His first tramway was built to convey stone from quarries at cliffs to the west of the town which was used in the construction of a harbour. It was only about 300 yards long and used wooden rails but was built to a gauge of 3 ft, a significant dimension which will figure much in later chapters of this book. Once the harbour was completed around 1750, a further tramway was built linking the harbour to coal deposits along the coast.

This operated until around 1780. At about the same time railways were in use in County Tyrone, again in relation to mining.

One of the few workable deposits of coal in Ireland was located near Coalisland in east Tyrone, close to the shores of Lough Neagh. While coal had been dug for local use, probably for several hundred years, in the 1720s shafts were sunk which revealed sufficient reserves of coal which led to the hope that the Tyrone coalfield could supply the needs of the growing city of Dublin. Supported by the Irish parliament, work began on the construction of a canal from Newry to Lough Neagh in 1731. The Newry Canal, which opened in 1742, was 18 miles long and had fourteen locks. The canal was wide enough to allow the passage of seagoing vessels which, loaded with coal and having passed through the canal, could continue down the east coast from Newry to Dublin. Ultimately, the coalfield never lived up to its early promise and most of Ireland's requirements continued to be imported from the other side of the Irish Sea, but as far as our story is concerned, the development of the Tyrone coalfield did lead to the building of another early railway. While the Newry Canal provided a means of transporting the coal to Dublin, it did not serve the collieries directly. To link them to this navigation, work began on a canal in 1733. However, what became the Coalisland Canal, a waterway only 4½ miles long, was not completed until 1787. In the absence of a workable waterway a tramway was constructed. This was the Drumglass Colliery Railway, built using wooden rails, which was opened in 1754 linking the pits to the navigation. It was still in existence in 1793 when the colliery was put up for sale, though it had probably fallen into disuse by this time.

It is probable that such rudimentary tramways operated in other parts of Ireland in connection with construction works, mineral extraction or quarrying. One such line which has been recorded was used to bring stone from granite quarries at Dalkey down to Kingstown where it was used in the construction of the new harbour there. This line, which was about 2 miles in length and used cast-iron rails on stone sleepers, opened in 1816 and was closed by 1836, though part of the trackbed was later used by the

Dublin & Kingstown Railway when this was extended to Dalkey in 1844. The first railway in the north of Ireland to be authorised by an Act of Parliament was also a mineral line. This was the Belfast & Cavehill Railway, which obtained parliamentary approval in 1832. Promoted to exploit the vast limestone deposits at the Cave Hill to the north of Belfast and convey these down to the shores of Belfast Lough for shipment, it was not until 1840, after years of painfully slow progress, that this line finally partially opened. As far as our narrative is concerned, it is sufficient to note that the pre-history of railways in Ireland is broadly similar to that in Britain, though the use of tramways and colliery lines was much more common there on account of the concentration of mineral wealth, especially coal, which powered the economy of western Europe from the late eighteenth century until the second half of the twentieth.

In Britain the transition from colliery and industrial tramways to the first public railways began in the late eighteenth century. The first prerequisite was the use of iron as opposed to wooden rails. These had first been recorded in what is now Cumbria as early as the 1720s. By the end of the century iron rails were increasingly common, with about twenty such lines operating in the Northumberland coalfield alone. Another significant development was the carriage of passengers by rail. In 1807, the line from Swansea to Oystermouth in south Wales was probably the first railway to carry fare-paying passengers. All the early lines used horsepower, though Richard Trevithick, a Cornish-born engineer, had successfully demonstrated as early as 1804 that a steam locomotive could pull a load greater than a horse. The price of horses and fodder rose dramatically during the Napoleonic Wars creating conditions which now encouraged the development of the steam locomotive. The first successful application of steam traction took place in 1812 on the Middleton Railway near Leeds. This line used a rack system, a precursor of the type of railway later used in mountainous terrain, with the rails having teeth which were engaged by a gear wheel on the locomotive. It was felt that a smooth wheel on an iron rail would not have sufficient adhesion to enable heavy loads to be pulled without the locomotives slipping to a standstill.

In 1814 the railway at Wylam colliery in Northumberland was converted to steam operation using conventional adhesion. This project was led by George Stephenson, who designed the locomotives used on the line. The success of steam locomotives at Wylam colliery led to several other lines in that part of the north-east of England being converted to steam power. Then in 1821 a railway was promoted to bring coal from the Durham coalfield to the coast for onward shipment. Stephenson was appointed engineer to this scheme which was opened in 1825 as the Stockton & Darlington Railway. This was the real beginning of the railway age in these islands. The s&D's goods traffic was steam worked from the outset, though its passenger services were horse drawn at first. The capital for the line was raised by offering shares to the public and it was sanctioned by an Act of Parliament which was necessary in order to allow it to be built along a route authorised by that Act which overrode the objections of any landowners who did not want it to cross their property. It may come as a surprise to some that in the year after the s&D opened in 1825, at the very dawn of the railway age as we know it, the first Act authorising the construction of a railway in Ireland was passed.

The Limerick & Waterford Railway Act received royal assent on 31 May 1826. The line authorised was to run from Limerick via Cahir and Clonmel to Carrick-on-Suir. There the line would divide with one branch serving Waterford, another heading north to Thurles and a third serving coalfields in County Tipperary near Killenaule and Ballingarry. It was clear that steam locomotives were to be used as the Act stipulated that they should 'consume their own smoke', a provision often included in early railway legislation which in effect meant that they burned coke rather than coal. The cost of the scheme was to be £350,000, a huge sum for the period. Setting a pattern which was sadly often repeated in the history of railway promotion in Ireland, it proved very difficult to raise the capital. Despite the Board of Public Works offering a loan, the first example of governmental involvement in railway building in Ireland in the nineteenth century, and a visit to Ireland by George Stephenson to conduct surveys on behalf of the L&W,

the company failed to lay a single yard of track and quietly faded from the scene.

Interest in railways at this time was not confined to the province of Munster. In the winter of 1824/25 two officials from the Liverpool & Manchester Railway, recognised as the world's first main line railway linking two major cities when it opened in 1830, came to Ireland to sell shares in the scheme. No less a figure than Daniel O'Connell was on the board of an 1825 company called the Leinster & Munster Railway which was established with the intention of providing 'a general railway communication with various parts of this Kingdom'. The first part of this grandiose project was to be a line linking Dublin with Belfast. While the L&M did not achieve any of its objectives, its significance in Irish railway history is that a number of its Dublin supporters were later active in the promotion of Ireland's first railway, the Dublin & Kingstown, which opened in 1834.

The idea of building a railway to link the new harbour at Kingstown to Dublin first emerged in a bill presented to parliament in 1825. The need for improved communications between the city and Kingstown came from the difficulties associated with access to Dublin along the River Liffey. The sandbanks and shallow waters of Dublin Bay had always made entry to the port hazardous. By 1800 ships of more than 200 tons could not get into the port. Passenger and mail vessels did not try to enter the river but used at various periods Ringsend and Howth, the latter from 1818. By the 1820s, with sail giving way to steam and ships getting much larger, the situation at Dublin Port had become impossible. An Act of 1815 created a Board of Commissioners for an Asylum Harbour. This was intended to be a refuge for ships waiting to go up the Liffey. Its location was to be the hitherto sleepy village of Dunleary, where the sands of Dublin Bay gave way to much deeper waters. To mark the use of the harbour by George IV in 1821, Dunleary was renamed Kingstown.

However, the problems with Dublin Port were unresolved and as Kingstown was some miles distant, attention was now turned to providing a link from there to the city. One option favoured was a grand ship canal, Captain Bligh of HMS *Bounty* fame being one of its advocates. However, the growing number of apparently successful railroads across the Irish Sea pointed to this as an alternative to the ship canal. The scheme promoted in 1825 for a railway from the harbour at Kingstown to a terminus near Mount Street in Dublin was rejected by parliament, but the project was revived in February 1831 when a provisional committee was formed to further the scheme and present a new bill to parliament once again. On 6 September 1831, the Act authorising the construction of the Dublin & Kingstown Railway received royal assent. The railway age in Ireland had begun.

Some of the men prominent in the unsuccessful L&M scheme were involved with the Dublin & Kingstown Railway. The company was promoted by a group of serious and influential Dublin businessmen, bankers and stockbrokers. One of the most prominent was the banker, James Pim, who became the treasurer of the company in May 1832 and gave it effective leadership for many years. The eminent Irish engineer, Charles Blacker Vignoles, became the D&K's engineer. One of Pim's first tasks was to lead negotiations with the Board of Public Works, who were eventually persuaded to assist the project with a loan of £75,000. The capital of the company was set at £150,000 and the contract to build the line, which was just over 5 miles in length, was given to a man who was to become a major figure in the construction of the Irish railway network, William Dargan. Before construction began the company conducted surveys of the traffic along the route over several months. All the vehicles passing through Blackrock were recorded and from this an extrapolation was made as to the revenues the railway could generate. From these it became clear that the main business of the line would be passenger traffic—in today's terms, commuters. This is still the case today over 170 years later, but there is a certain irony in that a scheme that was originally envisaged as an alternative to a ship canal should take on this character so quickly.

Built to a gauge of 4 ft 8½ in., this line, the first public railway in Ireland, opened on 17 December 1834. This modest beginning to the railway age in Ireland should be seen in context. In 1835 there were only 330 miles of railway in operation in the whole of the United Kingdom. Between 1833 and 1835 some of the major trunk routes in England such as the London & Birmingham (1833), the London & Southampton (1834) and the Great Western Railway from London to Bristol (1835) had been authorised, but were not yet open. Thus far, Ireland was keeping up with the rest of the kingdom. We should also respect the farsightedness of these early railway promoters. At this stage in the development of the railways, many aspects of what we would call today, the business plan, were still virtually untested. The ability and reliability of the early locomotives, braking and signalling, methods of track construction and even the most suitable gauge for railways were all open to debate. Building a railway anywhere in the early 1830s, let alone in Ireland, was a risky and capital-intensive venture. Many influential people were still unconvinced by the new technology and there were many pitfalls along the road for those involved.

Despite this, there occurred in the mid-1830s the first 'railway mania', and its effects were apparent in Ireland. The success of the world's first railway linking two major cities, the Liverpool & Manchester, which opened in 1830, showed that a railway on a large scale was viable and profitable. Political stability in the wake of the great Reform Act of 1832, which had broadened the franchise and general economic well-being at the time, encouraged the promotion of a large number of railway schemes throughout Britain. The passion for railways resulted in a number of very ambitious schemes being mooted in Ireland at this time. One such was the Grand Atlantic Railroad Company which intended to raise £2.4 million to build a railway from Dublin to the west of Ireland serving Galway, Sligo and Castlebar. Charles Vignoles, the D&K engineer, was involved with an ambitious scheme for a railway from Dublin to Valentia in County Kerry where a new port would be built to serve transatlantic shipping. Passengers and mail could then travel by rail across Ireland and reach Britain and the rest of Europe much more quickly than if they concluded their journey by sea. Similar schemes, all of them unsuccessful, emerged throughout the nineteenth century. In April 1835 Thomas Brodigan, a landowner who lived at Pilltown

House near Drogheda, published a pamphlet advocating a railway between Dublin and Drogheda and in the Belfast newspaper, the *Northern Whig*, an article was published in November of the same year announcing the formation of a company called the Grand Northern Irish Railway, with the aim of building a railway from Belfast to Armagh, with the ultimate aim of extending the line to the west coast, and in the autumn of 1835 preliminary steps were taken by the Great Leinster & Munster Railway Company to obtain an Act to build a line between Dublin and Cork.

The motivation of these early railway entrepreneurs is of interest. They were driven by a mixture of self-interest and a sense of duty to their districts and their country. The 1836 prospectus of the United Armagh, and Dublin & Drogheda Inland Railway Company described the line as a 'great national benefit'. A eulogy written by the directors of the D&K following James Pim's death in 1856 declared that his exertions on behalf of the company had been of national benefit in that it drew public notice to the advantages of railway communication and encouraged many people in Ireland to promote railways. George Greer, a director of the Ulster Railway, speaking in 1841, coupled private gain with public good. He said he had not expected more than 6, 7 or 8 per cent on his money invested in the company, but even had he expected nothing, he felt that he and his fellow directors could not 'sit quietly looking on whilst railroads were extending in England and on the continent, while doing nothing for this section of their country.' Sometimes the sentiment went a bit over the top, as in 1835 when the *Northern Whig* described the embryonic Ulster Railway as 'one of those great movements, to which we have longingly looked forward, when the province of Ulster, when the whole of Ireland shaking free of her inglorious Thraldom . . . would spring up into fresh and healthy vigour and secure for her children, the just character of a wise, a rich, enterprising and happy people.' This sense of railways representing progress, even the spirit of the age, appears again and again along with the notion that they are almost the mark of civilisation and that not to have a network of railways would mark Ireland out as a backwater lagging behind the rest of the kingdom.

The only railway schemes promoted in that first Irish railway mania of the mid-1830s that actually went on to build their lines were the Dublin & Drogheda and the Ulster Railway, the companies which were eventually to operate the northern and southern extremities of what was to become the main line between Dublin and Belfast. The main reason for the collapse in this cycle of railway speculation was a sudden economic downturn which began across the Irish Sea but soon affected Ireland. There was a bad harvest in 1836. This led to a financial crisis and a slowdown in trade and commerce. Out of this came a rise in unemployment which in turn created social discord and the beginnings of Chartism. In Ireland there was a serious run on the Agricultural and Commercial bank, which severely hit confidence and led to many of the railway schemes which had been filling the papers with their advertisements and prospecti being quietly dropped. The other reason for the end of this phase of railway speculation in Ireland was an announcement made in the House of Lords on 1 August 1836 by the Marquis of Lansdowne, who moved an address to the King 'to appoint proper persons to inquire and report upon the most advantageous lines of railway in Ireland'.

The immediate effect of the appointment of the Commissioners on a General System of Railways for Ireland, to give them their full title, was to create even further uncertainty in an already jittery market. The Commissioners were given the task of planning a system of railways for the whole of Ireland and thus railway promoters and speculators were immediately concerned that their schemes might not have a role in any government-planned and possibly sponsored national network. That uncertainty, against the prevailing poor economic climate, dampened down the final embers of the railway mania of the mid-1830s. The work of the Commissioners is of considerable importance to historians on a number of levels. While ultimately their recommendations were largely ignored, they collected a vast amount of information on the state of Ireland on the eve of the Great Famine, and their activities also show the beginnings of government involvement in trying to regulate the new and burgeoning railway industry.

In Britain, by the mid-1830s railways had emerged from the collieries on to the national scene. The prevailing economic ethos of the age was that of *laissez-faire*, unregulated capitalism and at first the official response to railways was pretty much this. However, even the most doctrinaire non-interventionists soon realised that the new railways had to be controlled and regulated in some way. An obvious example of the perils of letting the railway companies get on with it was the use of different gauges, especially in the south of England. The width between the tracks on most railways was 4 ft 8½ in. This had been used on many of the earlier colliery lines and some claim that the origins of this measurement go back to the ruts left by carts on Roman roads. Of course none of this cut any ice with one of the great geniuses of the Victorian age, Isambard Kingdom Brunel, the charismatic engineer of the Great Western Railway. Brunel ordained a gauge of 7 ft 0½ in. for his great main line from London to Bristol. This meant that where the GWR made a junction with other lines, as was to happen at many locations in the south and midlands of England, there would be a break of gauge and all kinds of problems in the transfer of goods and passengers from one line to another. This kind of chaos was already well under way in England when the government appointed the Irish Railway Commissioners to plan a network of lines for Ireland, and of equal importance, to recommend a gauge for the Irish railway network. In this way it was hoped that Ireland would avoid the problems already apparent in England. It was too late to do anything about the situation there, but with only the short Dublin & Kingstown line operating in Ireland, the Commissioners did have a chance to make a difference.

In terms of their contribution to the development of railways in Ireland, the Commission was a failure, but its report and atlas are a fabulous resource for the historian. The Commissioners' brief was to recommend a system of railways for the country. In order to do this they conducted a detailed economic and social survey of the country. Their main report is a window on an Ireland that was soon to disappear under the ravages of the Great Famine and the depopulation which followed in its wake. Had anyone at Westminster paid any attention to this report or that of the Irish Poor Inquiry which was published in 1836, alarm bells might have rung as to the parlous condition of the great mass of the population of Ireland, but no one did. What is apparent from the report of the Irish Railway Commissioners is that some of the patterns of economic activity which they recorded were changed radically by events of the 1840s. For example, the prospectus of the Ulster Railway Company issued in 1835 was quite clear that the company's main objective was a line from Belfast to Armagh with possible future extensions to Enniskillen, Sligo and Athlone. This focus on a line to the west, rather than to Dublin, was simply a reflection of the trading patterns of the time. Belfast was, by 1838, the busiest port in Ireland with trade worth over £8 million, of which the export of livestock, grain and dairy products amounted to nearly £1 million. The promoters of the UR saw their railway as a means to bring this great volume of agricultural wealth into the warehouses and ships of the Belfast merchants who backed the project. So much had changed in such a short time that by a supreme irony, when the Ulster Railway's line to Armagh was finally opened in 1848, among the goods traffic conveyed was corn imported to feed victims of the Famine.

The final report of the Irish Railway Commissioners, when it was published in 1838, provided a detailed economic survey of the condition of Ireland at that time down to an analysis of the traffic flows on existing roads and canals. It was generally pessimistic about the potential prosperity of railways in Ireland. It recommended the construction of two trunk routes from Dublin, one heading north-west and the other to the south-west, with some branches off these lines. It also proposed a cross-country line from Limerick to Waterford. There was no recommendation for a direct line from Dublin to Belfast; rather the northern trunk route was to run from Dublin to Armagh via Navan. Perhaps surprisingly there was no recommendation for a line from Dublin to the west coast, the Commissioners believing that the existing Royal and Grand canals were adequate for the traffic on offer in that direction. It had been hoped that the network laid down by the Commissioners would be supported by government money.

Their conclusion that railways in Ireland could not be funded by conventional methods led to their viewing Irish railways as public works rather than commercial enterprises, which would have to be backed by state funding. Unfortunately this enlightened opinion was not in keeping with the political culture of the time and realistically there was no chance that the government would provide any money to back the Commission's plans. So the great dream of a planned national system of railways for Ireland came to nought. The only part of the Commissioners' report which was acted upon was its recommendation as to the gauge which should be used in Ireland. It will be recalled that this part of its brief was a response to the different gauges already in use across the Irish Sea, which it was hoped could be avoided in Ireland. Only the UR adopted this gauge of 6 ft 2 in., a decision which, as we will see, was to cause major problems in the next decade.

The only railway promoted in the mania of the mid-1830s which actually opened for business in that decade was the first short section of the Ulster Railway from Belfast to Lisburn. On 19 May 1836 the Ulster Railway Act received royal assent. Shares in the company had gone on sale in January of that year and by the time the Act was approved were in such demand that £1 shares were attracting prices of between £8. 10s. and £10 in Belfast and Liverpool. Surveys were completed in 1836 and final plans were ready by early 1837. Tenders were sought and opened on 9 March 1837. The contract for the first section of the line was awarded to John Lynn, an Englishman who had been working in County Down for the previous twenty years. He was bound under a heavy penalty to have the line ready for traffic by 1 May 1839. Though bad weather in the winter of 1838 hampered construction work, on 30 July 1839 the first test runs began and the line opened to the public, without any of the ceremony and feasting that often accompanied railway openings in the nineteenth century, on 12 August. Around 3,000 passengers were carried that first day. Many more were turned away, such was the novelty of the affair, though the day was slightly marred by the derailment of one of the engines at the Belfast terminus. Despite the relatively high cost of land then as now between Belfast and Lisburn, the construction cost per mile of the 7½ miles between Belfast and Lisburn, including land, structures and track, was about £12,000, cheaper than the original estimate laid before parliament in 1836 and only about one-fifth of the cost per mile of Ireland's only other operating railway at that time, the D&K. With the opening of the country's second line, the railway age in Ireland was now well and truly under way. However, it was to be in the next decade that there would be a great expansion of the network, and that occurred against the background of the greatest disaster ever to befall the country.

Chapter 2

THE NATIONAL NETWORK EMERGES

As we have seen in the previous chapter, the worsening economic climate in the late 1830s and the uncertainty created among potential railway investors as they waited for the Irish Railway Commissioners to report effectively put an end to Ireland's first outbreak of railway speculation. However, the spine of the Irish railway network was laid down in the next decade. But before that happened, the one major railway controversy which had arisen in the 1830s, the course of the line which would connect Dublin and Belfast, had to be resolved.

When a railway between Dublin and Drogheda was first mooted in 1835, almost immediately discussion began as to whether the line should take an inland or a coastal route. One of the eminent English engineers of the era, William Cubitt, was invited to make a survey of both routes. His recommendation was in favour of the coastal route running north from Dublin via Malahide and Balbriggan. This led to a split in the camp and in January 1836 the dissenters launched the Dublin, Drogheda & Navan Inland Railway with William Bald as engineer. Born in Fife in 1789, Bald, best known for his work on the famous Antrim coast road from Larne to Ballycastle, was one of the few engineers working in Ireland at the time who had any practical experience of railways. On behalf of the Board of Works he had inspected the Belfast & Cavehill Railway, mentioned in the previous chapter, when its promoters had applied for a loan to aid its construction. He was one of three engineers named on the UR prospectus and had conducted surveys of the line from Belfast to Armagh on behalf of that company.

The battle between the parties advocating the inland and coastal routes was for more than the relatively short local line between Dublin and Drogheda, as both camps saw this as the first part of a route linking Dublin with Belfast. When the Dublin & Drogheda's bill for the coastal scheme was presented to parliament in 1836, there was vigorous opposition from those advocating the inland route. Debate raged for most of May and June 1836 before a parliamentary committee chaired by Daniel O'Connell, which eventually declared in favour of the bill which received royal assent on 13 August 1836. The cost of steering the bill through parliament in the face of so much opposition was around £30,000, a sum which would have built several miles of railway had it been used for that purpose. In order to get their bill through the House of Lords, the D&D directors gave an undertaking that if the recently appointed Irish Railway Commissioners proposed an inland route for a line to the north, they would not oppose it. This parliamentary setback did not stop the inland faction, for one month after the D&D Act was passed, the prospectus of the United Armagh, and Dublin and Drogheda Inland Railway Company was launched. The company proposed to raise £1.5 million and boasted sixteen peers and eleven MPs among its patrons. As well as a main line from Dublin to Armagh, the company planned to build branches to Navan and Drogheda. The company's intention was to introduce a bill in the next session of parliament. The D&D retaliated by depositing plans in December 1836 for a Grand Northern Railway which would extend the coastal route from Drogheda to Newry with possible future extensions to Armagh and Portadown. It looked as if another wasteful parliamentary battle between these two schemes was on the horizon.

This was an early manifestation of a phenomenon which occurred throughout the nineteenth century on both sides of the Irish Sea which can best be described as railway politics. In the context of an unregulated economy, these turf wars between competing companies for the right to build lines and control the traffic emanating from specific districts could be bitter and protracted affairs. Lines were sometimes built to defend a company's territory from the incursions of other railways, rather than for sound commercial reasons. One of the last significant new broad gauge lines to be built in Ireland, the Great Northern Railway's route from Castleblayney to Keady and Armagh, which was opened as late as 1909/10 and eventually completed in a roundabout sort of way the inland route from Dublin to Belfast some seventy years after it was promoted with such vigour in the 1830s, was built by the GNR solely to keep a competing railway, backed by the Midland Great Western Railway, out of its territory.

Back in the 1830s there was a final twist to the saga of the two competing routes north from Dublin. The appointment of the Irish Railway Commissioners put a brake on the speculation and this combined with the worsening economic situation caused the inland scheme to slip off the radar. The D&D, with its Act secured, began to prepare to build its line with the first construction contracts being awarded in early 1838. When the second report of the Commissioners was released in July 1838, the northern trunk route proposed was very similar to the inland route to Armagh. However, as it soon became clear that the government was not going to fund the national network proposed in the report, the potential hostage to fortune in the form of the undertaking given by the D&D to parliament not to oppose an inland route proposed by the Commissioners, was not invoked. In 1840 the company appointed John (later Sir John, knighted at the official opening of the line in 1844 by the Lord Lieutenant) MacNeill as engineer. Construction began in October 1840 and the line was sufficiently complete to allow the directors and the Lord Lieutenant to make a trip to Drogheda in March 1844. The official opening took place on 24 May 1844 from a temporary station and was preceded by the Lord Lieutenant, Earl de Gray, laying the foundation stone of the terminus at Amiens Street.

MacNeill, along with Dargan, is one of the towering figures of the first phase of the railway age in Ireland. Sir John Benjamin MacNeill was born near Dundalk in 1793. He began work as a surveyor, but on a visit to England in the 1820s he was introduced to Thomas Telford; under his influence, MacNeill's career began to turn towards civil engineering. He was for over ten years Telford's assistant on a variety of road and canal-building projects. He eventually succeeded Telford as the chief engineer on the project which will forever be associated with his mentor, the building of the Holyhead Road from Marble Arch in London to the dockside at Holyhead. After Telford's death in 1834, MacNeill became a consultant engineer and worked mainly on canal and railway projects in Scotland before returning to Ireland at the start of the first railway promotion mania. The Dublin to Portadown line is his major legacy. The great bridge across the Boyne, the Craigmore viaduct near Newry and the beautiful little bridge in the style of an ancient Egyptian pediment which still carries the line over the Newry to Bessbrook road are among his lasting monuments. In addition to this line, he was also the engineer for the Belfast & County Down Railway. His last railway commission was that of engineer of the first section of the Londonderry & Lough Swilly line in the early 1860s. MacNeill's other legacy was as a teacher of civil engineering: in 1842 he became the first professor of engineering at Trinity College Dublin, a position he held for ten years.

Meanwhile south of the River Liffey, Ireland's first railway, the Dublin & Kingstown, also had plans to expand, but it did so in a singular way by applying a technology which was briefly seen at the time as providing an alternative to the all-conquering steam locomotive. There are few reminders of this audacious experiment left today, but there is a lane in Dalkey called Atmospheric Road which gives a clue to what the directors of the D&K got up to over 160 years ago. It is a truism of popular science that nature abhors a vacuum. It was suggested as early as the seventeenth century that if a vacuum could be created and then broken, the inrush of air could propel a vehicle. Older readers may recall the contraptions used in shops and department stores years ago where sales dockets and change were conveyed to and from sales counters and the cash office by means of little containers inserted into tubes which worked on the same principle. The original concept seems to have envisaged some sort of vehicle in a large tube from which the air would be sucked, but this was later refined by a British inventor called Samuel Clegg to a railway carriage with a piston which was inserted into a large pipe between the rails. The pipe was sealed with a leather flap which closed behind the passage of the train maintaining the vacuum in the pipe, which was created by pumping stations built at intervals alongside the track.

Clegg's invention was taken up by a firm of London engineers, the Samuda Brothers, and a demonstration line was built in London in 1840. Called the atmospheric railway, among the visitors who came to see the system at work was James Pim and some of his fellow directors of the D&K. They had already been thinking of extending their line to Dalkey along the route of the tramway which had been built to bring stone down to Kingstown to build the harbour, and the bold decision was now made to apply the atmospheric system to the Dalkey extension. The line as built was separate from the original D&K; through running from Dublin to Dalkey was not possible. The 15 in. diameter cast-iron pipe in which the vacuum was created, lay between the rails. The leather seal on the top of the pipe, which was critical to the success of the whole operation, was held in place by iron plates riveted to the pipe. It was lubricated with tallow to keep it supple. If the seal was not immediately restored following the passage of a train, air would be admitted to the pipe and in extreme cases the system would not work. If it leaked, it meant that the steam engines at the pumping station, which extracted the air from the pipe and were located near the Dalkey terminus, had to work harder, burning more coal in the process. The line was uphill almost all the way from Kingstown to Dalkey, so atmospheric traction was only required in that direction; the trains free-wheeled back to Kingstown.

The line opened in March 1844 with trains running every half-hour. Clegg and his backers forswore royalties on their patents. The Dalkey line was to be a practical application of their system which could be used to demonstrate and ultimately sell the atmospheric railway principle to other interested parties. Many eminent visitors came to see it, including Isambard Kingdom

Brunel, who was so taken with it that he later applied the system to the South Devon Railway on which he was the engineer, to the detriment of its shareholders. Undoubtedly the atmospheric system could cope with stiffer gradients than the steam locomotives of the 1840s, so to this day the legacy of Brunel's flirtation with the atmospheric railway is a line with steep inclines, not much of a problem for today's diesels, but a nightmare for operators throughout the age of steam. The practical difficulties of maintaining the vacuum in the pipe was beyond the technology and materials of the time and in the end this proved to be a blind alley in terms of the development of railways. The Dalkey line lasted as an atmospheric railway until April 1854 when it was closed. It was rebuilt as a conventional railway when the line was extended by the Dublin & Wicklow Company. It lasted longer than the other applications in Devon and on the London & Croydon Railway, but for a brief time this short stretch of railway less than 2 miles long was seen to be at the cutting edge of railway science.

While the atmospheric railway is an interesting footnote in Irish railway history, at the same time that passengers were enjoying the novelty of being whisked up to Dalkey, another burst of railway speculation was getting under way which this time, unlike the railway mania of the 1830s, did give Ireland the core of a national railway network. Railway promotion throughout the nineteenth century was closely linked to the general condition of the national economy. The slump which had ended the speculation of the mid-1830s had, by the early 1840s, been replaced by a much more benign economic climate. This led to a second railway mania in Britain which also revived railway promotion in Ireland. The most significant scheme to emerge in the early 1840s was the Great Southern & Western Railway which was to some extent a resuscitation of the Great Leinster & Munster company of the 1830s. The GSWR planned no less than a great trunk line to the south and west to link Dublin, Limerick and Cork. A line to Galway was also mentioned in the early days but was not pursued. To do this the company had to raise capital of £1.3 million. Despite the huge sum required the shares were quickly taken up. The company had the backing of the directors of the London & Birmingham Railway which helped to sell the shares, and of Sir Robert Peel's Tory government that came to power in 1841 which allowed for the smooth passage of the GSWR bill through parliament in 1844. The ceremonial cutting of the first sod was done by the Duke of Leinster at Adamstown, near Lucan, in January 1845. Despite it being the setting for this historic event, Adamstown had to wait over 160 years to get its own station, opened by Iarnród Éireann in April 2007.

As well as the main line to Cork, the GSWR was authorised to make a branch to Carlow, diverging from the main line at Cherryville Junction near Kildare. The directors decided to complete the Carlow branch first. Construction proceeded rapidly, providing valuable employment against the background of the developing disaster of the potato blight which was spreading across the country. The 55 mile long line to Carlow opened for traffic in August 1846, though a shortage of rolling stock meant that only two trains ran daily at first. Meanwhile work progressed on the main line with trains serving Maryborough from June 1847, and Ballybrophy from September of that year. The original Act of 1844 had authorised a railway from Dublin to Cashel with a branch to Carlow. This was altered by a further Act obtained in 1845 which took the line away to the north-west of Cashel to run via Charleville and Mallow to Cork. This left Cashel some 5 miles from the nearest station on the main line, at Goold's Cross, from which a branch was eventually built, though it did not open until 1904!

Against the background of the Famine, the GSWR line inexorably pushed southwards. The contract worth £600,000 for the final section of the line, the 78 miles from Thurles to Cork, was given to William Dargan, who was already experienced from his work on other railways and had built sections of the GSWR line closer to Dublin. Dargan, who was born in County Carlow in 1799, was to become Ireland's greatest railway and public works contractor. He learned his trade in England working with that renowned builder of canals and the famous Holyhead Road, Thomas Telford. Dargan's achievements up to this time included work on the Ulster Canal, the D&K and the dredging of a new deep water channel, begun in 1839 though it was not completed until 1849, which allowed larger vessels to use the port of Belfast. The mud and spoil excavated in building this channel was used to create the Queen's Island (originally known as Dargan's Island but renamed following a royal visit), later the citadel of Harland & Wolff, the shipbuilders.

GSWR services commenced as far as Thurles from March 1848. Limerick Junction was reached in July 1848 and Mallow, 144 miles from Dublin, in March 1849. Trains finally served the temporary station at Blackpool on the outskirts of Cork from 29 October 1849. The remarkable achievements of the company at this time need to be put into context. The line from Dublin to Blackpool, the temporary Cork terminus up to 1855 when work was completed on the 1,335 yard long tunnel which brought the line into the city at Penrose Quay, was just over 160 miles long. At that time it was the longest line in the kingdom. Across the Irish Sea the two biggest railways operating were the London & Birmingham at 113 miles and the Great Western, from London to Bristol, 118 miles long. The GSWR had been built in its entirety in less than five years by a workforce that had no experience of railway construction and against the background of the social and economic catastrophe which was the Great Famine. The company did have some government assistance in the form of a loan of half a million pounds to employ victims of the Famine on construction work, but it also had to deal with attacks on staff and other effects of the terrible conditions of hunger, disease and social breakdown in which it was operating. The opening of such a long railway in such a short time, against this background, was nothing short of astonishing.

Given the prevailing conditions, looking back at the 1840s, it is remarkable the amount of progress that was made in laying down the foundations of a national network of railways. As with the GSWR, some of these schemes harked back to earlier proposals, none more so than that of the Waterford & Limerick Railway, which was authorised in July 1845, a revival of the first Irish railway to get parliamentary approval back in 1826. A provisional committee had been formed in Waterford in 1844 with Charles Vignoles as engineer. To build the line via Carrick-on-Suir, Clonmel and Tipperary, capital of £750,000 had to be raised. The W&L line was to cross the GSWR route near Tipperary at that famous location known ever since as Limerick Junction. The W&L was actually the first to reach the junction with goods services commencing between Limerick and Tipperary in April 1848, passenger trains first running the following month. Thereafter progress was slow, the line to Waterford not being completed until 1854. Limerick Junction has been a source of bewilderment for many observers since it first opened. Worse, it has been the subject of many ill-informed jokes told to show Ireland and its railways in an unfavourable light. The reason for this is that from the opening of both the GSWR and W&L lines in 1848, up to 1967 when CIÉ installed a new track layout, all passenger trains serving the Junction had to reverse to reach the station's one lengthy island platform. Trains from Dublin and Cork reversed into their respective sections of the main line side of the platform, which did not have track the whole length of its face but was split with cross-overs in the centre. Trains from Waterford crossed the GSWR line on the level just north of the platform and then reversed into their bay at the north end of the platform. Trains from Limerick to Waterford traversed a through road parallel to the Dublin to Cork line and then reversed into a south-facing bay platform. While these manoeuvres were a nuisance for the operators, it meant that all the trains serving Limerick Junction ended up on either side of one large platform providing the most convenient of interchanges for passengers in both directions on the two lines.

One of the most surprising aspects of the final report of the Irish Railway Commissioners, when it was published in 1838, was their view that a line from Dublin to the west of Ireland would not be viable and that the existing Grand and Royal canals would be able to deal with any traffic on offer from this direction. The initial proposals of the GSWR did include a line to Galway but this was not pursued, leading to the resignation of several members of the provisional committee led by John Ennis, who set up a provisional committee of their own to build a line to the west under the title of the Midland Great Western Railway. At first it was proposed that this line should diverge from the GSWR route near Sallins, but soon the idea of an independent line from Dublin via Mullingar and Athlone to Galway took shape. John MacNeill had already conducted preliminary surveys of this route and it may have been he who first suggested that the new company should acquire the Royal Canal. Building the railway alongside the canal was a stroke of genius, for its course was level most of the way and putting a railway on Royal Canal land avoided arguments with landowners which often held up railway schemes. After some negotiation the directors of the canal company agreed to the MGWR's offer of £40 for every £100 of Royal Canal stock. No sooner was the MGWR prospectus issued in the autumn of 1844 than a rival scheme was set up called the Irish Great Western Railway. This scheme, which had the backing of the GSWR, was for a line from Portarlington to Athlone, Ballinasloe and Galway. The MGWR Act of July 1845 authorised the company to raise £1 million to build a line from Dublin to Mullingar and Longford. There was no mention of Galway at this stage as the company had agreed to drop its branch from Mullingar to Athlone in order to get its main line authorised. However, the IGW bill was rejected by parliament and the MGWR revived its aspirations for a line to Galway which was eventually authorised in 1847, as was a GSWR line from Portarlington to Tullamore. This early spat between the GSWR and the MGWR was to flare up again in the years ahead as the two companies jostled for territory and traffic in the midlands and west of Ireland. As a footnote to all of this, trains from Dublin to Galway have, since the 1980s, travelled via the Cork line, branching off at Portarlington and joining the former MGWR Galway line at Athlone. The old MGWR main line from Mullingar to Athlone is still in existence but has not seen regular traffic for many years.

Once the railway politics had settled down, the MGWR began to construct the first part of its line from Dublin to Enfield. The ceremony of turning the first sod was performed by the Lord Lieutenant on 12 January 1846 at the site of the company's Dublin terminus at the Broadstone in Phibsboro. As with the GSWR line, construction proceeded with remarkable speed. The engineer Hemans reported to the board in September 1846 that 15 miles of track had been laid and ballasted. The 26 miles to Enfield were opened on 28 June 1847 and trains started operating on the full 50 miles to Mullingar from 2 October 1848. The works were conducted against the background of the Famine and one small personal tragedy will perhaps serve to highlight the distress of many thousands.

Ernie Shepherd, the historian of the MGWR, recounts an inquest held in Mullingar in March 1847 into the death of Michael Kelly, a labourer employed on the railway who died of starvation. His widow, who was left with five children to support, told the inquest that the family had moved from County Offaly to find work on the railway. Kelly was paid 11 shillings a week in summer but only 9 shillings in winter. He died in his sleep on the Monday night, having worked on the railway all day without eating anything. The doctor who performed the post-mortem reported that his stomach and intestines were 'perfectly empty' and he had the appearance of a man who had not eaten for some time. Much of the Irish railway network on which we travel today was built in the 1840s by men like Michael Kelly, though the employment created through railway construction did undoubtedly save many more from his fate.

Apart from the fate of men like the unfortunate Michael Kelly, victims of the hunger and disease which marked this terrible period in Irish history, the building of major public works such as the railways were always attended with great peril for those engaged on them, in an age when any real concern for the health and safety of the workforce was unheard of. Many men were killed building the railways throughout the country during the nineteenth century. This is not surprising as large numbers of men were employed and used work practices which were inherently hazardous, such as the use of explosives to shift rock formations which were in the way. The building of steep embankments and deep cuttings, often in wet weather which made these features potentially unstable, also led to many deaths and injuries during the construction phase.

Building the railway network in the nineteenth century called for the manipulation of the natural landscape on a grand scale to create a level formation on which the tracks could be laid. A few examples from the building of the MGWR line from Mullingar to Athlone may suffice to show the sort of incidents which were common as railways spread across the country. Returns for August 1850 show that a total of 1,059 men were engaged in building the railway between Moate and Athlone. On one occasion when the formation was being excavated, part of a bank on which a group of men were working gave way and four of them were asphyxiated. On the same day another man was killed when a wagon ran over him—an all too common occurrence during the construction phase. Human life was cheap, and by November 1850 no fewer than twelve men had died in accidents associated with the construction of the Midland line through County Westmeath alone.

So far we have concentrated on lines promoted in the south of the country, but the core of Ulster's railway network was also laid down in this decade. The UR, which had opened the first section of its line to Lisburn in 1839, awarded the contract for the line from Lisburn to Portadown to William Dargan in the spring of 1840. The contract, which included earthworks, ballasting and the permanent way, was worth £90,000. Once again, as we have seen further south, progress was rapid. The extension was about 17 miles long. Part of the new line as far as the Maze, 3 miles beyond Lisburn, was temporarily opened in July 1841 to bring passengers to the races held there. A total of 18,603 travelled by train to the Maze during that race week. Services as far as Lurgan commenced in November 1841 and the entire line, to a temporary terminus at Seagoe just outside Portadown, was open from 31 January 1842. Trains ran through to the town once its station had been completed in September of that year. Discussions on extending the line to the company's original planned destination, Armagh, began almost immediately. By this time the powers granted to build the line to Armagh in the original UR Act of 1836 had lapsed. Preliminary work began in 1844. New surveys were conducted which estimated the cost of the line at £10,000 per mile. The bill for the Armagh extension received royal assent on 21 June 1845. Dargan's tender to build the line was accepted in September and the original intentions of the promoters of the UR were finally fulfilled, thirteen years after the company was formed, on 1 March 1848, when a service of six passenger and two goods trains commenced daily between Belfast and Armagh.

The only major engineering work on the route was the bridge spanning the River Bann at Portadown which was completed in October 1847. The testing of the bridge was described in detail in the Belfast paper, the *Northern Whig*. This was conducted in a way which was common in the nineteenth century and which might seem strange, if not positively hazardous, to us today.

> The *Vulcan* engine with a flag at her funnel, and her shrill whistle extensively proclaiming her triumphant progress, moved slowly and majestically over amid the cheers of a crowd of people, principally the men on the works who hoisted several flags. She returned at a quicker pace, and afterwards, passed three or four times over at varied velocities. The trial was perfectly satisfactory. Mr Godwin [the UR engineer] and Mr Dargan and others attentively viewed the structure at different places, as the engine passed and not even the slightest shaking of the framing or tension rods could be detected.

One wonders what would have happened to the *Vulcan*, Messrs Dargan, Godwin and others, had there been a problem with the bridge!

While the UR was still looking west rather than south, a line to bridge the gap between the UR and the D&D linking Belfast and Dublin was also authorised in the 1840s. A new company, the Dublin & Belfast Junction Railway, formed to build the 55 mile long line between Drogheda and Portadown, obtained its Act in 1845 which also authorised a branch from Drogheda to Navan. This branch opened before the main line in February 1850, though by that time this line had been passed to the D&D, with the D&BJR concentrating its efforts on the main line. The promotion

of the Dublin to Belfast connection was a stimulus to another
spate of railway promotion to bring the iron road into the interior
of the province of Ulster. Back in 1836 in the frenzy of schemes
being promoted at the time, a prospectus was published for the
Londonderry & Enniskillen Railway which would link the towns
in its title via Strabane and Omagh. The route was surveyed in
1837 by George Stephenson, but the scheme was not pursued with
the worsening economic conditions of the late 1830s. It was
revived in 1845 and this time began to construct its line, the first
section from Derry to Strabane opening in April 1847. Across on
the east coast, at around the same time, two companies were
promoted to provide lines which would branch off the D&BJR
route. These companies were the Dundalk & Enniskillen and the
Newry & Enniskillen. The first section of the D&E, from a station
at Barrack Street in Dundalk to Castleblayney, opened on the
same day as D&BJ services to Dundalk began, 15 February 1849.
The location of the D&E's station, to the east of the main line,
meant that its trains had to cross the Dublin line on the level. The
painfully slow expansion of both the D&E and the L&E to an
eventual junction at Enniskillen belongs to Chapter 4, and while
they did eventually achieve their original objectives, the same
could not be said for the third line promoted on the east coast at
this time, the Newry & Enniskillen.

Newry had grown in importance as a port from the 1730s
onwards, which the opening of the Newry Canal linking the town
to Lough Neagh in 1742 had reinforced, though by the 1840s it was
already being eclipsed by the growth of the port of Belfast. In fact
two railways were promoted based at Newry in the mid-1840s.
One of these, the Newry, Warrenpoint & Rostrevor, was a short
local line authorised in 1846 which opened in 1849 between Newry
and Warrenpoint but never actually reached Rostrevor. The other
company, the N&E, had a much more chequered history.
Authorised by an Act of Parliament in July 1845, the company
planned a line over 70 miles long to reach Enniskillen via Armagh
and Clones. Parliament insisted that the section from Enniskillen
to Clones should be built first, in collaboration with the D&E.
Construction began in 1846 on a short line, less than 4 miles in

length, from Newry to a junction with the D&BJ at Goraghwood. While the speed of construction of some Irish lines has been mentioned elsewhere, incredibly this short stretch of track did not open until March 1854.

Further north, more foundations of the national network were laid down in the 1840s. The Belfast & County Down Railway was incorporated by an Act of January 1846 to build a main line from Belfast to Downpatrick with a branch to Holywood on the shores of Belfast Lough. The Holywood line opened in August 1848 with the first section of the BCDR main line as far as Comber following in May 1850. The first parts of what was to become an extensive system of lines serving much of the counties of Antrim and Londonderry were built by the Belfast & Ballymena Railway Company. This was another scheme which had been proposed in the 1830s and revived in the 1840s. Authorised in 1845, by 1848 lines had been opened from its station at York Road in Belfast to Carrickfergus, Ballymena and Randalstown.

In addition to all the lines which emerged from the railway mania of the 1840s, many more were promoted but failed to achieve their objectives. In 1846 some seventy-eight Irish railway companies were presenting schemes to parliament. Some of these, for example the lines proposed in mid-Down, centred on Banbridge, were built later in the century. Others were frankly mad, such as the plans of the Kilrush, Dublin & Belfast Junction Railway, which hoped to raise £1.5 million to link the small port of Kilrush on the Shannon Estuary in County Clare with the country's two largest cities. Other schemes seemed slightly suspect. Two companies were promoted in 1845 to build similar sounding railways to connect Limerick and Belfast. One of these, the Limerick & Belfast Direct Railway, drew protests from two peers, Lord Bloomfield and Lord Rossmore, and nine other gentlemen, whose names appeared on the prospectus of the company but who denied any connection with the scheme.

All this activity, it must be remembered, took place against the background of the Famine and with a minimum of support from the government. The 1840s also saw the resolution of another major issue in relation to Ireland's railways, the legacy of which is still with us to this day. Ireland's railways are unique from those in the rest of western Europe, apart from the systems on the Iberian Peninsula, in one major respect. The gauge of Irish railways is 5 ft 3 in.; in Britain and across the English Channel a gauge of 4 ft 8½ in. is used. How this came about is the subject of the next part of this narrative.

Chapter 3 ∾

HOW IRELAND GOT ITS GAUGE

The single most important measurement on any line of railway is the gauge, the distance between the rails. On a practical level, if the gauge is not maintained rigorously, derailments and accidents can result. When a line is being built, the gauge selected has a bearing on the costs of constructing the railway in terms of the amount of land which has to be acquired on which to build the track, and on the speed and volume of traffic it can carry. Looking back at the era when the railway age was beginning to build up momentum, from the perspective of the twenty-first century, with the human race having put men on the moon and many of us possessing cars which can easily, if illegally, travel in excess of 100 mph, it is hard for us to realise the effect which the first railways had on our ancestors, who had to come to terms for the first time in recorded history with a technology which permitted travel at speeds hitherto unknown. For the ordinary citizen, the first railways were probably as awesome and incomprehensible as space travel is to the rest of us today.

The rapid rise of railways from the obscurity of the collieries and other industrial settings to providing a means of connecting major cities, a process which took less than twenty years to achieve, meant that a lot had to be learned very quickly. It also meant that the lumbering government process had to come to terms with both the technology and a whole range of new financial and regulatory issues which it had not previously confronted. The main problem was there were few people around who knew very much about railways and this led to a whole host of problems which were only really resolved as the century progressed. On the crucial issue of the best gauge for railways, in Britain the protagonists quickly settled into two camps: one backing Isambard Kingdom Brunel and the 7 ft gauge which he set for the Great Western Railway and its satellites; and the rest supporting the standard or narrow gauge of 4 ft 8½ in. which was used on most other lines elsewhere in the country outside the realm of the GWR. Already by the late 1830s it was clear the use of two gauges in England was going to cause major problems wherever there was a junction between the GWR and other lines. In order to avoid similar issues in Ireland, the Irish Railway Commissioners were asked to recommend a gauge which would be used throughout Ireland.

The Commissioners consulted widely among those whom today we would call the great and the good and their recommendation, published in their second report in 1838, was for a gauge of 6 ft 2 in. At this time in Ireland only the short D&K line was operating. Though built to a gauge of 4 ft 8½ in., converting the D&K to the new Irish standard gauge of 6 ft 2 in. would not present any insurmountable problems if it was ever extended to make a junction with another line. The directors of the Ulster Railway Company had been awaiting the Commissioners' report and had not decided on a gauge for their line up to this date. They were happy to accept the recommended gauge and informed UR shareholders in September 1838: 'In pursuance of the recommendations of the Irish Railway Commissioners, a gauge of 6 ft 2 in. will be used as the breadth of way between the rails.'

The initial section of the UR, from Belfast to Lisburn, and the extension to Portadown were duly built to the 6 ft 2 in. gauge. The method of track construction adopted by the UR was not that with which we are familiar today, with cross sleepers to which the rails are fixed by chairs or clips. Rather, the track was laid in a fashion similar to that used by Brunel on the GWR in England, the rails being fixed to longitudinal timbers with the gauge being maintained by cross ties. The operation of the line drew favourable reactions. The Belfast *News Letter* reported in September 1839 that there was 'universal gratification at the smoothness of the motion'. Another paper reported that the extreme steadiness with which the trains were found to travel was attributed to the wide gauge. The matter of the gauge used in Ireland should have rested there and the country today would be operating trains on the widest gauge in the world. But this was far from the case.

After many difficulties involving finance, engineers and contractors, the Dublin & Drogheda Railway had by 1842 issued contracts for the whole of its route, with construction starting from the Dublin end. In 1838 the D&D directors had agreed to build their line to the Irish Railway Commissioners' gauge of 6 ft 2 in. However, by the end of 1841 they were clearly having second thoughts about this and their engineer, John MacNeill, was having consultations with English engineers on the question. In September 1842 the secretary of the UR, J. G. Smith, wrote to the D&D board to enquire whether there was any truth in reports reaching Belfast that they planned to use a different gauge to that of the UR. Surviving D&D minute books do not show clearly when this decision was made, but the UR directors reported to their shareholders in March 1843 that they had become aware of this in September 1842, at the time Smith wrote to the D&D directors. MacNeill's report on the gauge to be used was not presented until December 1842, but this may have been a formality, rubber stamping a decision which had already been made. MacNeill advocated a gauge of 5 ft 2 in. and in January 1843 the D&D board formally accepted this recommendation. As there was every likelihood that a line linking Dublin and Belfast would be built, Ireland was now faced with the very situation which the government, through the appointment of the Irish Railway Commissioners, had hoped to avoid, a break of gauge on a major main line. The arguments started almost immediately and involved not just the fortunes of the two companies concerned, but broadened to focus on the role of the government through its agency, the Board of Trade, in regulating the affairs of private railway companies.

The UR referred the matter of the gauge to the Board of Trade. While they were investigating, the protagonists in Ireland were active in publicising their respective points of view. MacNeill's arguments for the 5 ft 2 in. gauge were wide ranging. He claimed that there would be savings of £6,000 in the costs of laying the track between Dublin and Drogheda to the narrower gauge. The earthworks and embankments for this line had been built to take the 6 ft 2 in. gauge, so there would be no cost savings there, though this argument would apply to the construction of future lines. MacNeill's most contentious opinions related to the savings made by locomotives and carriages which would be smaller and lighter than those built for a wider gauge. He claimed an annual saving of £3,000 on operating the Dublin to Drogheda line if built to his gauge.

The UR camp did not attack MacNeill's gauge, rather, they argued that while 5 ft 2 in. would probably be perfectly acceptable, so was their gauge. The UR line had been using the 6 ft 2 in. gauge for several years without the slightest problem, so why change it? The UR engineer, John Godwin, did dispute the £3,000 operational savings claimed by MacNeill by stating that the UR's entire locomotive operating costs the previous year, when the line had conveyed 353,000 passengers and 20,000 tons of freight, had only amounted to £4,000.

The Board of Trade's Inspector of Railways, Major-General Pasley, made his decision in March 1843. His recommendation was that an extra inch should be added to MacNeill's gauge and that the D&D be built to a gauge of 5 ft 3 in. This was communicated to the D&D directors in a letter from the secretary of the Board of Trade which was discussed at a D&D board meeting on 31 March. The letter stated: 'The Lords of the Committee of the Privy Council for Trade have adopted the recommendation of Major-General Pasley that a gauge of 5 ft 3 in. is, under all circumstances, the best for general adoption in Ireland.' It went on to express their lordships' hope 'that the directors of this company will feel no difficulty in adopting it as it

differs so slightly from the gauge recommended by their engineer'.
Not surprisingly the D&D directors resolved to 'cheerfully adopt'
the 5 ft 3 in. gauge and to be 'at all times ready to promote any
reasonable arrangements for securing an uninterrupted
communication between Dublin and Belfast when a line of
railway shall be made to connect those two places'. Equally
unsurprisingly Major-General Pasley's recommendation was not
so warmly received in Belfast.

The directors of the UR and their supporters were outraged at
the decision. Firstly, the new gauge was completely untried
anywhere and it was also alleged that Pasley had only consulted
those associated with the narrower gauges in Britain and had
ignored Brunel and advocates of the 7 ft gauge on the GWR, only
seeking the opinion of those wedded to the narrow gauge such as
George and Robert Stephenson and John Gooch, who worked for
the London & South Western Railway, the GWR's principal narrow
gauge competitor in the south of England. The UR directors felt
that their point of view had been completely ignored and they
had strong support from those who were uneasy with the role of
the Board of Trade in the matter. The influential journal, *The
Railway Times*, joined the battle on behalf of the UR, but also
attacked the Board of Trade and the whole issue of government
interference with private railway companies. In September 1843
The Railway Times described Major-General Pasley as 'this old
gentleman, a mere tyro in the science settling offhand a question
upon which the most eminent professional men in the Kingdom
are at issue'.

For some commentators at the time, the imposition of a new
gauge on the UR could set a precedent for further interference in
the affairs of railway companies. If the Board of Trade as
constituted in 1843 could make this decision now, which changed
the earlier judgment of another government body, what was to
stop the government making a further change at some time in the
future? One of the first attempts at controlling the new form of
transport was the Railway Regulation Act of 1840 which set up the
Railway Department at the Board of Trade to collect statistics and
inspect and approve new lines before they were opened. The first

inspector general of Railways was Lieutenant-Colonel Sir Frederick Smith. In time this body was to be responsible for many of the major improvements in railway safety, their recommendations coming mostly in the wake of their investigations into railway accidents. As we will see later, one of the gravest of these accidents occurred in Ireland in 1889, and as a consequence of this the government was forced to act quickly to pass an Act which imposed radical measures to force the railway companies to improve their operating practices. From 1840 onwards and for most of the next 150 years, the inspecting officers were drawn from the ranks of the Royal Engineers. However, in 1843 the Board of Trade and its railway inspectors did not have the respect in the railway world which they were later to gain. Their pronouncements often involved sending hurried and not necessarily helpful advice to railway companies in the aftermath of accidents. The targets of their concern in the mid-1840s included the use of four coupled engines, engines running tender first and the locking of carriage doors, the latter particularly irrelevant when most Third-Class carriages, if they were available to the poorest of travellers at all, amounted to little more than open wagons with hard, wooden seats.

While such interference would be judged reasonable and necessary today and has been so for many decades, in the context of the 1840s, for many this was not how it would have been viewed. The prevailing ethos of the day was expressed in 1848 by the political philosopher, John Stuart Mill, who wrote: '*Laissez-faire* . . . should be the general practice. Every departure from it, unless required by some great good, is a certain evil.' Self-regulation through competition was generally thought sufficient to control the railways. If the government could determine the gauge to be used in Ireland now, what was to stop it imposing fare structures or attempting to control the amount of profit a company might make in the future? Indeed the arguments over the Board of Trade's right to impose a gauge on the private railway companies of Ireland was an early salvo in a battle which raged throughout much of the nineteenth century. It was followed shortly by Gladstone's Regulation of Railways Act of

1844 which attempted to impose restrictions on excessive dividends and fares and introduced the requirement of what later became known as the parliamentary train. This forced every company to run at least one train a day along the full length of its lines, stopping at all stations, with a fare of no more than one penny per mile. This established the principle of Third-Class travel and proved a boon to the poor, giving them a means of using the railways at fares they could just about afford. This was of particular relevance to Ireland where there was no shortage of poor and destitute people in the wake of the Great Famine. Indeed a trip on a parliamentary train to a port was often the first stage of the journey which led countless thousands of emigrants to join the great Irish diaspora of the second half of the nineteenth century.

The Dublin & Drogheda opened its line for traffic on the new 5 ft 3 in. gauge in May 1844, the first railway in the world to use this gauge. In 1846 the branch line from Howth Junction opened as far as Sutton and reached Howth the following year. There was no immediate pressing need to convert the UR line as the two components of what was to become the Dublin to Belfast main line were still many miles apart. In April 1843 the Board of Trade had accepted, in a letter to the UR, the need to compensate the company if it had to change its gauge and hinted that such a claim for compensation might involve the expenditure of government funds. For the time, this was fairly radical as it was generally accepted that public money was not to be used to subsidise railway companies, though some Irish companies had already by this time had the benefit of government loans. In 1845, Acts of Parliament granted to several companies planning to build lines in the north of Ireland included clauses stipulating that they should be built to the new gauge and that these companies should contribute to the expenses incurred by the UR in altering its gauge. The companies affected were the Dundalk & Enniskillen, the Newry & Enniskillen and the Dublin & Belfast Junction Railway. In addition, the Act renewing the UR's powers to extend its line to Armagh included a clause asserting that it be built to a gauge of 5 ft 3 in.

The days of the 6 ft 2 in. gauge were now clearly numbered. The UR began changing its gauge in 1845. The earthworks for the line to Portadown had been built to take two tracks, though initially only one line was put down. By March 1846 a second line laid to 5 ft 3 in. had been virtually completed as far as Portadown. Traffic began to be worked on the new gauge from 4 January 1847, and by September the original track had been regauged and all the line's traffic was being worked on 5 ft 3 in. tracks. The UR's accounts show that the cost of altering the track and rolling stock amounted to £19,246. Their solicitor approached the Board of Trade to obtain a settlement from the companies whose Acts made them liable to contribute to the UR's costs. The companies concerned began at once to prevaricate. The secretary of the D&E, A. J. Macrory, declined to contribute on behalf of his directors on the unlikely basis that 'it never can be necessary or expedient that their company should run any of their engines, carriages or wagons upon any portion of the Ulster Railway'. The directors of the D&BJR, while accepting their responsibility to contribute, tried to pass the bulk of their liability on to the D&D on the basis that it was their decision to change the gauge which caused the problem in the first place. The correspondence between the various companies dragged on for over a year, with the UR trying to extract as much money as it could and the other companies trying to give as little as possible. In the end Captain Simmons of the Board of Trade was appointed to act as arbitrator. He determined that the UR had spent £15,563 changing its gauge and apportioned the amount payable in compensation to the UR by four companies, including the D&D. Proceedings had to be initiated by the UR against the D&E and the N&E in 1851 to obtain payment. In November 1851 the impecunious N&E made an application to the Court of Chancery for an injunction to restrain the UR from taking proceedings against them for recovery of this money, and it was not until April 1853 that the D&E was forced to pay up.

The only place in the world where the 6 ft 2 in. gauge was ever used was between Belfast and Portadown on the Ulster Railway between 1839 and 1847. Had it survived, it would have been the widest gauge in use anywhere in the world today. Let us imagine

turning up at Belfast Central or Dublin Heuston in the early years
of the twenty-first century to be whisked to our destinations in
high, wide and spacious trains at speeds of up to 200 mph. Or
would the costs of building non-standard rolling stock and
maintaining the infrastructure required for such a wide gauge
have meant the closing down of the last railways in Ireland in the
1960s? In retrospect, it is probably fair to say that the 6 ft 2 in.
gauge was too grand for Ireland. Had it survived, it might have
been a cost which railways in a poor country, economically
devastated by the Great Famine and its consequences, could not
have borne. The Irish standard gauge railway system would
probably have been smaller and perhaps many more lines would
have been built to narrower gauges later in the nineteenth century
in order to save money on construction costs.

The historic consequences of the events which led to the
introduction of the 5 ft 3 in. gauge in Ireland are also extremely
significant. This was an early example of successful government-
imposed control and regulation on private companies in an age of
laissez-faire. This process eventually led to major advances in
railway safety which were to benefit passengers and staff as the
railway age grew towards maturity.

Emboldened by the Board of Trade's success in settling the
gauge to be used in Ireland, the government belatedly tried to
tackle the issue of the competing gauges in Britain, where by this
time there were already over thirty locations where a break of
gauge occurred. A royal commission was set up in 1845 to
investigate the merits of the two gauges, Brunel's 7 ft gauge and
the narrow or 4 ft 8½ in. gauge. The Commission concluded that
the narrow gauge was best suited to the long-term needs of the
country. It expressed the aspiration that broad gauge lines should
be converted to the newly ordained standard gauge, but in the
absence of any public money to bring this about, this hope
remained unrealised. One practical consequence of these debates
was the passing in 1846 of the Gauge Act which stipulated that the
4 ft 8½ in. gauge was to be used for all future railways in Britain,
though there were loopholes which allowed the GWR and its
allies to continue to extend their broad gauge network. The last

new 7 ft gauge line, a branch from St Erth to St Ives in Cornwall, was opened as late as 1877, and the broad gauge was not finally abandoned until 1892.

As a footnote to this chapter, the 5 ft 3 in. gauge, known in some quarters for obvious reasons as the Irish gauge, was used in two other places in the world. In Victoria and South Australia there are around 2,970 kilometres of 1600 mm (5 ft 3 in.) gauge track. The first railway to open in Australia, which started operations on 12 September 1854, was a short 5 ft 3 in. gauge line from the famous Flinders Street station in Melbourne to Port Melbourne. The engineer was an Irishman, Francis Webb Shields. In Brazil there are around 5,290 kilometres of 1600 mm (5 ft 3 in.) gauge track. There must be an Irish connection there somewhere, though I have been unable to find it! So we are not quite unique with our gauge, but not far off it.

Chapter 4 ❧

CONSOLIDATION AND EXPANSION (1850–1880)

B y 1850 the gauge question had been settled and the roots of the national network had been laid down. The next thirty years were to see a steady expansion of railways into most parts of Ireland. In this chapter we will follow this process and some of the vicissitudes which were experienced along the way. The choosing of this period is not an arbitrary one, for by 1880 the network had probably reached the greatest extent which conventional methods of railway promotion could have given Ireland. This still left many parts of the country, especially in the poorer and more remote areas of the south and west, without the benefit of access to a railway. The final major phase of railway expansion, in the last two decades of the nineteenth century, was effected by changes in government policy towards the development of the Irish economy which, as we will see later, led to the construction of many miles of railway. Rather than try to present the expansion of the network in the years up to 1880 chronologically, which would mean jumping all over the country all the time, it seems logical that this survey should adopt a geographical progression, starting in the south and gradually working our way northwards.

The first railway to open in County Cork was the GSWR main line from Dublin which reached Mallow in March 1849, and in September of that year the temporary terminus at Blackpool (or Cork Victoria as the GSWR referred to it) on the northern outskirts of Cork city. While the line from Dublin was being built, railway promoters in County Cork had not been idle. Two companies were authorised to build railways in 1845 and 1846. The latter was the Cork, Blackrock & Passage Railway which opened its short 6½ mile line from a terminus at Victoria Road in the city to Passage in June 1850. (The rather more interesting later history of this line is told in Chapter 5.) The line authorised in 1845 was the Cork & Bandon which began the construction of its 20 mile route from the Bandon end. The first sod was cut by the Earl of Bandon at a ceremony on 16 September 1845 after which, as often happened at such events in the nineteenth century, the directors and their guests retired to an adjacent pavilion to partake of *déjeuner* and toast the success of the project. The line from Bandon to Ballinhassig opened in 1849 and included the 135 yard long Kilpatrick tunnel, the first in Ireland to be used by passenger trains. Services on the final section to Cork Albert Quay station, which included another tunnel, the much longer 900 yard Goggins Hill tunnel, and the superb lofty Chetwynd viaduct, 90 ft high and consisting of four 110 ft long iron spans which is still in existence, commenced in December 1851. The first addition to the C&B system was a branch promoted by a separate company, the Cork & Kinsale Junction Railway, authorised in 1859, opened in 1863 and worked by the C&B, which left the main line at Kinsale Junction and ran the 11 miles to the fishing port of Kinsale on the south coast. The main line was also gradually extended west from Bandon. The West Cork Railway opened a line 18 miles long from Bandon to Dunmanway in 1866. Another independent company, the Ilen Valley Railway, further extended this line to Skibbereen in 1877. (The final extensions to the railway network of west Cork are discussed in Chapter 6.)

One other independent railway company in County Cork should be mentioned here. This was the Cork & Macroom Direct Railway which was authorised in 1861 to build a line from Cork to the small market town of Macroom 24 miles to the west of the city. The line opened in 1866 and sensibly its trains shared the C&B station at Albert Quay, joining C&B metals at Ballyphehane Junction a mile out from the terminus and paying the Bandon company £2,000 per year for this arrangement. However, disputes between the two companies soon arose, with the C&MDR believing it was paying too much for the use of the C&B's facilities, the latter predictably being of the opinion that the Macroom company was not paying enough. Traffic on the two lines was not particularly heavy, with about six trains a day on both of them. Despite this, they were unable to come to an equitable agreement, the C&B declining arbitration offered by the Board of Trade. The result was that the C&MDR sought authorisation in 1877 to build its own line into the city, and in 1879 it opened a terminus at Capwell some distance from the city centre. The junction at Ballyphehane was severed and the Macroom line continued in splendid isolation until a connection with the Bandon line was re-established during the First World War. The lack of any kind of planning or overall strategy in the way Ireland got its railway system had resulted in Cork city having, by 1879, no less than five separate railway stations, four of them termini, only two of which were linked to each other.

The next part of the story is dominated by the activities of the Great Southern & Western Railway, Ireland's largest railway company, which came to occupy much of a huge swathe of territory on either side of its Dublin to Cork main line, through which a number of lines were built in this period which were either owned or worked by the GSWR. The building of its main line, over 160 miles in length, in the space of less than five years against the background of the Famine, was a fine achievement. Its future expansion was largely driven by buying up smaller companies at bargain prices, many of whose lines the GSWR had previously worked. The final part of the main line, from Blackpool to Penrose Quay, was opened in 1855. The delay had been due to the construction of the 1,355 yard long tunnel needed to bring the line into the city. The line through the tunnel was built on a gradient of 1 in 60 and 1 in 70, which meant that in the days of steam most trains leaving Cork required two locomotives. Two branches were later built which extended the main line beyond Cork. These were built by an independent company, the Cork & Youghal. The C&Y had originally intended to make a line connecting Cork and Waterford via Dungarvan and though this was never realised, a line as far as Youghal was opened in 1860. From the late 1850s transatlantic liners began to call at Queenstown in Cork Harbour and a branch was built by the c&y to the port, opening in 1862, which diverged from the Youghal line at Queenstown Junction. The c&y terminus in Cork was at Summerhill which overlooked the gswr station. It was not at first linked to the gswr line, but when that company bought the c&y in 1866 for about half the amount it took to build the lines in the first place, a link was built from Grattan Hill to Penrose Quay. Summerhill continued in use until 1893 when all services from these lines were diverted into the gswr's new Cork station.

Moving north up the gswr main line we come to the important junction of Mallow. In 1846 the Killarney Junction Railway was authorised to build a line from Mallow to Killarney, already a popular destination for tourists. The kjr had the strong backing of the gswr, who took up shares in the company to the value of £100,000. The line was just short of 40 miles in length and opened in 1853. It was built by William Dargan at the very low cost of less than £5,000 per mile. The kjr had one other claim to fame in that in 1854 it opened the first railway-owned hotel in Ireland at Killarney, which was later known as the Great Southern Hotel. Once the line to Killarney had been completed, a separate company backed by the kjr and the gswr was formed to extend the line to Tralee. The Tralee & Killarney Railway, also built by Dargan, opened in 1859. One minor irritation still evident today stems from the decision to start the line to Tralee from a point east of the Killarney terminus of the original line from Mallow. This meant that all trains serving Killarney, in effect almost all passenger workings on the line from 1859 to the present day, have had to reverse in and out of Killarney station before resuming their journey to either Mallow or Tralee. Towards the end of the century several branches were built off the Mallow to Tralee line, to which we will return later in the book. Only one of these was built within the time frame of this chapter, the short 4½ mile line from Gortalea, 7 miles from Tralee, to Castleisland. This was promoted by an independent company, the Castleisland Railway, and opened in August 1875. It was worked from the start by the GSWR who acquired the line in 1879. At first passenger traffic was so modest that the GSWR had built a combined engine and coach at Inchicore to work the branch. As traffic developed, more conventional methods were adopted and the coach was removed from the engine leaving a small 0-6-0 tank engine No. 90. Against all the odds, No. 90 survived until virtually the end of steam on CIÉ in the 1960s and was subsequently preserved by the company, initially on a plinth at Mallow. Now owned by IÉ, the locomotive is on permanent loan to the Downpatrick & County Down Railway where it can be seen at work hauling passenger trains once again.

Mallow became a two-way junction in 1860 when a 17 mile long line east to the town of Fermoy was opened. This route was one actually built by the GSWR who had bought out the promoting company, the Mallow & Fermoy Railway, before construction work began. In 1872 the line was extended to Lismore by the Fermoy & Lismore Railway. Then in 1878 it was further extended the 43 miles to a station known as Waterford South, on the southern side of the River Suir, by the Waterford, Dungarvan & Lismore Railway. All this activity was achieving on a step by step basis the establishment of a through route from Cork to Waterford, as had originally been envisaged in an Act of 1845 which authorised the Cork & Waterford Railway to build this line, though via Youghal. When this scheme failed, it had been revived in a much more modest form as the Cork & Youghal Railway, mentioned above. The final part of this saga was not to unfold until the early years of the twentieth century, and we will return to this line in Chapter 6.

It will be recalled that the GSWR had arrived at Limerick Junction just after the Waterford & Limerick line opened in 1848. Passengers wishing to travel from Dublin or Cork to Limerick had to change at the junction into a connecting W&L service. This dependence on another company seemed to have irked the GSWR, for it made attempts to reach Limerick independently from both Dublin and Cork, though neither of the lines which resulted were ever as well used as the connection from the Junction. The line from Cork to Limerick was promoted by the Cork & Limerick Direct Railway with the backing of the GSWR. It left the main line at Charleville Junction about a mile north of Charleville station and ran 17½ miles north to make a junction at Patrickswell with the Limerick & Foynes Railway, over which C&LDR trains had running powers to Limerick. The line, which opened in 1862, was worked by the GSWR from the outset and acquired by the company in 1871. Though initially some trains did run through from Limerick to Cork following the GSWR takeover, most terminated at Charleville where through passengers would change on to main line services.

The direct GSWR line to Limerick from the north was a rather more complicated affair. It began as two separate branches built by two independent companies. The first of these was the Roscrea & Parsonstown Railway which was authorised in 1854 and had the backing of the GSWR. Parsonstown, which has been known as Birr for over a hundred years and whose station was renamed as long ago as 1900, was the home of the Earls of Rosse, one of whom was famed for the great astronomical telescope built in the grounds of Birr Castle in the middle of the nineteenth century. The line took time to build, not being fully opened until 1858. Meanwhile, closer to Limerick, at the same time, the Limerick, Castleconnell & Killaloe Railway was building a line which was to terminate at Killaloe Pier on the River Shannon, which was served by steamers. The line which reached Castleconnell in 1858, Birdhill in 1860 and Killaloe in 1862, was worked by the Waterford & Limerick. To bridge the gap between Roscrea and Birdhill, put the sizeable town of Nenagh on the railway map and complete the GSWR route to Limerick, the company promoted an extension which was opened in 1864. At Ballybrophy, where this line met the Dublin to Cork route, trains terminated in a bay platform so through running towards Dublin was not possible, and even though this route to Limerick was about 6 miles shorter than the original one via Limerick Junction, the fastest and most frequent services between Dublin and Limerick from 1864 to the present day have always been via the Junction. The building of this through route had the consequence of creating branches at both ends. The original line to Birr now became a branch leaving the new line at Roscrea. At the other end of the line, until the early years of the last century, GSWR trains did not run through to Limerick but terminated at Birdhill where they connected with W&L services to and from the Killaloe line, which was now left as a 4 mile long branch from Birdhill. Ironically, the GSWR's alternative route to Limerick was still dependent on the W&L for the last part of the journey.

The arrival of the railway at Parsonstown gave rise to one of the most ill-starred lines ever to operate in Ireland, the Parsonstown & Portumna Bridge Railway, sometimes referred to as the 'stolen railway'. Many of the railway schemes in the midlands in the middle of the nineteenth century endeavoured to connect with traffic on the extensive waterway which was the River Shannon, its lakes and tributaries. This was the impetus behind the P&PBR which was authorised in 1861 to build a line from the recently opened branch to Parsonstown the 12 miles to Portumna. This small town on the Shannon was actually in County Galway and the site of a road bridge over the river. When the line was eventually opened in 1868, it made a trailing connection on to the existing line at Parsonstown and terminated on the Tipperary side of the Shannon opposite Portumna, about a mile from the town. The intention of the company was to build a bridge across the river and into Portumna itself, but this never happened. The GSWR agreed to work the line for ten years, but a service of only two trains per day was provided and receipts were poor. There seems to have been little exchange of traffic with steamers on the waterway. In 1878 the GSWR refused to continue to work the line on the grounds that it was losing money and it closed to all traffic in December of that year. The Public Works Loan Commissioners, who had given financial support to the company, repossessed the line, but other than appoint caretakers made no attempt to work it. Though several efforts were made to revive the line, the Commissioners washed their hands of it in 1883 and withdrew their staff. This was the signal to the locals to remove its effects piecemeal. The timber station buildings at Portumna Bridge were demolished and removed, along with rails, signals

and anything else portable and, indeed, not obviously portable. In
the latter category was an attempt to use a crane to remove a six
span iron bridge over the Little Brosna river at Riverstown, which
was allegedly foiled by the police. The railway was literally stolen,
and thus ended the brief ignoble career of perhaps the most
unsuccessful railway company ever to operate in Ireland.

The progress made by the Waterford & Limerick Railway after
it reached Limerick Junction and Tipperary in 1848 was more
measured. With the aid of a loan of £120,000 from the Public
Works Loan Commissioners, Clonmel was reached in 1852 and
trains began to run to a station at Newrath, on the western
outskirts of Waterford, in September 1854. The line was built by
Dargan who also for a time entered into a contract with the
company to work it. w&l trains did not reach the site of the
present Waterford station, close to the road bridge over the Suir,
until 1864. The w&l was in fact Waterford's second railway. The
year before the w&l reached Newrath and the Waterford &
Kilkenny provided the city with a service to Dublin via Kilkenny,
on the opposite side of the river the short 7 mile long Waterford
& Tramore Railway opened for business. This line was unique in
a number of ways. Firstly, in its early years it was very prosperous,
paying dividends of over 7 per cent. The w&t had no
intermediate stations and no passing places and its profits were
due to the large number of tourists heading for the fleshpots of
Tramore. Its terminus, Waterford Manor, was over a mile away
from the main station in the city, and for the entire length of its
existence it remained physically isolated from the rest of the Irish
railway network. Its inaccessibility meant it was operated up to
the 1920s with rolling relics in the form of locomotives and
carriages dating from the 1850s and 60s.

In the nineteenth century there was just one branch off
the entire Limerick to Waterford route, the line from Clonmel
to Thurles. This had first been promoted as long ago as 1846,
but nothing came of it. Then in 1865 the imposingly titled
Southern Railway was formed to build this 25 mile long link
which offered, in theory at any rate, a much quicker route from
Clonmel to Dublin than the trek via Limerick Junction. The usual

catalogue of financial difficulties plagued the company, which in the end needed substantial loans from the Public Works Loan Commissioners to complete the construction of its line, which was opened as far as Fethard in 1879 and through to a junction with the GSWR main line at Thurles in July 1880. The SR was worked from the outset by the W&L, but by 1884 it was insolvent and ownership passed to the Board of Works though the W&L continued to provide the service on its behalf.

The main thrust of the expansion of the W&L was centred on Limerick which the company turned into a major railway centre. By the time it had reached its greatest extent, the W&L was the fourth largest railway in Ireland. However, its main line from Limerick to Waterford was only 77 miles long and its growth was due to it absorbing smaller concerns or working their routes. The lines which spread south-west from Limerick, and took nearly thirty years to reach Tralee eventually in 1880, illustrate this process well. The first part of this line was opened from Limerick to Ballingrane in 1856 by the Limerick & Foynes Railway, reaching Foynes two years later. This line was extended a further 10 miles to Newcastle West in 1867 by a separate company, the Rathkeale & Newcastle Junction. This left Ballingrane as the junction for the port of Foynes on the Shannon Estuary. Both these lines were worked by the W&L. Yet another company, the Limerick & North Kerry, was authorised in 1873 to build a line 42½ miles long from Newcastle to Tralee. The W&L agreed to provide £25,000 of the company's £260,000 capital on condition that it worked the line. The North Kerry line, as it came to be known, was a difficult one to construct. L&NK tracks did not make an end-on junction with the existing line at Newcastle West, which remained a terminal. This meant that the locomotives of through workings had to run round their stock before continuing. From Newcastle West to Barnagh the line climbed on gradients as steep as 1 in 81 and 1 in 61 to pass through a 110 yard long tunnel at Barnagh, the only one on the entire W&L system. Just beyond the tunnel a summit of 630 ft above sea level, the highest point on an Irish standard gauge railway, was reached.

The W&L also began to expand north from Limerick in a

similar fashion to that which took its trains into Kerry. The first part of this expansion came with the opening of the Limerick & Ennis Railway in 1859. The line was authorised in 1853, but in true Irish fashion difficulties in raising the capital soon emerged and the company had run out of funds by 1856. The original English contractors were replaced by William Dargan and in 1857 the Public Works Loan Commissioners once again rode to the rescue of a faltering Irish railway company with a loan of £40,000. This line, which was worked by the W&L from the outset, was absorbed by that company in 1874. As the Ennis line was stuttering towards completion, a new company was incorporated to continue this route north to make a junction at Athenry with the MGWR's Galway to Dublin line. This was the Athenry & Ennis Junction Railway, which though it was incorporated in 1860 did not open its 36 mile long line until 1869, once again with the aid of loans from the Public Works Loan Commissioners. The A&EJR was also worked by the W&L which was eventually, like the L&E, absorbed by the W&L. North from Athenry a line had been opened to Tuam by the Athenry & Tuam Railway in 1860. This was worked initially by the MGWR but later by the W&L, which used it as a springboard for a further extension to the north which eventually, as we will see in Chapter 6, was to bring its trains to Sligo.

The GSWR was also active in expanding its activities to the east of its main line. It will be recalled that the branch to Carlow was actually the first part of the GSWR system to open, in August 1846. This line was quickly extended to the important town of Kilkenny in 1850 by the Irish South Eastern Railway, effectively a GSWR satellite. The ISER was formally taken over by the GSWR in 1863. Kilkenny had already been reached two years before by the Waterford & Kilkenny company and the ISER trains used the existing W&K station. Through travel by rail from Dublin to Waterford was now possible. A further line was built from Kilkenny in the 1860s. This was a route north to Maryborough via Abbeyleix which was opened by the Kilkenny Junction Railway in 1867. Eventually this fell into the hands of the GSWR as well, but not until 1900. Another direction which attracted the interests of the GSWR was a route down the valley of the River Barrow towards Wexford.

In 1854 the Bagenalstown & Wexford Railway was incorporated to build this line. Involved in the promotion and direction of this company was one of the most remarkable Irishmen of the era, Arthur MacMurrough Kavanagh. Born in 1831 with only stumps for arms and legs, Kavanagh, who liked to trace his family's ancestry back to the twelfth-century King of Leinster, Dermot MacMurrough, nevertheless managed to overcome his disabilities and was able to ride, shoot and fish like any other country gentleman of the time. He also travelled extensively in the Middle East, Persia and India, returning to Ireland in 1853 on the death of his brother to run the family's estates. As well as being at times a Justice of the Peace and High Sheriff of both Carlow and Kilkenny, he was also a Member of Parliament from 1866 until 1880. Despite the involvement of this energetic and distinguished man, the B&W was a far from successful venture.

Though the company had the financial backing of the GSWR, progress was slow. Borris, 12 miles from Bagenalstown, was reached in 1858 and Ballywilliam, a further 12 miles on, in 1862 and there the line and its funds ran out and the B&W was declared insolvent. Receipts were poor and the GSWR, which had been working the train service, pulled out in 1864. The bankrupt concern was put up for auction and was bought by the unlikely figure of a London barrister with the equally unlikely name of Standish H. Motte. His plan, to extend the existing line to both Waterford and Wexford, was authorised in an Act of 1866 for the Waterford, New Ross & Wexford Junction Railway. In 1870 an extension of the existing line about 15 miles long from Ballywilliam to Palace East and to a temporary terminus at Sparrowland was opened. This was in anticipation of the Dublin, Wicklow & Wexford Railway opening their route to Wexford, which had been authorised in 1868. The DW&W line opened in 1872 and in the following year a junction between the two lines was established at Macmine. Motte engaged the GSWR to resume the train service, which they did for three years from 1870 to 1873, when that company again withdrew their services. By now the colourful barrister's dream of a railway empire in the south-east of Ireland had faded, but the future of the line was finally secured when it was bought jointly by the DW&W and the GSWR. In time the GSWR worked the line from Bagenalstown through to Palace East, with the DW&W handling trains from there to Macmine Junction. The through inland route to Wexford was at last realised twenty years after it was first mooted, though despite the high hopes of the original promoters back in the 1850s, it remained a rural backwater and never competed with the direct route to Wexford down the east coast.

The first mention in these pages of the Dublin, Wicklow & Wexford Railway brings us to the story of the railways which were built from the 1850s onwards down the east coast through the counties of Wicklow and Wexford. When we left the Dublin & Kingstown Railway it was operating its original line by steam power and the short extension to Dalkey on the atmospheric system. To understand what followed, we have to briefly return to the 1840s. Other interests were eyeing up the potential of extending into County Wicklow and beyond. The English Great Western Railway, through its subsidiary, the South Wales Railway, was looking to establish a port in west Wales linked to a new port which was to be established south of Wexford to grab a share of the lucrative traffic across the Irish Sea. On the Irish side, this port would have to be connected to Dublin by rail. As the D&K began to plan an extension to Bray in 1846, a company bearing the catchy name of the Waterford, Wexford, Wicklow & Dublin Railway, with a capital of £2 million, backed by the GWR and with Isambard Kingdom Brunel as its engineer, was authorised to connect the districts in its title. At the same time another company, the Dublin, Dundrum & Rathfarnham, was incorporated to build a line from a site at Harcourt Road in Dublin to serve those habitations. The Dublin & Kingstown had by now obtained powers to extend their line down the coast to Bray. A further Act of 1847 allowed the D&K to sell their Bray line to the WWW&D, which in turn would lease the original D&K line. Construction of the line began in 1848, but the pace soon slowed due to a shortage of funds. By this time the SWR was also in some trouble across the water and looked unlikely to extend its line beyond Swansea. With Dargan as its contractor, work started in

1849 on the first section of the DD&R line, which included the impressive nine-arch viaduct over the River Dodder at Milltown. Gradually reality crept up on the WWW&D. The great scheme for lines to Wexford and Waterford and the new port was officially dropped in an Act of 1851 which changed the name of the company to the Dublin & Wicklow Railway, reflecting its current plans and reducing its capital to £500,000. Another Act changed the name of the DD&R to the Dublin & Bray and paved the way for an amalgamation of the two companies. The two lines to Bray were eventually opened by the D&W on 10 July 1854 and the original line from Dublin to Kingstown was regauged from 4 ft 8½ in. to 5 ft 3 in. in 1855, allowing through running from Dublin to Bray along the coastal route. In the same year the line from Bray to Wicklow was opened, and in 1859 the inland route was brought closer to the city centre in Dublin when a new station was opened at Harcourt Street.

The line from Wicklow was in time extended down the east coast. The company had another name change in 1859 when it became the Dublin, Wicklow & Wexford, reflecting its intended destination. Enniscorthy was reached in 1863 and Wexford finally in 1872 over twenty years behind schedule. This railway, starting in the Dublin suburbs with the original D&K line hugging the coast, perched on a ledge above the sea between Dalkey and Killiney, followed by the climb around Bray Head then sweeping through the Vale of Avoca and along the banks of the Slaney to Wexford, is one of the most picturesque stretches of railway in Ireland. There were just two branches off the over 90 miles between Westland Row station in Dublin and Wexford. The first, only about a quarter of a mile long, really more of a siding than a branch, opened in 1859, but was a very important one. This was the link from the main line to the pier at Kingstown, which allowed trains to connect directly with the steamers from Holyhead. The other branch, a proper one this time, was the 16 mile long line from Woodenbridge Junction to Shillelagh which opened in 1865. The final additions to the DW&W network were not completed until some years later. There was one further development in the south-east at this time. In 1863 the Waterford & Wexford Railway was incorporated to build a line linking those towns and with a branch to Greenore where a pier was to be constructed. Greenore soon came to be known as Rosslare. Construction proceeded at a snail's pace and the only parts of the scheme completed were the pier and a line linking Rosslare to the DW&W along the quays at Wexford which opened in 1882. The line was worked by the DW&W, but receipts were so poor the service was suspended in 1889. The real significance of this line had to await later events (described in Chapter 6).

We have alluded to railway politics earlier in the book and one of the bitterest feuds between two Irish companies was that waged between the GSWR and the MGWR in the 1850s. Its origins can probably be traced back to the Irish Railway Commissioners of the 1830s who believed that the west of Ireland was best served by the existing canals and did not need a railway. Despite initial thoughts of a line to the west as well as to Cork, the embryonic GSWR did not pursue this, and this led to one of its directors, John Ennis, leaving to promote such a line through a new company, the Midland Great Western Railway. When we left the MGWR in 1848, it was open for traffic as far as Mullingar and had been given the authorisation to build a line to Galway. The GSWR had also obtained powers to build a branch from Portarlington to Tullamore, which it saw as a staging post for an extension to Athlone where it could encroach on the Midland's Galway traffic or build lines to other western counties. Another factor which had arisen since the early 1840s was the possibility that Galway or another location on the west coast would be developed as a packet station for trade and mails to the Americas which could have generated a lot of traffic as mails were rushed across Ireland by rail to the east coast for the short sea journey on to Britain. Both lines were delayed by the appalling economic conditions in the country in the immediate aftermath of the Famine, but in June 1849 the MGWR, arguing that railway construction could be used to help relieve the distress, obtained a government loan of half a million pounds to assist in the building of the Galway line. The company appointed William Dargan as the contractor for the whole route from Mullingar to Galway, and in September 1850 the

1 A marble bust of William Dargan, 1799–1867, who was responsible for building over 800 miles of railway in the mid nineteenth century as well as undertaking many other significant public works including the Ulster Canal and what became the Queen's Island in Belfast. (*National Gallery of Ireland*)

2 This depiction of railway construction in the mid nineteenth century is notable for the absence of any mechanical assistance for the navvies, apart from the steam locomotive. When the formation was hacked out of the landscape, temporary track were at first laid to aid the construction work. This was later replaced by the permanent way, a term still used today to describe the track on which the trains run. (*Alan Fearnley*)

LOCOMOTIVE ENGINE—DUBLIN AND KINSTOWN RAILWAY

3 This early woodcut shows one of the first railway locomotives to run in Ireland. *Hibernia* was built in Manchester by Sharp, Roberts & Company for the commencement of services on the Dublin & Kingstown Railway in 1834. *Hibernia* withdrew herself from service when her boiler blew up at Kingstown in October 1842. (*Author's collection*)

4 In the next thirty years, the size of locomotives increased exponentially. This is one of a trio of 2-4-0 locos built by Beyer Peacock in Manchester in 1866 for use on the passenger trains of the Dublin & Belfast Junction Railway. Steam locos were often long-lived. The last of these machines was not withdrawn by the GNR until 1920. (*Author's collection*)

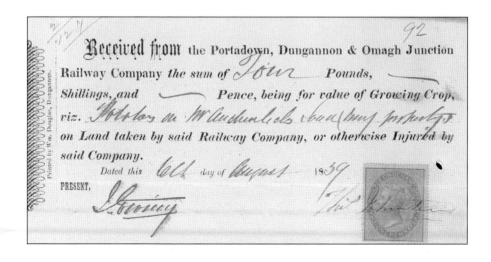

Portadown, Dungannon, and Omagh Junction Railway.

MEMORANDUM OF AN AGREEMENT,

Made and entered into the _25th_ day of _July_ &c one thousand eight hundred and _fifty nine_ Between _Daniel Denny Henry Denny_ &c

of _Omagh_ in the County of _Tyrone Gentleman_ hereinafter called "THE VENDOR," of the one part, and "THE PORTADOWN, DUNGANNON, AND OMAGH JUNCTION RAILWAY COMPANY," established, incorporated, and empowered by the Portadown and Dungannon Railway Acts, 1847 and 1853, and the Portadown, Dungannon, and Omagh Junction Railway Act, 1857, and hereinafter called "The Company" of the other part—

Whereas, the vendor is or claims to be entitled to the Lands and Hereditaments hereinafter set forth for an Estate _Dergmoney &c as Tenant from year to year under Alex Jo Stuart Esqr_

and has agreed to sell and dispose of the same to the Company, on the terms hereinafter mentioned. NOW THESE PRESENTS WITNESS, that the vendor doth hereby agree to Grant, Sell, Assign, Release, and Convey unto the Company, with the right of immediate entry thereon, ALL THAT AND THOSE, that part of the Townland of _Dergmoney Lower_ &c

5 & 6 Every railway company was empowered by its Act of Parliament with the right to acquire the land needed for its construction from landowners often reluctant to co-operate. The construction of each line could lead to hundreds of transactions to acquire the relatively small linear pieces of land which were needed to lay the tracks. These examples of some of the paperwork involved relate to the Portadown, Dungannon & Omagh Junction Railway which was constructed between 1858 and 1862. They show a Memorandum of Agreement between the company and a landowner in the townland of Dergmoney Lower, near Omagh, and a receipt for £4, compensation for crops damaged in the course of the construction work.

Received from the Portadown, Dungannon & Omagh Junction Railway Company _the sum of Four_ Pounds, Shillings, and Pence, being for value of Growing Crop, viz. _Potatoes on Mr Auchinleck's &c_ on Land taken by said Railway Company, or otherwise Injured by said Company.

Dated this _6th_ day of _August_ 18_59_

PRESENT,

Printed by Wm. Douglas, Dungannon.

7 This was the aftermath of the Armagh disaster of 12 June 1889, with the engine of the 10.35 am regular passenger train, into which the runaway carriages crashed, derailed by the force of the impact and thrown onto its side. The scarcely recognisable remains of the wooden carriages reduced to matchwood in the crash are seen littering the embankment. The events leading up to this defining moment in the railway history of these islands are described on pages 156–8. (PRONI)

8 Despite improvements to the braking of passenger trains imposed by parliament after the Armagh disaster, the same could not be said of broad gauge goods trains which mostly consisted of wagons equipped only with handbrakes, right through to the end of the age of steam. Inadequate braking meant that runaways were not uncommon. On St Valentine's Day in 1900, a cattle special from Enniscorthy made up of twenty-nine cattle wagons and a brake van failed to stop as it approached Harcourt Street station in Dublin, with the spectacular consequences seen here. No. 17 *Wicklow*, an 0-6-0 tender engine which was built at Grand Canal Street works by the DW&W only the year before, crashed through the wall of the station and is seen here sticking out into Hatch Street, precariously balanced on the buffer stops which were unable to halt its progress. The locomotive was repaired and remained in service until 1929.

9 This late-nineteenth-century view at Limerick Junction shows Waterford, Limerick & Western 4-4-0 No. 55 *Bernard*, built in 1897, at the head of a train for Limerick. Trains from both Dublin and Cork used the other face of this platform; those for Waterford ran down the line in the foreground and reversed into a south-facing bay platform beyond the station buildings. The singular platform layout at Limerick Junction meant that all services calling there used different parts of the one island platform, making interchange for passengers extremely convenient. (*Author's collection*)

10 The main line side of Limerick Junction is seen in CIÉ days. The train is arriving at the station from the Cork direction. It will pass the photographer and reverse onto the line in the foreground beside the platform. This is one of the mail trains with a travelling post office at the front, complete with the nets needed to collect mail bags from the line side at certain places, without having to stop. Also of interest is the third carriage, one of only three Pullman cars ever to run in Ireland, though by this time it had long lost that elevated status. (*Author's collection*)

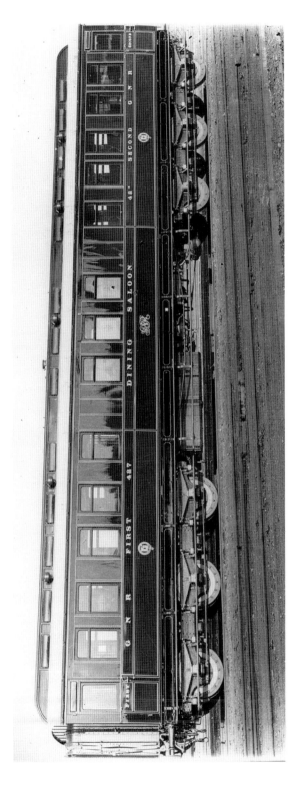

11 Late Victorian elegance on the GNR. This twelve-wheeled dining car, No. 427, was built at Dundalk works in 1900, its body being made from Honduran mahogany. It accommodated both First and Second Class passengers. Apparently Third-Class riff-raff were allowed in to dine only on payment of a supplement. (*Courtesy of Seán Kennedy*)

12 The elegant Belfast terminus of the Great Northern Railway in Great Victoria Street is seen at the end of the nineteenth century before the city's street tramways were electrified. The *porte cochère* in front of the station where carriages and cabs could pull up under cover was a feature of some of the more impressive railway termini. Whilst happily for the convenience of passengers, Great Victoria Street station was reopened in 1995 following the closure and demolition of this station in the 1970s, the present adjunct to the adjacent bus station is a far cry from the splendour of the original building. (*National Library of Ireland*)

13 Broadstone is Dublin's forgotten railway terminus. It is now over seventy years since it last saw passenger trains, the GSR transferring services off the former Midland lines to Westland Row in January 1937. The train sheds in the background in this early-twentieth-century view, are used today as workshops to maintain Bus Éireann vehicles. (*Author's collection*)

14 One of the most spectacular of the Balfour lines was the 39 mile long branch from Farranfore to Valentia Harbour in County Kerry which opened in 1893. A mixed train with a brake coach and some open-topped cattle wagons at the rear, heads on to the viaduct at Cahirciveen. (*National Library of Ireland*)

GREAT NORTHERN RAILWAY COMPANY (I.)

WORKING TIME TABLE

OF

SUTTON AND HOWTH

ELECTRIC TRAMWAY

To operate from Monday, 8th Sept., 1952
until further notice

R. CARSWELL AND SON, LTD., QUEEN STREET, BELFAST.

15 & 16 All the railway companies published two types of timetable, the public timetable and the working timetable. The former was widely disseminated for the benefit of prospective passengers; the latter were closely guarded and, as in the case of the one shown here, restricted to the sight of the company's servants only. There were often differences in the timings of passenger trains shown in the two, and the working timetables contained information on the running of goods and cattle trains and spare paths for special workings. Even the GNR's Hill of Howth Tramway had its own working timetable; part of the September 1952 issue is illustrated here.

Sutton Station to Hill of Howth and Howth Station.
SUNDAYS.

		1	2	3	4	5	6	7	8	9	10	11	12	13	14	15	16	17	18
		A	A	B	A	B	A	B	A		C		C	C	C			C	C
		a.m.	a.m.	a.m.	a.m.	a.m.	a.m.	p.m.	p.m.		p.m.		p.m.	p.m.	p.m.			p.m.	p.m.
DUBLIN (Eden Quay)	Omnibus dep.	...	...	9 0	9 40	10 20	11 20	12 20	1 20	...	3 20		5 20	6 20	7 40	...		9 0	10 0
SUTTON CROSS	„ arr.	...	...	9 30	10 10	10 50	11 50	12 50	1 50	...	3 50		5 50	6 50	8 10	...		9 30	10 30
SUTTON STATION	Tram dep.	7 40	9 0	9 43	10 15	10 50	11 50	12 50	1 50	...	3 50		6 0	6 52	8 15		...	9 39	10 35
No. 1 Loop Sutton Cr. Rd.	„ „	7 42	9 2	9 45	10 17	10 52	11 52	12 52	1 52	...	3 52		6 2	6 54	8 17		...	9 41	10 37
„ 2 „ Strand Road	„ „	7 45	9 5	9 48	10 20	10 55	11 55	12 55	1 55	...	3 55		6 5	6 57	8 20		...	9 44	10 40
„ 3 „ Howth Demesne	„ „	7 48	9 8	9 51	10 23	10 57	11 57	12 57	1 57	...	3 57		6 8	6 59	8 22		...	9 47	10 43
„ 4 „ St. Fintan's	„ „	7 51	9 11	9 54	10 26	11 0	12 0	1 0	2 0	...	4 0		6 11	7 2	8 25		...	9 50	10 46
„ 5 „ Barren Hill	„ „	7 54	9 14	9 57	10 29	11 3	12 3	1 3	2 3	...	4 3		6 14	7 5	8 28		...	9 53	10 49
„ 6 „ Baily P.O.	„ „	7 57	9 17	10 0	10 32	11 6	12 6	1 6	2 6	...	4 6		6 17	7 8	8 31		...	9 56	10 52
„ 7 „ Stella Maris	„ „	8 0	9 20	10 3	10 35	11 9	12 9	1 9	2 9	...	4 9		6 20	7 11	8 34		...	9 59	10 55
HILL OF HOWTH	„ arr.	8 3	9 23	10 6	10 37	11 12	12 12	1 12	2 12	...	4 12		6 23	7 14	8 37		...	10 2	10 58
HILL OF HOWTH	„ dep.				10 39	11 12	12 45	1 45	2 45		4 15				8 45				
No. 9 Loop Dungriffan Road	„ „				10 43	11 16	12 49	1 49	2 48		4 18				8 48				
HOWTH STATION	„ arr.				10 50	11 23	12 55	1 55	2 55		4 25				8 55				
HOWTH (East Pier)	Omnibus dep.			9 40	11 0	11 40	12 20	1 0	2 0	3 0		4 40				9 0			
DUBLIN (Eden Quay)	„ arr.			10 20	11 40	12 20	1 40	2 40	3 40		5 20				9 40				

17 The coming of war in 1914 was marked by a great increase in military traffic on the railways from garrison towns the length and breadth of the country. Here, soldiers board a train at Omagh station. (*Author's collection*)

18 Judging from the photographic evidence, the external condition of many steam locomotives in the years before 1914 was superb, as is evidenced by this view of one of the four 2-4-2 tank locos built by Beyer Peacock in 1897 for the BCDR. This was a mainly passenger railway most of whose locomotives were tank engines, ideal for short suburban runs with quick turn-arounds where a tank, as opposed to a tender engine, did not need to be turned on a turntable. (*Author's collection*)

19 Two contrasting types of BCDR tank engines are seen outside Queen's Quay station in Belfast in June 1938. In the background is No. 1, a 4-4-2T dating from 1909; closest to the camera is No. 25, one of a quartet of large 4-6-4 tanks delivered by Beyer Peacock in 1920. Handsome and purposeful machines, the only examples of this type ever to run on the Irish broad gauge, in service, they were notorious for their insatiable appetite for coal. (*H.C. Casserley*)

20 The parting gift of the LMS to its satellite in Northern Ireland was the WT class of 2-6-4 tank engines. Between 1946 and 1950, seventeen of these machines were built and such was their strength and versatility they were soon affectionately nicknamed 'the Jeeps'. No. 4, seen here at York Road in NCC livery and one of the first to be delivered, was built at Derby works in 1946. A few survivors of the class, including No. 4, which was subsequently preserved, remained on the books of Northern Ireland Railways until 1971, to become the last steam locomotives in service in these islands. (*Author's collection*)

21 This view along the Boyne viaduct on the GNR main line at Drogheda shows the structure after it had been rebuilt in the 1930s. The original viaduct had been built for double track but, with the rebuilding, the two tracks were interlaced or gauntleted. The rebuilding, which took place without traffic being interrupted, allowed heavier and more powerful locomotives to be used on the line. (*Welch Collection, Ulster Museum*)

22 A tramcar hauling a couple of trailers leaves a bustling Portrush to head for the Giant's Causeway. Before overhead electric current collection was introduced in 1899, steam tramway locomotives, their motion hidden by metal screens to protect other road users, were used to haul the trams on the final stretch through the streets of Portrush to the BNCR station. (*Author's collection*)

23 The narrowest gauge of all was that of the Lartigue monorail on the Listowel & Ballybunion in County Kerry. One of the astonishing looking twin-boilered locos is seen at Ballybunion. The section of monorail in front of the loco was a point which could switch trains from one line to another. (*Author's collection*)

24 A train on the Schull & Skibbereen Tramway which opened in 1886, one of the lines promoted with the aid of barorial guarantees, is photographed on the magnificent 12-arch viaduct at Ballydehob which took the line over the shallows of Roaringwater Bay. (*National Library of Ireland*)

25 The Irish narrow gauge provided unlikely places such as the small village of Aughnacloy in County Tyrone with the status of being the locations for railway workshops. In the works yard at Aughnacloy, three of the Clogher Valley Railway's 0-4-2 tank engines are seen resting between duties. Because the line ran mainly alongside the public road, the legislation governing such lines stipulated that the wheels and motions of the locos had to be enclosed so as not to harm or alarm other road users. (*Author's collection*)

26 There was convenient interchange for passengers between the two gauges at Ennis. In CIÉ days, a train from Limerick to Galway is about to depart, whilst the connecting West Clare service is headed by the now preserved No. 5, formerly named *Slieve Callan*. The first two carriages on the narrow gauge train are a pair of the splendid Tourist saloons built at the WCR workshops in Ennis between 1904 and 1910. (*Author's collection*)

company reported that 9,000 men were engaged on the works. The line was completed when the great bridge over the Shannon at Athlone was finished in July 1851 and trains began running between Dublin and Galway in August 1851, five months ahead of schedule.

The GSWR line to Tullamore, which opened in October 1854, was seen by the MGWR as a direct threat to its fiefdom and it did all in its power to obstruct its further progress. The MGWR attacked on two fronts. While publicly in favour of a connection between their Galway line and the GSWR branch, the Midland suggested that the junction for the two lines should not be at Athlone, which the GSWR wanted, but at Mullingar, Moate or Streamstown. These options were in fact designed to keep the GSWR away from Athlone. The other front involved the Grand Canal. This waterway, which pre-dated the Royal Canal which the MGWR now owned, had been opened from Dublin to Shannon Harbour in 1802 and followed a more southerly, east-west course than the Royal Canal. Both the Midland and the GSWR entered joint negotiations with the Grand Canal Company in 1852 with a view to buying or leasing the waterway. Before these were concluded, it emerged that the Midland had made an offer to buy the canal, which the Grand Canal Company had accepted. As the Grand Canal served districts which the GSWR perceived as its territory, the company vigorously opposed the purchase and persuaded parliament to limit the MGWR to a seven year lease on the canal. At this point in its history the MGWR operated more miles of canal than railway! The GSWR then backed a scheme called the Grand Junction Railway which planned to build a line from Tullamore to Athlone and then on to Sligo, Ballina and Westport, in other words, deep into Midland territory. Though the GJR bill was thrown out by parliament in 1854, hostilities continued. In response to the GSWR cutting its rates, the Grand Canal, now controlled by the MGWR, followed suit. As part of its battle with the GSWR, the Midland offered some fairly improbable connections such as through fares from Dublin to Limerick, greatly undercutting the GSWR rail fare, though the MGWR option meant a rail journey to Athlone and the rest of the way down the

Shannon by steamer, a trip for those with time on their hands.
They also advertised a fare from Dublin to Killarney at exactly
half that charged by the GSWR. This involved a steamer to the
north Kerry shore of the Shannon Estuary and then, presumably,
some sort of road vehicle the rest of the way—not a journey for
the faint hearted, given the probable state of the roads in Kerry at
the time.

Meanwhile the Midland had decided to press on with an
extension of its existing line from Mullingar to Longford and
Cavan. The latter route was promoted with a view to eventually
making a junction with the Ulster Railway, which had always
intended to extend towards the west and was slowly heading that
way, reaching Monaghan in May 1858. The Longford line had the
advantage of putting the MGWR in a position to repel invasion
from the south in the form of the GJR or another GSWR-backed
Trojan horse, as this line could be extended from Longford
towards Sligo. The section from Mullingar to Longford opened in
1855 and services commenced on the Cavan line, which diverged
at a place which was originally called Cavan Junction in July 1856
(from 1878 it was renamed Inny Junction). Then the Midland
finally took steps to extend the line on from Longford to Sligo.
The Sligo Extension Act of 1857 allowed the company to raise an
extra £580,000 to build the 58 mile long route. The MGWR's second
main line finally opened for traffic in December 1862.

The GSWR-sponsored Grand Junction Company, which had
slipped beneath the waves in 1854, was partly an attempt to get at
the Midland, but it also reflected a growing demand for railways
to serve County Mayo. At this point enter Lord Lucan. This multi-
talented toff had chaired a meeting at Castlebar in October 1852 to
discuss this very subject. He then took time out from his railway
activities to preside, in October 1854, over perhaps the greatest
British military disaster of the nineteenth century when he
ordered his light cavalry regiment to charge Russian gun
emplacements in the Crimea. He returned to railway promotion
in 1855 when he appeared along with John Ennis of the MGWR on
the provisional committee of the North Western Railway of
Ireland which planned to build a line to Castlebar from

Strokestown, where it would be met by an MGWR-built line from Longford. This scheme was rejected by parliament in 1856, but its successor, again with Lucan at the helm, the Great Northern & Western, was authorised in 1857 to raise £240,000 to build lines which the Midland was to work, originating in Athlone and going to Castlebar, Westport and Ballina. The line opened in stages, reaching Castlerea in 1861, Claremorris and Castlebar in 1862 and Westport in 1866. Ballina had to wait until 1873 when the branch off this line, from Manulla Junction, reached the town.

In 1857 parliament finally authorised the GSWR to complete its long-desired branch to Athlone. The Act however insisted that the GSWR line was not to cross the Shannon at Athlone, so it had to have its own station there to the east of the river. At the same time it authorised the MGWR to build its connection off the Mullingar line from Streamstown, not to Tullamore as planned, but to Clara. Peace eventually broke out between the two companies in 1860 when they agreed to allow two distinguished English railway managers to act as arbitrators in relation to their grievances against each other. The main consequence of this was that a line of demarcation was established defining their respective spheres of influence. This ran roughly across the centre of Ireland from Dublin to Athlone and down the Shannon to its estuary. The MGWR was to stay to the north of this, and the GSWR to the south and south-east, and they were prohibited from promoting lines or funding satellite companies in each other's territories. The closest equivalent to this type of deal can only be found in diplomatic relations between sovereign countries and it shows just how complex and fraught relations between companies could be at this stage in the railway age. By and large both companies stuck to the agreement throughout their independent existence. In the 1870s the agreement was cited by the GSWR as preventing them from assisting the ill-fated Parsonstown & Portumna Bridge Railway from extending its line across the Shannon at Portumna, though perhaps the GSWR directors saw which way the wind was blowing in relation to that particular disaster on rails and found the agreement of 1860 a convenient excuse. The closing act of this saga was the building of the MGWR line from Streamstown to

Clara. This had been promoted by the Midland for purely strategic purposes, designed to thwart their rival's drive to Athlone. Once arbitration had been accepted, the MGWR tried to get out of building this branch, but they were forced to go ahead with it. This now fairly pointless 8 mile long line with just the one intermediate station at Horseleap eventually opened in 1863 and quickly took on the character of a country branch line with very modest receipts to show for all the fuss there had been over its conception.

The Midland was a geographically compact system and relatively few branches off its main lines were built between 1850 and 1880. The first such line to the west of Dublin was the Dublin & Meath Railway which received royal assent in 1858 to build a line from a junction with the MGWR near Clonsilla to Navan, with a branch off this line from Kilmessan Junction to Athboy. The line, which was worked by the MGWR, opened to Navan in 1862, with the branch to Trim and Athboy following in 1864. In 1869 the line was extended to make a junction with the Dublin & Drogheda line which had reached Navan in 1850, which itself was extended to meet the D&M line at Navan Junction. In 1864 a separate company, the Navan & Kingscourt, was empowered to build a line from what became Navan Junction to Kingscourt in County Cavan. The poor state of the national economy in the late 1860s meant that finance was slow in coming forward and it was not until 1872 that the first section to Kilmainham Wood was opened, and this after three visits from the Board of Trade inspector, which says something about the state of the construction work and permanent way. Kingscourt was finally reached in 1875. The N&K, with the backing of the MGWR which also worked this line and later bought both the D&M and the N&K, planned to go further north with extensions to Carrickmacross or Castleblayney. These did not materialise in the 1870s, but their revival later in the century led to another spat of railway politics, this time involving the Midland and the Great Northern.

The next branch line encountered after Clonsilla was that to Edenderry, which left the main line at Nesbitt Junction, just west of Enfield, some 28 miles from the Dublin terminus of the MGWR at the Broadstone. This 10 mile long branch to the small market town of Edenderry, which had one intermediate station at Carbury, was opened in April 1877. The proposal to build a line to the town was floundering on the usual and fundamental difficulty which dogged so many of the schemes discussed in these pages— the raising of capital, in this case over £20,000. The impasse was resolved through the generosity of a local landowner, a Miss Nesbitt, who offered £10,000 towards the cost of the line. In grateful thanks for her largesse, the junction was named after her. Apart from the line to Cavan mentioned earlier, which was more of a secondary route rather than a branch, the only other branch line off the MGWR built in this period was not encountered until Kilfree Junction in County Sligo was reached, 112 miles from Dublin. This served the small County Roscommon town of Ballaghaderreen. The Sligo & Ballaghaderreen Junction railway was incorporated in 1863 to build a branch from the town to the Midland's Sligo line. The branch would be about 10 miles long and the MGWR engineer estimated it could be built at a cost of around £40,000. By this stage readers can probably fill in the next bit for themselves. The 1860s was not a good decade in which to raise money for railway construction, especially in the west of Ireland. The company had to return to parliament in both 1865 and 1871 to have the time allowed for construction extended. Work finally got under way in 1869, but shortly afterwards it stopped when bailiffs seized some of the company's assets at the behest of a creditor. After an unfavourable report from Colonel Hutchinson of the Board of Trade which called for much remedial work to be done before the line was safe to open to the public, services finally got under way at the end of 1874. The line was worked by the MGWR, but receipts were poor and they decided to withdraw at the end of 1875 when the line temporarily closed. With no other real options on the horizon, in March 1876 the S&BJ directors agreed to sell their line to the Midland for £24,000, and it reopened as part of the Broadstone empire.

The years between 1850 and 1880 would also see railways extended into many parts of north Leinster and Ulster. The most important element of this was the completion of the line between

Dublin and Belfast. There are two major engineering works on the former D&BJR line, the majestic eighteen-arch Craigmore viaduct near Newry, the highest on the Irish railway network, and the viaduct spanning the River Boyne at Drogheda. Trains also have to face a stiff climb in both directions to a summit at milepost 65½ near Newry, so this was not an easy line to build or operate. The first section, from a temporary terminus at Newfoundwell, just north of Drogheda, to Dundalk, opened in February 1849 and was extended to a remote temporary station at Wellington Inn, just north of the present-day border, in July 1850. With the completion of the Craigmore viaduct in 1852, trains from Newfoundwell could run through to Portadown. However, through running between Belfast and Dublin was still not possible until the Boyne viaduct at Drogheda was completed. In 1853 William Dargan was instrumental in organising and financing a great industrial exhibition in Dublin modelled on the one held in London in 1851 and in order to encourage visitors from the north to attend, a temporary timber viaduct was built over the Boyne, opening on 22 June 1853, which for the first time allowed railway passengers an uninterrupted journey between Ireland's two biggest cities. The timber viaduct was later replaced by an iron structure which opened in April 1855. Also in 1853 the branch to Navan, originally promoted by the D&BJR but now in the hands of the D&D, was extended to Kells, 26 miles from Drogheda. A further 13 miles were added to this branch in 1863 when Oldcastle was reached.

At Dundalk the first section of the Dundalk & Enniskillen Railway as far as Castleblayney opened with the commencement of D&BJR services in 1849. Thereafter progress was slow and several return visits to parliament were required to renew its powers. Ballybay was reached in 1854, Newbliss in 1855, Clones in 1858 and finally Enniskillen in 1859. One branch 8 miles long was built at this time from Shantonagh Junction to Cootehill, which opened in 1860. The original intention had been to extend this to Cavan, but the finances of the D&E were not up to this. At Enniskillen the D&E made a junction with the Londonderry & Enniskillen which had reached the county town of Fermanagh in

1854. Like so many Irish lines, the L&E struggled to raise the capital to build its line, taking seven years to construct about 60 route miles of track. When the line reached the small County Tyrone village of Fintona in 1853, construction stopped for about a year while the company gathered its breath. When work resumed the following year, it was decided to carry on towards Enniskillen from a point about a mile from the village, leaving it on the end of a very short branch. To work the line economically, from what became Fintona Junction to the village, the company was permitted to use horse traction, and from then until the closure of the line in 1957 the branch was the preserve of the Fintona horse tram whose motive power was a series of geldings, all of which are believed to have carried the name, Dick. Shortly after the line opened, a special train from Derry to Enniskillen carrying supporters of the loyal order, the Apprentice Boys of Derry, was maliciously derailed near Trillick when it ran into large stones prised off the parapet of a nearby bridge. An engine driver was killed, but despite the offer of a reward, no one was indicted for the crime. Occasionally when looking at the history of Ireland's railways, the wider divisions of Irish society impose themselves on the story, as in this instance. There were just two lines branching off the L&E line. The first of these was the Finn Valley Railway from Strabane to Stranorlar which opened in 1863, of which much more will be heard in Chapter 5. The other was a line 35 miles long from Bundoran Junction, about 8 miles north of Enniskillen, to the seaside town on the Atlantic coast at the southern tip of County Donegal. This line was built by an independent company, the Enniskillen, Bundoran & Sligo. Its name reflected its intention to extend the railway through easy country the 20 or so miles to Sligo. The extension, authorised in 1862, was never built and is one of the great might-have-beens of Irish railway history, for it would have completed in time a railway down the whole west coast from Derry to Limerick. When one reflects on some of the very marginal lines which were built at great expense in other parts of the country, the absence of this link is all the more inexplicable.

One interesting new company which emerged in this part of

the world in the 1870s was the Sligo, Leitrim & Northern Counties
Railway. The purpose of the line was to link Enniskillen and Sligo
via Manorhamilton and in the process bring the railway to a poor
and remote part of north Leitrim. Local landowners were the
main backers for the line which was authorised in 1875 with a
share capital of £200,000 and additional powers to borrow up to
£100,000. It was to be 42 miles in length with running powers
from its junction with the MGWR at Carrignagat a further 5 miles
into Sligo. The line opened in 1879 from Enniskillen to Belcoo on
the Leitrim/Fermanagh border and reached Manorhamilton in
1880. Problems raising the capital led to a return to parliament in
1880 for additional time to build the line and powers to raise more
capital to complete the works, the borrowing powers in the
original Act having been used to obtain a loan of £100,000 from
the Board of Works. SLNCR trains began running through to Sligo
in 1882, but as evidence of the company's impoverished state, all
its rolling stock was hired from one of its shareholders. Such were
the company's debts, it was put into receivership in 1890 and the
Board of Works threatened to sell it to the two companies whose
lines it linked. Despite this it managed to retain its independence
and, as we shall see later, was to become one of the last
independent railway companies operating in these islands.

Having achieved its first objective in 1848 with the opening of
its line to Armagh, the Ulster Railway began to follow the plan set
out in its original prospectus of 1835 to head west. The first
extension was to Monaghan, opened in May 1858, and the UR
main line reached Clones in 1863, where it made a junction with
the D&E. To continue the line to Cavan, the Clones & Cavan
Extension Railway had been established under the wing of the
D&E. However the UR, D&BJR and the D&D between them
contributed £70,000 to the cost of this 15 mile line. At Cavan this
line made a junction with the MGWR, which had reached the town
from the south, in 1856. The UR was also behind the building of a
line from Portadown to Dungannon and Omagh, which opened
to Dungannon in 1858 and through to Omagh in 1861. There was
only one branch off this line, that from Dungannon to
Cookstown which opened in 1879. At Omagh this line made a

junction with the L&E line from Derry and provided a second through route between Belfast and Londonderry. The Portadown, Dungannon & Omagh Railway, nominally independent, was strongly backed by the UR who took a lease of the line for a term of 999 years in 1861. Sadly the line was only to see out 104 years of this term, another victim of that serial killer of railways, the Ulster Transport Authority, which closed the line in February 1965. As an Omagh man, over forty years on I am still clearly bitter about this.

Going back to the Dublin to Belfast main line, when we last discussed the affairs of the Newry & Enniskillen Railway, it had taken the company eight years to scrape up enough funds to build the 4 miles from Newry to a junction with the D&BJR at Goraghwood. It had planned to reach Enniskillen via Armagh and Clones. Apart from this being a roundabout route over difficult terrain, the section from Enniskillen to Clones was to be made jointly with the D&E. The delays in getting even as far as Goraghwood left the company in a state of crisis. The powers for the Enniskillen part of its route lapsed and this was eventually built by the D&E. Therefore in 1857 the company changed its name to the Newry & Armagh and embarked on an 18 mile extension to join the UR there. The line was marked by steep banks, one of which was to help change the course of railway history in 1889, and also required two tunnels. Lisummon tunnel, between Goraghwood and Markethill, at 1,759 yards, was the longest railway tunnel in all of Ireland. The long drawn out saga of the N&E/N&A finally reached some sort of conclusion when the line to Armagh opened in 1864.

Newry now had connections to both Armagh and, dating back to 1849, to Warrenpoint. In the 1870s a further railway, in some ways one of the most singular ever to operate in Ireland, also reached the town. This was the Dundalk, Newry & Greenore which had two lines, one from Dundalk to the port of Greenore which opened in 1873, and the line from Greenore to Newry which followed in 1877. The DN&G was a child of the English railway company which liked to style itself the 'Premier Line', the London & North Western Railway. From its headquarters at Euston station in London, LNWR trains served many of the major

towns and cities in the midlands and north-west of England as far
north as Carlisle, including Birmingham and Manchester and
through its satellite company, the Chester & Holyhead Railway,
north Wales, Holyhead and the most direct route to Ireland. In
the light of subsequent political developments it is easy to forget
that in the nineteenth century Dublin was the second city in the
British Empire and just how important, extensive and lucrative
the traffic across the Irish Sea was. The main English railway
companies which served the west coast, including the Midland
and the Great Western, strove to get a share of this traffic which
was dominated by the LNWR with its Holyhead route. Interested
parties on both sides of the Irish Sea, including the Dundalk &
Enniskillen and the LNWR, began to focus on Greenore on
Carlingford Lough as a possible site which could be developed as
a port which would need railway links north to Newry and also to
Dundalk. Separate companies were set up to build the two lines,
but these were amalgamated before the Act authorising the DN&G
Company was passed in 1863. As the Irish partner in the scheme
was in some financial difficulty at the time, the cost of building
and equipping the railway and developing the harbour fell to the
LNWR. What resulted was a 5 ft 3 in. gauge version of the LNWR on
Irish soil. The original locomotives and carriages, some of which
survived until after the closure of both lines in 1952, were of LNWR
designs and carried LNWR livery long after that company had lost
its identity across the water in 1923. Everything from signals to
signage followed the same pattern. The company opened a hotel
and a golf course at Greenore and there were hopes that it could
be developed as a holiday destination as well as a port. Steamer
services from Greenore to Holyhead began in 1870 and when the
line to Newry was open, boat trains could run through from
Belfast to connect with these. Despite all of this, Greenore never
came close to usurping the established routes such as Holyhead to
Dublin or Belfast to Fleetwood, which were also shorter and more
convenient.

There had been frenzied speculation in the late 1840s centred
on railways running through County Down to make a connection
with the D&BJR. The UR had generally opposed these as it suited

it well for the connection to Dublin to branch off its main line at Portadown, which meant that Dublin traffic would spend more time on its metals, a fact which would be reflected in its receipts. However, once the main line was opened, railways began to reach into the south and west of the county. The first of these was a short local line, the Banbridge Junction Railway, which opened a branch 7 miles long in 1859 from the D&BJR at Scarva to Banbridge. This line was worked and leased by the Junction company. Banbridge got a connection to the north in 1863 with the opening of the Banbridge, Lisburn & Belfast Railway. Backed by the UR, this line left the main line at Knockmore Junction just west of Lisburn. It was extended 10 miles south of Banbridge to Ballyroney in 1880. Knockmore became a three-way junction in 1871 when another UR satellite, the Dublin & Antrim Junction Railway, opened an 18 mile line which ended at a bay platform at the Belfast & Northern Counties station at Antrim providing a useful link between the two systems. Both of these lines were worked by the UR.

The next major developments were institutional rather than involving the laying of track. In 1860 the D&E leased the L&E, and to reflect the fact that its activities now went far beyond the towns in its title, changed its name in 1862 to the Irish North Western Railway. In addition to the Dundalk to Derry line, the INWR worked the FVR in Country Donegal, the line to Bundoran and that from Clones to Cavan. However, it was far from prosperous and made an operating loss in 1874. An amalgamation of the D&D and the D&BJR had been authorised in 1847 but had never taken place. It was anomalous that the Belfast to Dublin line was worked by three separate companies. Discussions took place between these companies and the UR in 1868, but the UR was doing very nicely on its own and was reluctant to get involved with its less affluent southern neighbours. The issue was revived in the early 1870s and finally in 1875 the D&D and the D&BJR merged to form the Northern Railway. The increasingly financially challenged INWR amalgamated with the NR on 1 January 1876, INWR ordinary shareholders losing five-sixths of the value of their shares in the transaction. The UR now felt it had to get involved with the amalgamations. At its final half-yearly meeting in February 1876, it declared a dividend of 7½ per cent, providing a rare note of financial success from an Irish railway company in an era which had so often produced a catalogue of fiscal disasters. An extraordinary general meeting followed at which approval was given for the UR to become part of a new company which was to be for many, in the seven decades ahead of it, quite simply the most enterprising and progressive railway operator in Ireland, the Great Northern Railway. The amalgamation took effect on 1 April 1876 and to induce the UR to participate, each £100 of UR shares was exchanged for stock worth £124. 10s. in the new company. The Newry & Armagh shortly afterwards also joined the club and became part of the GNR in 1879, though inevitably those unfortunate enough to have invested in it did a lot less well than the UR shareholders.

What turned out to be one of the most useful stretches of railway in the whole of Ulster was built by a company which was a failure both in financial terms and because it did not achieve one of its major objectives. This was the Belfast Central Railway authorised by an Act of 1864 to build a line linking the three existing termini in the city and a central station to be used by all three companies. The site proposed for this station was near High Street. The BCR ran from a junction with the UR, just outside Great Victoria Street station, to the Albert Bridge and across the River Lagan to join the BCDR at Ballymacarrett Junction, a short distance out from Queen's Quay station. Construction began in 1865, but with the economic crisis of the 1860s it was difficult to raise the capital. Eventually in 1878 a passenger service began from the junction with what was now the GNR to a station at Oxford Street beside the Queen's Bridge. The line was eventually extended through a short tunnel under the western end of the bridge to reach Donegall Quay, where tenuous contact with the BNCR was made over dockside tramways owned by Belfast Harbour Commissioners. The BCR had a final fling of the dice in an Act of 1880 which proposed a series of 3 ft gauge steam tramways to various parts of the expanding city such as the Falls, the Shankill and Ligoniel and also into east Belfast, none of which were ever built. It was the misfortune of the BCR to commence its passenger service just as the first horse-powered street tramways were opening in the city. The company was sold to the GNR in 1885 who promptly stopped the passenger service, but for the next eighty years the BCR was a vital link for goods tranfers between the Belfast railways, and passenger excursions were run from the former GNR system to Bangor up to the closure of the line in 1965. By this time the Lagan viaduct was known as the 'shaky bridge', and only the lightest ex-GNR locomotives were allowed across it.

By 1850 the Belfast & County Down Railway's trains were running to Holywood and Comber, the latter the first part of its planned main line to the old episcopal town of Downpatrick where the body of Ireland's patron saint was alleged to be buried. A branch from Comber to Newtownards was also opened in 1850, but the line did not reach Downpatrick until 1859. From Ballynahinch Junction, on the way to Downpatrick, a short branch 3½ miles long served Ballynahinch. The BCDR rather lost its way in the middle of the nineteenth century and became seduced by an Admiralty-sponsored scheme to establish a short sea passage from Ireland to Scotland. On the Irish side the facilities at Donaghadee and Bangor were candidates for development with Portpatrick in Galloway, the port favoured on the Scottish side. In 1858 the Admiralty chose Donaghadee and the BCDR quickly extended the line from Newtownards there in 1861. However, across the Irish Sea, Portpatrick proved to be a disappointment as a port and after only two years the steamers to the north of Ireland were transferred to Stranraer, which is still used to this day. By this time the BCDR was in a parlous financial state and only a government loan of £160,000 kept the wolf from the door. With all its focus on Donaghadee, the company had lost sight of a much more promising extension, that of the existing Holywood line to the growing town of Bangor. In 1860 a separate company, the Belfast, Holywood & Bangor Railway, was incorporated to build this line which opened in 1865. The BCDR leased the Holywood line to the Bangor company in 1865 and turned its focus back to extending the main line to the seaside resort of Newcastle, which was reached in 1869.

The final major company to be considered in this survey is the Belfast & Northern Counties Railway which had a virtual monopoly of rail services in the counties of Antrim and Londonderry. The BNCR was the name adopted in 1860 by the Belfast & Ballymena Railway, which had been incorporated in 1845 and was, by 1848, operating services from its Belfast terminus at York Road to Carrickfergus, Ballymena and Randalstown. The branch to Randalstown was extended by the B&B to Cookstown in County Tyrone in 1856. Trains to Ballymena had to reverse to continue the journey north at Greenisland on the Carrickfergus line. The reason for this was concern that the locomotives of this early period would be unable to cope with the severe gradients if a more direct route had been followed. At what was to become the other end of the BNCR system, the Londonderry & Coleraine Railway was floated in 1845, but construction of this line did not begin until the 1850s. A line from Londonderry reached Limavady in 1852 and was completed from what became Limavady Junction to Coleraine in 1853, leaving Limavady on the end of a 3 mile long branch from the main line. The gap between Coleraine and Ballymena was filled by a company with one of the most long-winded names in the whole of Irish railway history, the Ballymena, Ballymoney, Coleraine & Portrush Junction Railway. Incorporated in 1853, the line to Portrush was built quickly, with traffic operating over the whole 34 miles by December 1855. Through running from Belfast to Londonderry was still not possible as the L&C station at Coleraine was on the west bank of the River Bann and that of the BBC&PJ was on the other. The river was not bridged by the railway until 1860.

Having assumed its new identity in 1860, the BNCR began to take the other railways in its area under its wing. The BBC&PJ was acquired in 1861, and in the same year the company leased the L&C, taking it over ten years later in 1871. An Act of Parliament in May 1860 authorised the Carrickfergus & Larne Railway to build a line the 14 miles from Carrick to Larne Harbour. This was a separate company, but the line was worked by the BNCR from its opening in October 1862 and it was eventually absorbed by the BNCR in 1890. The line to Larne Harbour profited from the traffic generated by the transfer of the steamer services from Portpatrick to Stranraer in the year the line opened. The final addition to the BNCR system in this period was also built by an independent company, the Derry Central Railway. This line diverged from the BNCR Cookstown branch at Magherafelt and ran for 29 miles through a largely rural district with no major towns, roughly parallel to but to the west of the River Bann, to meet the BNCR main line at Macfin Junction 3 miles from Coleraine. The Derry Central opened throughout in February 1880. From the commencement of services the line was worked by the BNCR and was later acquired by the company in 1895.

At the start of the 1850s there were about 800 miles of railway open in Ireland. By 1880 this had risen to around 2,400 route miles of standard gauge track. Railways now served virtually all the country's major towns and cities and also penetrated many rural districts. However, as we have seen, a large number of companies had needed substantial loans from the Treasury to complete their lines. Even a company such as the Belfast & County Down, which had originally been profitable, was in need of such assistance to keep afloat in the 1860s. Despite this and the fact that investment in many Irish railway schemes had proved to be far from profitable, there was still a large number of route miles to be built before the national network was to reach its greatest extent. How this came about is the subject of the next two chapters.

Chapter 5

THE RISE AND FALL OF
NARROW GAUGE

A s we saw in the previous chapter, the Irish railway network expanded steadily from the 1850s through to the start of the 1870s, by which time a total of just over 2,000 miles of 5 ft 3 in. gauge tracks were operating throughout the country. By 1880 almost all the major towns and cities had a railway station. There were however large areas of the country which had no railways at all. The most obvious gaps in the geographical coverage were down the west coast. Apart from short broad gauge lines from Derry to Buncrana, Strabane to Stranorlar and the stretch of the former Londonderry & Enniskillen (by now GNR) line which ran along the edge of the county between Strabane and Derry, there were no railways at all in County Donegal. The MGWR reached Sligo in 1863, Westport in 1866 and Ballina in 1873, but these were the only lines in the counties of Sligo and Mayo. There was no line to the west of Galway city, and in County Clare only the Limerick to Athenry line had been built. In County Kerry, Tralee had been reached by a line from Mallow in 1859 and in 1880 by the straggling North Kerry line which started from Limerick, but apart from these lines, and the short Castleisland branch, there were no other railways in the county. In west Cork the railway reached Skibbereen in 1873 but went no further until the 1890s.

The reasons why there were such large tracts of the country without railways are not hard to fathom. Railways were capital intensive businesses and the money to build them had to be raised by selling shares with the promise of dividends from the profits which accrued once the line was opened for traffic. While the government through the Board of Works had been providing loans to help railway construction since the 1830s, these were commercial transactions on which interest had to be paid and the loans ultimately had to be paid off by the recipients. Put yourself in the place of a nineteenth-century investor with money to put into railway schemes. You have the choice of buying shares in a line in a populous part of Britain, perhaps with coalfields or other mineral deposits which the line could tap, and a railway in a remote part of Ireland where the population had been on the decline since the 1850s and with no apparent mineral wealth. The answer to this rhetorical question is very obvious: the Irish scheme would clearly not look an attractive proposition and could struggle to raise capital on the commercial markets.

Arguably, the Irish railway network by 1880 was probably as big as it could get if its expansion was to be financed solely by conventional methods of raising capital. To fill in the gaps in the national network, two questions had to be addressed. One was of course how do you find a way of raising the money to build additional lines in unpromising parts of the country, from the point of view of their potential to generate traffic and thus profit? Allied to this was a desire to explore whether less expensive types of railways could be constructed, which could cope with the more modest levels of traffic which might be expected in areas to which the commercial market had failed to date to deliver any railways. Positive answers to these questions helped to fuel a minor railway mania (pun intended) in the 1880s which provided many parts of Ireland with a new network of lines, all different and individualistic. The only things they had in common was a gauge of 3 ft and a reliance on what were effectively subsidies from the ratepayers in the districts they served to begin with and, latterly, towards the end of this phase of railway expansion, outright grants from the government. National politics, local rivalries, great expectations and monumental incompetence all played their part in the fascinating story of the rise and ultimate decline of the Irish narrow gauge, the subject of this part of our narrative.

No one involved in the debate which surrounded the choice of gauge for the national network in the 1840s (*see* Chapter 3) had argued that there was any benefit from having other than one gauge for the whole country. Yet in the 1880s a whole batch of 3 ft gauge lines was promoted, most of which would make a connection into existing standard gauge lines with all the inevitable disruption caused by the need for both goods and passengers to be trans-shipped from one gauge to the other at junctions between the two. Furthermore, initially at least, the narrow gauge was being advanced with indirect official encouragement. The reason for this volte-face was purely economic. Narrow gauge lines were cheaper to construct and operate and it was felt that the benefits which sprang from having a railway in a district, where previously there was none, far outweighed any disadvantages caused by the break of gauge, such was the perception in the late nineteenth century of the economic boons which a railway of any sort would bring to the area it served.

The first narrow gauge railways were almost as old as the railway age itself. The acknowledged pioneer was the Festiniog Railway which was authorised by parliament in 1832 to build a line with a gauge of 1 ft 11½ in. from Portmadoc on the coast of Tremadoc Bay in north Wales to Blaenau Festiniog. There was a strong Irish connection with this line in the person of Henry Archer, a wealthy Dubliner who lived in this part of north Wales. He became in effect the line's managing director, also buying shares in the company to the value of £8,000. Indeed most of the shares were taken by investors in Dublin, and reflecting the heavy Irish financial involvement in the company, its registered office was at No. 41 Dame Street in the city. It is odd in some ways that, given the endemic difficulties in raising capital which dogged so many railway schemes promoted in Ireland throughout the nineteenth century, an early line such as the Festiniog in a remote part of north Wales was built largely with Irish capital. The purpose of the line was to bring slate from quarries at Blaenau down to the coast for shipping to meet the seemingly never ending demand for slate to roof the rapidly expanding towns and cities of Victorian Britain. The FR was uphill all the way to Blaenau, which was fortunately the direction of travel for the empty wagons which were hauled by horses. The animals then hitched a ride back to Portmadoc in special wagons coupled to the loaded slate trains which ran by gravity. This method of working was carried on from the line's opening in 1836 until 1863 when steam locomotives were used for the first time. Steam-operated narrow gauge lines were being built by the 1860s in parts of the British Empire such as New Zealand and Queensland in Australia and significantly, as far as Ireland was concerned, much closer to home on the Isle of Man, where the first part of the island's extensive 3 ft gauge system, a line from Douglas to Peel, opened in July 1873. The year before, Ireland's first 3 ft gauge line had quietly opened for business. I say quietly because, as it ran on private land and did not infringe the property rights of others, it required no Act of Parliament. With hindsight, its brief career was not an auspicious beginning for this new chapter in Irish railway history.

The line was built by the Glenariff Iron Ore & Harbour Company to exploit deposits of iron ore found at the head of Glenariff in County Antrim and bring them down to a pier which was constructed near Waterfoot. To this day a few remnants of the pier and the remains of the White Arch, which carried the line over the Antrim coast road and down to the pier, stand in silent testimony to this ill-starred venture. The line was about 4½ miles long and was worked by two four coupled steam engines built by Robert Stephenson & Company, Ireland's first 3 ft gauge locomotives. If the company had spent more time doing thorough geological surveys and less building its railway it might have fared better, for the extensive iron ore deposits which the line was supposed to exploit proved to be illusory. Within three years of the railway opening, all the high grade ore had been extracted and both the mines and the railway were forced to close. The engines and the railway lingered on until 1885 when the Earl of Antrim, on whose lands the whole operation had been conducted, obtained a judgment against the company for monies owed to him, and the assets of the company, including the engines, were sold to meet this liability.

While the sheep in Glenariff were being frightened out of their diminutive wits by the sight and sounds of steam locomotives and long before the high hopes of the GIO&HC were to be dashed by geological mishaps, Ireland's second narrow gauge railway to be authorised by an Act of Parliament and the first to actually be built, was being promoted in the same area and with the same intent as the Glenariff line. The Ballymena, Cushendall & Red Bay Railway obtained its Act in July 1872. There was a growing demand at this time for iron ore from the industrial centres across the Irish Sea in the west of Scotland and in what is now Cumbria, and there was ore in the Antrim Glens north-east of Ballymena. The BC&RB was built to bring this ore down to Ballymena for onward transport through the ports of Belfast or Larne. The company's Act stipulated a gauge of between 2 ft and 3 ft. There is no surviving document which explains why the 3 ft gauge was adopted, but there is plenty of circumstantial evidence linking the Red Bay line to the use of this gauge on the Isle of Man and indeed to that pioneering narrow gauge line, the Festiniog Railway in north Wales. The engineer of the Isle of Man Railways, Henry Vignoles, had visited the Festiniog Railway before the first Manx line was constructed. There he met Charles Easton Spooner, the Festiniog general manager, an enthusiastic advocate of the narrow gauge who had been responsible for the introduction of steam traction on the Welsh line in 1863. Henry Vignoles was the son of Charles Blacker Vignoles, whom we encountered earlier as the engineer of the Dublin & Kingstown and Waterford & Limerick Railways. It was Henry Vignoles who advocated the use of the 3 ft gauge on the Isle of Man and given its close proximity to Ireland and the links provided by coastal shipping, it is inconceivable that the directors of the GIO&HC and the BC&RB were not influenced by the decision to use the 3 ft gauge there. Further circumstantial evidence is found in the locomotive fleet of Antrim's second 3 ft gauge line, the Ballymena & Larne Railway which opened in 1878. The B&L acquired several 2-4-0 tank engines from Beyer Peacock in Manchester which were virtually identical to locomotives provided by the same builder for the Isle of Man Railways from 1873 onwards, some of which are still active on the island to this day.

The BC&RB had problems raising the capital to build its line, a recurring theme in Irish railway history, and it was not until 1875 that it opened for traffic as far as Cargan, 11 miles from Ballymena. It was extended to Parkmore (13½ miles) and Retreat (16½ miles) in the course of the following year. The line climbed virtually all the way from Ballymena and reached the highest point on any Irish railway at Essathohan siding, 1,045 ft above sea level. The other problem which the BC&RB had was geographical. Its terminus at Retreat, while affording fine views of both Cushendall and Red Bay, was about 1,000 ft above sea level and it was impossible to find a way to bring the railway down Glenballyemon on gradients that were other than suicidal to reach the agreeable village of Cushendall at the bottom of the glen. Plans to make a connection from Parkmore to the abandoned Glenariff line which did reach, all too briefly, the shores of Red Bay, came to naught. The BC&RB was probably unique in that it managed to serve only one of the three places mentioned in its title. Various tramways met the line bringing iron ore down from the mines and quarries along Glen Ravel. At first the BC&RD carried huge tonnages of iron ore: in 1880/81 an average of 100,000 tons were transported along the line. The iron ore was initially transferred to broad gauge wagons at Ballymena for onward transit along the B&NCR line to Belfast, but with the opening of Antrim's third 3 ft gauge line, the ore was diverted to the port of Larne.

The Ballymena & Larne Railway Company was authorised in August 1874 to build a 24 mile long line linking the two towns in its title which this time was accomplished, though at first its Ballymena terminus was at Harryville on the outskirts of the town. The line was extended in 1880 to the town's broad gauge station, where it also made an end-on junction with the BC&RD. There was also a short branch from what was called at first Ballyclare Junction (from 1889 it was renamed Ballyboley Junction) to Ballyclare. This branch was extended to Doagh in

1884. The share capital of the B&L was £136,000 with additional powers to raise up to £45,000 in loans. The first part of the line, from Larne to Ballyclare, opened for goods traffic in September 1877 with passenger traffic commencing in August of the following year. It took several visits before the Board of Trade's inspector, Colonel Rich, was prepared to allow the company to open the rest of the line from the junction to Harryville. The B&L was a steeply graded line. From sea level at Larne Harbour it climbed 12 miles to a summit of 660 ft at Ballynashee on gradients as stiff as 1 in 36. Sadly for both the BC&RB and the B&L, the boom in iron ore was short lived. A trade depression in the mid-1880s greatly reduced the demand for Antrim ores and by the time the economic tide had turned, cheaper and richer ores were being imported from Spain. The BC&RD was forced to agree to a takeover by its broad gauge neighbour, the Belfast & Northern Counties Railway, in 1884 and the B&L followed suit in 1889. While the B&L had carried passengers from the outset, the independent BC&RD had been a goods only line. From 1886 the BNCR began to operate passenger services in stages along the former BC&RD line. These reached Parkmore in August 1888 but went no further. The final section of the line from Parkmore to the terminus at Retreat Castle was only ever served by goods and mineral trains.

A further 3 ft gauge line opened in County Antrim in 1880 to complete the mini narrow gauge boom in this north-eastern county. The Ballycastle Railway was authorised in 1875 to build a 16 mile line from a junction with the BNCR at Ballymoney to its terminus in the seaside town on the north coast which had seen some of the first documented railway activity in Ireland way back in the 1740s (see Chapter 1). Not all the company's £90,000 capital was taken up when the line was promoted and this meant that the BR had to take out loans to complete the works. The lack of funds meant that the line was built as cheaply as possible using very light track to save money. The cost of replacing this after a few years of traffic was a severe imposition on the BR's limited resources. The interest payments on the loans was another burden on the company's finances and meant that even in the years before the Great War when the railways had a virtual monopoly of the traffic on offer, the line failed to prosper. It almost became the first 3 ft gauge line in Ireland to close down when in March 1924 the directors suspended the service. It was rescued by what was probably the biggest railway company in the world at the time, the London Midland & Scottish Railway, formed at the grouping of Britain's railways the previous year and now the owner of the BNCR. Services resumed in August 1924 in time for the famous Auld Lamass Fair, which to this day still attracts enormous crowds to Ballycastle. In the end the Ballycastle line was the last of the Antrim lines to run passenger trains, these lasting until July 1950 when it was closed by the Ulster Transport Authority. This is the second reference in these pages to the UTA, though sadly it will not be the last, an organisation whose conduct and reputation is still so reviled by those who love the railways of Ireland that by comparison the onslaught of the Mongol horde on the lands it conquered seems benign. Suffice to say at this point that the busmen of the UTA closed the Ballycastle line the month before the Auld Lamass Fair of 1950, just in case anyone wanted to use the train to visit this great event in the town's year.

The Antrim narrow gauge lines were unique in Ireland in that they were promoted and financed in the time-honoured way, with authorisation by an Act of Parliament and their capital being raised in the commercial market through the sale of shares. The BC&RD and to a lesser extent the B&L were also unusual in that they were originally associated with the transport of mineral traffic in the form of iron ore from the glens. In the few other parts of the British Isles where narrow gauge lines were promoted, notably in north Wales, there was often a mineral flow such as slate underwriting the operating costs of the line. The Antrim lines came on the scene before other factors conspired to give the promotion of narrow gauge lines in Ireland an enormous boost, and the case of the BR was an object lesson in how difficult it was to finance and operate profitably a small line in a remote part of the country. As these pioneering schemes were opened before the bulk of the lines described in this chapter, let us follow their history through to the end of their existence before considering the narrow gauge companies which followed them on to the scene. The fate of the BR at the hands of the UTA has been recounted above, but what of the lines centred on Ballymena?

With the trade in iron ore in decline within a few years of the lines opening, under the ownership of the B&NCR, the erstwhile BC&RD and the B&L lines became normal minor routes serving the communities through which they passed. In order to stimulate traffic on the Parkmore line, the B&NCR began to promote the line to tourists. The company rented part of Glenariff, which was close to Parkmore station, and turned it into what might be described as a nineteenth-century equivalent of one of today's theme parks. Instead of erecting roller coasters, in 1889 the B&NCR engineer Berkeley Deane Wise laid out a series of rustic paths and bridges through the glen. A tea room was built; there was even a dark room which could be used by photographers. Visitors were met at Parkmore by a variety of cars and charabancs which took them to Glenariff or on tours of scenic parts of the glens, of which there are many. Some of these trips would have covered part of the Antrim coast road which was not far away. While the line continued to carry some iron ore traffic, though only a shadow of the amounts conveyed in those hectic years following its opening, without the tourist traffic the modest transport needs of villages such as Rathkenny, Cargan and Martinstown would hardly have justified keeping the line open. In the years following the Great War the tourist traffic fell away. During the time of the troubles, on 25 March 1921 the railway buildings at Cargan, Parkmore and Retreat were destroyed by fire. Passenger and goods services lingered on for a few more years, but the last passenger train to Parkmore ran on 1 October 1930, and in April 1937 the section from Rathkenny to Retreat was closed completely. Goods trains continued to serve a creamery at Rathkenny up to June 1940. With the end of this traffic, the whole of the former BC&RD was closed for good. Today, from the road between Ballymena and Cushendall, a surprising amount of the trackbed, abandoned in the 1930s, can still be seen, especially north of Cargan. Parkmore station itself, rebuilt in sturdy concrete following its destruction in 1921 and with its brick-built water tower still in place, is remarkably well preserved, hidden from the road by a belt of conifers. Even its concrete nameboard is still in place nearly eighty years after it saw its last passenger train. In recent times the elaborate paths and bridges close to the waterfalls in Glenariff, which had fallen into disuse once the railway company lost interest in the place, have been carefully restored and visitors can once again experience this truly spectacular and beautiful glen in the way that their forebears would have done, though of course in the twenty-first century the car park is full and the sight and sound of a narrow gauge engine working hard on the long haul up to Parkmore is something we can only imagine.

Unlike the Parkmore line, the B&L route had carried passengers from the outset. It served a more densely populated part of the county, terminated at a major port and boasted boat trains to connect with the steamers to Scotland from Larne. Passenger numbers declined as road transport took off in Ireland in the years following the First World War, and in 1930, at the same time as passenger services ended on the former BC&RB line, they were also withdrawn between Ballyclare and Doagh. However, in 1928 the LMS, which had managed the line since 1923, provided a new set of coaches for the Ballymena to Larne boat trains. These were by far the most elaborate vehicles ever to run on the Irish 3 ft gauge and they brought contemporary main line standards of comfort and even luxury in the form of electric lighting, steam heating, corridor connections and lavatories. The boat trains ran non-stop and covered the 25 miles or so between Ballymena and Larne in an hour. However, the new carriages only ran until 1933 when, during the course of a bitter railway strike in Northern Ireland provoked as management tried to impose pay cuts on railway workers, it was announced that passenger services between Ballymena and Larne and Ballyboley Junction and Ballyclare were to be abandoned. At the same time the section from Ballyclare to Doagh was closed completely. Goods services on the main line continued to run until 1940 and up to 1950 between Larne and Ballyclare to serve a paper mill located there. Final closure occurred on the same day as the Ballycastle line, bringing an end to these pioneering 3 ft gauge lines in County Antrim.

Though they were pioneers, the Antrim lines were not typical of the rest of the 3 ft gauge lines in Ireland which owed their existence to a different set of circumstances. Before exploring the reasons for this, there was another line, fortuitously for the continuity of this narrative, located in the neighbouring county of Londonderry, which can be seen as acting as a bridge between the two. The story of the Portstewart Tramway can be told very briefly. When the railway was extended from Coleraine to Portrush in 1855, the local landowner refused to allow it to go anywhere near the little coastal village of Portstewart. The result was that while Portrush prospered, even boomed, one of a string of seaside resorts dotted around Ireland's coasts created by the arrival of the railway, Portstewart lagged behind, a mile and a half from a distant station supposed to serve the town. Several abortive attempts were made to promote a branch or a tramway from the main line to Portstewart. Then in 1875 the government passed a Tramways Act, one of several legislative attempts to ease the promotion of minor lines such as this. The Act allowed the use of steam traction on tramways and also introduced procedures whereby promoters of local lines in Ireland could bypass the complex and costly business of getting an Act of Parliament and instead obtain authorisation to build their line by applying to the Lord Lieutenant of Ireland for an Order in Council. The latter is precisely what the Portstewart Tramway Company did. They were granted an Order in Council in 1880 and opened their 1 mile 62 chains long 3 ft gauge line in June 1882. The track ran along the side of the road most of the way from the town to the station. Steam tram engines, their motion cloaked in metal skirts, hauled one or two tramcars and perhaps a van for goods and parcels to and from the station to connect with main line trains.

The line was one of the least successful ever to run in Ireland. It was in receivership by 1892 and was rescued by the B&NCR, to whom it was of value as a feeder service to their broad gauge trains. By 1925 the track was in poor order and even at that date it must have seemed to its new owners (since 1923), the LMS, that a short length of steam tramway such as this was a bit of an anachronism. Even though the LMS had saved the Ballycastle line the previous year, there was no attempt to rescue or modernise the Portstewart tramway and for the first time, the first of many, many times in the history of Irish railways since that date, the train service was replaced by a bus from 1 February 1926. The significance of the Portstewart Tramway is that for the first time the effect of government legislation helped to make possible the construction of a minor Irish railway. While the Tramways Act of 1875 had a limited effect beyond this line, a later Act which followed in 1883 changed matters radically and was responsible for creating the bulk of Ireland's narrow gauge network. But before exploring that Act and its effects, the legislation needs to be seen in the context of the politics of the time.

In the relative prosperity of the first decade of the twenty-first century, it is difficult for us to imagine the bleak and devastated condition of most of Ireland in the decades following the Great Famine. This is not the place to provide a social and economic history of the country in those years, but a few telling statistics will set the scene. The census of 1841 recorded that the population of Ireland was just over 8 million. Had the existing rate of growth continued, in 1851 the population would have been around 9 million. In fact it was just over 6½ million. It was calculated that the immediate effects of the Great Famine through starvation, disease and emigration, had reduced the population of Ireland by around one million in the space of a few years, and this was not the end of this demographic and economic catastrophe. By 1881 the population had fallen to just over 5 million and while the population of what became Northern Ireland had begun to show a small increase by the end of the 1930s, that of the Free State/Irish Republic continued to decline until the mid-1960s. Emigration became the only option for millions. The Irish left their homeland and spread across the world in a biblical-like diaspora. In the 1850s over 900,000 people emigrated to the United States alone. Not far short of another million crossed the Atlantic between 1861 and 1880, and there was another spike in the figures in the 1880s when over 650,000 emigrants headed west.

There was little doubt in the minds of most people in Ireland that the British government was largely culpable for the disaster. During the years when blight was ravaging the potato crop on which millions depended for their subsistence, food exports were pouring out of the country. The government, faced with a catastrophe on an unprecedented scale and blinkered by the *laissez-faire*, non-interventionist philosophy of the time, was largely ineffective in providing relief to the victims of the Famine. More people were probably rescued from starvation by the work of voluntary agencies such as the Society of Friends than by the government. This left a legacy of bitterness and anger towards the union with Britain which began to be expressed in the years to come, not just in a growing demand for Home Rule but, at the extremes, in the legitimising of the use of violence as a means to political ends. This had been largely dormant since the rebellion of the United Irishmen in 1798, but expressed itself again as soon after the Famine as the abortive insurrection of the Young Irelanders in 1849.

While the official response to the Famine in the 1840s had been limited and grudging, ironically, in the following decades British government policy towards Ireland shifted radically. Partly from a realisation of its guilt through inactivity in the events of the 1840s and a desire to prevent such a disaster happening again, and partly from a more pragmatic aspiration to steer Ireland away from political separatism, British government policy tilted towards a much more interventionist approach to the Irish economy. Some cynics later described this as an attempt to kill Home Rule with kindness. Less-jaundiced historians have referred to this change in policy as constructive unionism. Whatever its motivation, this policy shift played a major role in the development of narrow gauge railways in many parts of Ireland. Railway construction was one of a number of strategies used in an attempt to improve economic conditions, especially in the west of Ireland. The most significant of these in the long term was the series of Land Acts passed from the 1870s through to the first decade of the twentieth century, which transformed the farmers of rural Ireland from being the tenants of landlords to peasant proprietors in the space of a generation. The state provided the finance to buy land from the landlords and then sold it on to the incumbents who paid for it by an annual rent until eventually they would come to own their farms. Various initiatives were undertaken by the Board of Works and other agencies to improve roads, introduce more progressive agricultural practices and develop fisheries.

Perhaps the best known of these late nineteenth-century government bodies was the Congested Districts Board, established in 1891 when Arthur Balfour was Chief Secretary for Ireland. The term 'congested district' is a strange one to use in the context of what the board was about, as the areas it was set up to assist had less than the average national population density. These districts were defined by their low rateable value and amounted to about one-sixth of the land mass of Ireland with a population, at the turn of the century, of around one million. The congested districts stretched down the west coast and included all or part of the counties of Donegal, Sligo, Leitrim, Roscommon, Mayo, Galway, Clare, Limerick, Kerry and Cork. Initially funded from the disestablishment of the Church of Ireland, the board built harbours and promoted the development of fisheries, led initiatives to improve agriculture, laid down roads and encouraged the construction of railways. By the early twentieth century its main function, and perhaps its lasting legacy, came from its work in purchasing and redistributing land. It had dealt with over two million acres by the time of its dissolution in 1923. It was against this background, in the context of a political culture which had changed dramatically from that which was prevalent in the middle of the nineteenth century, and as part of the attempt to resuscitate economically disadvantaged parts of the country, that narrow gauge railways came to the fore in Ireland.

The Tramways Act of 1883 was the catalyst which led to this happening. The full title of the Act, which also tied up some loose administrative ends in other areas, was: 'An Act for promoting the extension of Tramway communication in Ireland and for assisting Emigration and for extending certain provisions of the Land Law (Ireland) Act 1881, to the case of Public Companies.' I quote its full title because, arguably, one of the effects of expanding the railway network into the remoter parts of Ireland, was to accelerate emigration or at least migration, though this link in the 1883 Act was unintentional. The Act attempted to provide a stimulus to railway construction in disadvantaged areas by allowing the promoters of a line to approach a county's Grand Jury to seek financial support for their scheme. The Grand Juries dated back to the time of Charles I and remained in being until they were replaced by county and district councils in 1898. They were responsible for the administration of a county and the levying of the county cess or rate. The Grand Juries were unelected bodies dominated by landowners. Each county was subdivided into districts or baronies which gave rise to an instrument associated with many of the railways which will be discussed, the baronial guarantee. Under the Act of 1883, if a railway scheme met the approval of the Grand Jury, it could undertake to guarantee the interest on the capital employed to build the line and stipulate the baronies that would benefit from the building of the line which were to fund this. The Act itself made no mention of what gauge should be used, but in the General Tramways Order issued by the Lord Lieutenant the same year, the gauge of the tramways was specified as being three foot. This gave promoters a good nudge in that direction and obviously, as narrow gauge lines were much cheaper to construct than broad gauge ones and with construction costs a critical part of the process, this was why many promoters opted for the narrow gauge. Interest on the capital employed in railway construction was guaranteed at up to 5 per cent. Suddenly the promotion of a line, providing it was narrow gauge, in a rural backwater in Ireland, was transformed from a highly risky enterprise into a gilt-edged investment for both private investors and bankers. To put this in perspective, of the forty Irish railway companies included in the Board of Trade returns for 1882, twenty-three paid no dividends at all on their ordinary capital, while nine paid under 4 per cent and only eight exceeded that amount. William F. Bailey, a barrister, addressing the Statistical and Social Inquiry Society of Ireland in June 1884, pointed out another potential problem with the provisions of the Tramways Act:

It seems hard on the heavily burthened ratepayer that he should be expected to guarantee a dividend of 5 per cent, to the shareholders of a private company which, if it really had a good prospect of paying, would assuredly have been undertaken on its merits by some shrewd and enterprising body of capitalists. Naturally, numberless companies will be found willing to undertake any scheme, no matter what its ultimate prospects of success, if a certain return is guaranteed them. Five per cent, will be paid no matter what is earned, and it is needless to say that under such a state of affairs the zealousness and constant vigilance so characteristic of private undertakings will in all likelihood be altogether wanting.

This was the inherent flaw in the process which led in time to monumental rows in connection with the management of lines in different parts of Ireland. The Tramways Act, with its financial incentive in the form of the baronial guarantee, had no quality threshold as to who were fit and proper persons to promote and build a railway. Its construction was often seen as being of most benefit to the landowners who ran the un-elected Grand Juries, while the cost of the baronial guarantees had to be met by the ordinary ratepayers in the districts served by the line. The baronial underwriting of these schemes was virtually open ended and an unwisely promoted or badly run railway, rather than being a boon to a district, could become a serious financial burden for the unfortunate ratepayers who had to keep picking up the tab for the folly or incompetence of others. The seeds of potential conflict were clearly there and often germinated.

The Tramways Act of 1883 was the first of three significant pieces of legislation in this period which have a bearing on Ireland's railways. In 1889 the Light Railways (Ireland) Act became law. This contained clauses which allowed the government to provide direct funding for lines which the Lord Lieutenant deemed to be in the public interest. This Act did not restrict the financial assistance available to narrow gauge lines, and as we will see in the next chapter, it actually led to the construction of more broad gauge than narrow gauge lines. The final Act which encouraged the railway promotion was the Railways (Ireland) Act of 1896. This allowed the Treasury to provide grants from the public purse to fund the construction of railways in areas where the government felt they were needed. Nothing like this level of total financial support was offered elsewhere in the kingdom and the main beneficiary of this largesse, as we will see, was north Donegal. The effect of all this was to create a network of narrow gauge lines throughout the country which consisted of over 500 route miles of 3 ft gauge track at their peak. These lines offered all the services that one would expect on a standard gauge line. They were common carriers conveying passengers, goods, livestock and any other traffic on offer; the only difference from the rest of the network was their gauge and, in turn, a smaller loading gauge and lower speeds. This brief survey of these lines will follow a roughly south to north progression, starting in County Cork where one of the first lines out of the traps following the passing of the 1883 Act was the grandly named West Carbery Light Railways and Tramways Ltd set up in that year to build two lines centred on Skibbereen in the west of the county.

One of these which was to head east towards Clonakilty was never built, but the other line which was renamed in due course the Schull & Skibbereen Tramway was partly built, though the original intention to take the line down to Crookhaven at the bottom of the Mizen Peninsula was never realised. In March 1884, the Cork Grand Jury agreed to guarantee the interest on £57,000 of the company's proposed capital of £95,000 and an Order in Council authorising the line's construction was granted in 1885. It took two years to build the 15 mile long tramway to Schull, most of the route being beside the public road. The only significant engineering feature on the line, a fine twelve-arch viaduct at Ballydehob which took the line over the waters of an inlet of Roaringwater Bay, can still be admired to this day. The quality of the work on the line must have been suspect for the Board of Trade inspector, Major General Hutchinson, refused to pass the line for public service on his first inspection in August 1886.

Following another inspection, he agreed to allow the line to open to the public, but his imposition of a 15 mph speed limit on the trains suggests that the work was far from sound. Things went from bad to worse soon after the opening in September 1886. The three 0-4-0 tramway engines acquired by the company were underpowered and prone to derailments on the dodgy track. Services were briefly suspended the month after opening, and again in 1887. By this time some ratepayers had become so exasperated that they petitioned the Lord Lieutenant to investigate the company. This resulted in another visit from the major general and a damning report highlighting shortcomings in the way the line was being maintained and operated. Losses and a poor service continued until in 1892 the Grand Jury appointed a committee of management which effectively took over the line from the West Carbery Company. The only extension of the line, opened in 1893, was a short branch from the station at Schull to its pier; by this time all thoughts of the Crookhaven extension had been laid to rest. The line never made a profit. It was calculated that between its opening and 1922, operating losses and the payment of baronial guarantees on the capital amounted to over £150,000, a heavy price to pay for a line of about 15 miles in length operating two or three services per day. Taken over by the Great Southern Railways in 1925, the line fell victim to fuel shortages during the Emergency in 1944 when services were suspended though, perhaps surprisingly, they resumed in 1945 and lingered on until January 1947 when the tramway was closed entirely by Córas Iompair Éireann.

There were two other narrow gauge lines in County Cork, very different in their character and origins though they ultimately suffered the same fate. The first of these companies dated back to 1850 and was one of three lines in Ireland which began life as broad gauge routes, converting to the 3 ft gauge towards the end of the nineteenth century. A line from Cork to the port of Passage on the shores of Cork Harbour was first mooted in 1837 and revived and authorised in 1846. With Sir John MacNeill as its engineer and William Dargan its builder, the line which was only about 6 miles long opened on 8 June 1850, its trains hauled for all of its existence as a 5 ft 3 in. line by the three 2-2-2 well tanks supplied for the opening by Sharp Brothers of Manchester. In addition to its trains, the company operated steamer services to various destinations around that great expanse of sheltered water which is Cork Harbour. Over the years there were plans to extend the line to Monkstown and Crosshaven, but these came to naught. Then in 1896 the directors took the plunge and decided both to build a 9½ mile extension to Crosshaven and to convert the existing line to the 3 ft gauge on the grounds that this would save £30,000 on the cost of constructing the new line. The Cork, Blackrock & Passage Railway Extension Act was passed in 1896 and the first 3 ft gauge trains ran on the original line from Cork to Passage in October 1900. There were no baronial guarantees around here, it will be noted; the Crosshaven extension was promoted and financed in the traditional way, probably to the regret of the directors of the company, for it proved a very expensive undertaking. It was a difficult line to construct with a 500 yard long tunnel, the only one found on an Irish 3 ft gauge line, between Passage and Glenbrook stations and a substantial four-span girder viaduct near Crosshaven. The company had to seek a loan from the Public Works Commissioners in 1901 to complete the line and in the end the cost of the Crosshaven extension, which was eventually opened by the Lord Lieutenant, the Earl of Dudley, on 1 June 1904, was £200,093, much more than had been originally anticipated.

The CB&P was quite different from the rest of the Irish narrow gauge lines in the nature of its traffic. This was essentially a commuter line serving the suburbs of a large city, not a tramway meandering through some rural backwater. When the original line was converted to the narrow gauge, double 3 ft gauge tracks were laid from the Albert Street terminus in Cork to Blackrock, the only such instance in the whole of Ireland. The regular service was hourly, but in the summer timetable of 1905 the most intensive service ever seen on the Irish 3 ft gauge was offered. On Sunday mornings a half-hourly service was operated to take legions of Corkonians to enjoy the coast and the harbour. The fastest weekday limited-stop trains on the line took thirty-six minutes for the 16 miles from Crosshaven to the city, running at a creditable average speed of over 26 mph. No sooner was the line reopened on the 3 ft gauge than the city's electric tramways were extended and began to bite into the commuter traffic on the part of the line closest to the city. Then in August 1914, with the start of the First World War, the British naval facilities in Cork Harbour became of enormous strategic importance and the company's trains and steamers were pressed into service to deal with the huge amount of extra traffic generated by the naval base at Haulbowline. The CB&P's heavy excursion traffic was cut back to cope with the extra military requirements. In 1916 the company was unable to meet the repayments from the 1901 loan, and even though it had record receipts of £45,000 in 1918, the costs of wages and coal were escalating greatly on account of wartime inflation, leaving its finances in a parlous state. Worse was to follow with the Civil War. In 1922 Free State forces landed at Passage to mount an attack on rebels holding the city of Cork. To impede the government forces, the insurgents inflicted a catalogue of destruction on the railway which culminated in the blowing up of the Douglas viaduct near Rochestown station on 8 August 1922. The line was taken over by the GSR in 1925 and losses began to occur on a yearly basis as lorries and buses began to eat into its traffic. It did manage to see off the Cork electric trams, which ceased running in 1931, but only just. The last train left Albert Street on 10 September 1932 bringing an end to a unique line, even by the standards of the Irish narrow gauge. The company only ever owned a total of seven locomotives throughout its existence, three broad gauge and four narrow gauge machines. Even though the line closed in 1932, as we will see, its speedy and powerful quartet of 2-4-2 tank engines outlasted it by over twenty-five years.

Cork's other narrow gauge system was much more typical of the Irish 3 ft gauge network as a whole than the CB&P. The Cork & Muskerry Light Railway was built to serve the rural districts to the north and west of the city and took its name from the barony of Muskerry. Promoted in the wake of the Tramways Act, the scheme was approved by the Cork Grand Jury in 1884, though there was some delay in obtaining the necessary legal authority to proceed, so construction did not begin until February 1887. When work did eventually start, it progressed very quickly. The main line was to run from a terminus at Western Road in Cork city to Coachford, a distance of 15½ miles, with a short branch from Coachford Junction to Blarney, famous for its castle and still today a magnet for tourists in search of eloquence. Trains began to operate to Blarney in August 1887 and the line to Coachford was opened in March 1888. There was a further addition to the system with a line from St Anns, between Coachford Junction and Blarney, to Donoughmore. This was built by a nominally separate company, the Donoughmore Extension Light Railway, but it was always operated by the c&MR. The Donoughmore line was approved by the Privy Council in June 1891 and the 8½ mile line opened for traffic in May 1893.

One unusual feature of this line was that after leaving its Western Road terminus in Cork, trains ran along Western Road itself. That road was shared by the normal road traffic, the city's electric trams and the Muskerry's steam trains. Once it had left the city behind, the track continued to skirt the public road on a long straight run of about 2½ miles until it reached Carrigrohane. The locomotives were fitted with bells and cowcatchers because they ran beside and in the middle of the road. Just imagine the reaction if such a layout for a new railway was proposed today. While it may have been a hazard to road users in and around Cork, the c&M was less of a hazard to the local ratepayers than many of the other lines discussed in this chapter which, like it, were underwritten with their assistance, willingly given or otherwise. In its most prosperous year, 1913, the profit generated by the company was sufficient to pay the interest on its capital without the need to resort to the Grand Jury, a rare occurrence in the history of such lines and worth noting because of that. The c&M, as was the case with the CB&P and many other lines around the country, passed through the War of Independence largely unscathed, but suffered serious damage during the Civil War when its bridge over the River Lee at Leemount, just outside the city, was blown up. The story from the 1920s onwards is all too familiar. In 1924, the year before it was taken over by the GSR, the line sustained losses of £2,799. Being so close to a large centre of population, where the roads were generally better than out in the sticks, the unchecked rise of the bus and the lorry after the war made the C&M particularly vulnerable. Even if road transport had grown at a more restrained rate, it could not have been long before there would have been sustained hostility to steam trains clattering along a major artery into the city, as the Muskerry trains had to do to reach their terminus. The whole system was closed by the GSR on the last day of December 1934.

Heading north-west from Cork, we come to one of the most famous or notorious of all the narrow gauge lines in Ireland, the Tralee & Dingle Railway. The GSWR reached Tralee from Killarney in 1859 and the circuitous 70 mile long route from Limerick that was the North Kerry line, worked by the Waterford & Limerick Railway, made an end-on junction with the GSWR line at Tralee from 1880. At that time there was no railway to the west of Tralee, but the Tramways Act of 1883 gave life to a proposal to build a line down the Dingle Peninsula the following year. This first scheme was approved by the Privy Council but was not proceeded with. It was revived in 1888 and this time the Grand Jury was persuaded to guarantee at 4 per cent interest £120,000 of the £150,000 capital required for the line. The building of the line was entrusted to Robert Worthington, an experienced contractor whose contribution to the last great flourishing of railway building in Ireland at the end of the nineteenth century was akin to that of Dargan earlier in the century. Worthington urged the directors of the railway to build the line to the 5 ft 3 in. gauge as the earlier restriction of baronial guarantees to narrow gauge lines only had by now been lifted. However, this advice was ignored and while the cost of building the T&D was incredibly low at £2,700 per mile, the root of the line's many problems in later years lay in what turned out to be this very false economy. The consequence of the low construction costs were gradients as steep as 1 in 29 and over seventy level crossings on a system only 38½ miles long and for the permanent way, the use of poor ballast and very light rail weighing 45 lb per yard.

The T&D consisted of a main line from Tralee to Dingle of 32 miles and a short branch 6 miles long from Camp (later renamed Castlegregory) Junction to Castlegregory. From Dingle station the main line continued down to the harbour and at the other end of the line, while there were interchange sidings with the broad gauge in the GSWR yard, passengers had to walk the several hundred yards between the town's broad and narrow gauge stations. To understand the problems which the operation of the line posed, one can do no better than look at its gradient profile. Leaving Tralee, the line was mostly level, indeed prone to flooding for the first few miles out to Blennerville station and beyond to Castlegregory Junction 10 miles from Tralee. Then the fun started! In a little over 4 miles, the line climbed from just above sea level at the Junction to a summit of 680 ft at Glenagalt Bridge. Like a roller coaster, it then plunged downwards for 6 miles to Emylough and Annascaul, the latter station the same height above sea level as Castlegregory Junction. From Annascaul the climbing started again for some 4 miles to a second summit at Garrynadur, from which it descended steeply on gradients of mostly 1 in 29 to reach, over a curving viaduct, Lispole station. The remaining 5 miles or so to Dingle had relatively easy grades compared to what went before. Add to the gradients many severe curves, a line which skirted the public road for part of the way, level crossings which had limited sighting for both road users and trains and it can easily be imagined why a passenger train from Tralee to Dingle, with lengthy stops to shunt wagons at stations along the way, took around two and a half hours to complete its 32 mile run.

Major General Hutchinson of the Board of Trade made several visits to inspect the line before he felt able to allow it to be opened to the public, inauspiciously perhaps, on 1 April 1891. The problems started almost immediately as it quickly became apparent that the receipts from traffic were not sufficient to pay for the operating costs and the poor unfortunate ratepayers of the baronies of Corkaguiney, Trughanacmy, Clanmaurice and Tralee itself had to pay up right from the start for the pleasure of having the T&D in their midst. The ratepayers demanded a Board of

Trade inquiry and Major General Hutchinson was summoned back to Tralee to conduct this in March 1893. While some malpractices were brought to light, the next episode in the eventful early history of the T&D overshadowed this when, on 22 May of that year, a pig special from a fair at Dingle ran out of control on the bank from Glenagalt down to Camp Junction and derailed on Curraduff Bridge. The driver and two other members of staff were killed in the smash. Some years later a deviation was built, including a new Curraduff viaduct, to make the gradients and curves on this part of the line less hazardous. Two further serious accidents occurred on the line. In 1898 at Baunogue, an exposed location near Garrynadur summit, a passenger was killed when a carriage on a train from Dingle was derailed in a gale, though the Board of Trade inquiry also hinted at deficiencies in the track. A further accident occurred at Lispole in 1907, very similar to the Curraduff incident, when a train went out of control on a descent and derailed near the viaduct.

An account of what travel was like on the Tralee & Dingle has been left by the writer, J. M. Synge, who arrived at the GSWR station in Tralee on what was probably a market day in the first years of the last century:

> At Tralee station—I was on my way to a village many miles beyond Dingle—I found a boy who carried my bag some way along the road to an open yard, where the light railway starts for the west. There was a confused mass of peasants struggling on the platform, with all sort of baggage, which the people lifted into the train for themselves as well as they were able. The seats ran up either side of the cars, and the space between them was soon filled with sacks of flour, cases of porter, chairs rolled in straw, and other household goods. A drunken young man got in just before we started, and sang songs for a few coppers, telling us that he had spent all his money, and had nothing left to pay for his ticket. Then, when the carriage was closely packed, we moved slowly out of the station. At my side there was an old man who explained the Irish names of the places that we came to, and

pointed out the Seven Pigs, a group of islands in the bay; Kerry Head, further off; and many distant mountains. Beyond him a dozen big women in shawls were crowded together; and just opposite me there was a young woman wearing a wedding ring, who was one of the peculiarly refined women of Kerry, with supreme charm in every movement and expression. The big woman talked to her about some elderly man who had been sick—her husband, it was likely—and some young man who had gone away to England, and was breaking his heart with loneliness.

Even in this short extract there is a reference to the pain which was caused by emigration which seemed to infuse most accounts of railway journeys recorded in the second half of the nineteenth century and beyond. An example of the type of narrow gauge carriage used on the T&D described by Synge, with its wooden longitudinal seats, has survived and is preserved at the narrow gauge station at Dromod in County Leitrim.

The discontent as to the way the railway was being run boiled up again in 1896. Under the terms of the baronial guarantees, if a railway thus supported failed to meet its operating costs for four consecutive years, control passed from the company to the Grand Jury. This happened in 1896, though apart from the name over the door, so to speak, little else changed as the same staff operated the same trains on the same cheaply constructed railway. A committee of management was formed, but in the first year of its stewardship the ratepayers of the baronies still had to stump up £7,000 for the dubious honour of having the T&D on their doorsteps. Protests were now directed at Westminster for its parsimony and in 1898 the government did make a one-off payment of £80,000 which reduced but far from removed the imposition on the ratepayers. Further government funding of £23,000 in 1907 allowed the construction of the new line at Curraduff. In 1898 the Grand Juries in Ireland were replaced with elected county councils and from around this time onwards the turmoil which had swirled around the T&D began to die down, though in 1910 a Ratepayers' Association in Corkaguiney alleged serious inadequacies in the company's accounting procedures. The relative calm which surrounded the railway was shattered by the War of Independence and the Civil War which saw bridges blown up, stock damaged and services periodically suspended. Still being run by the committee of management, the line was handed over to the GSR on 1 January 1925, and to greet the new owners, a train hit a car at Glenmore crossing on the same day!

The GSR imposed some economies such as the rundown of the workshops at Tralee with locomotives now being overhauled at Limerick or Inchicore works. Because all the Irish narrow gauge lines were not connected to each other, every one of them had to have their own workshops to repair their rolling stock, and because they all developed independently, there was little or no standardisation. They all had their own types of locomotives and rolling stock, and keeping these on the road as they got older was an increasingly burdensome task. On most of the lines, even when they had a virtual monopoly in their catchment areas, before the Great War there was never enough revenue coming in to allow for the regular renewal of track and rolling stock and this meant that they increasingly had to make do and mend with what they had. Given the bleak economic landscape in the early decades of the Free State's existence, the GSR had to continue patching up what they had inherited from the independent companies and there was never any serious attempt to implement a programme of sustained investment for main line railways, let alone the likes of the T&D.

For the Dingle train, road improvements in the 1930s meant that a bus could do the run down the peninsula about an hour quicker than the train. The branch to Castlegregory was closed completely on 17 April 1939, and at the same time passenger services were withdrawn from the main line. Goods trains continued to run until March 1947 when the chronic coal shortages of the post-war years led to their withdrawal. That however was not quite the end of the story. The line's latest lucky owners, CIÉ, ran a monthly cattle special in connection with the fair at Dingle. These trains became the stuff of legend as worn out engines running on life-expired track charged the banks once a month for another six years. Railway enthusiasts came from far and wide to record these trains and hitch a ride on them; paradoxically, more photographs and cine film was used to record the T&D in these last years than in the whole of its previous existence. The last of these trains ran in June 1953 and the line was officially closed by CIÉ on 1 July of that year. Even that was not quite the end. Several of the locomotives found work on other surviving CIÉ narrow gauge lines and one locomotive, 2-6-2 tank No. 5, built in Leeds in 1892, was eventually preserved by a railroad museum in Vermont in the United States. In 1986, No. 5 was repatriated and restored to working order on a short section of rebuilt track from the outskirts of Tralee to Blennerville, which opened in July 1993, forty years after the line closed. While the level run to Blennerville in a coach which came from a metre gauge line in Spain and with door handles that might have originated in your local DIY store is a far cry from the heroics required to get trains to and from Dingle in years gone by, this unlikely revival at least keeps the sheep in that small part of Kerry on their toes and brings the often turbulent story of the T&D to a restful, pipe and slippers sort of conclusion.

We now head north from Tralee and cross the estuary of the Shannon to the southern shore of County Clare for the next instalment of our narrow gauge odyssey. But first of all I suppose we had better get Percy French and that song out of the way, for it is all but impossible to discuss the West and South Clare Railways without reference to it. William Percy French was born in County Roscommon in 1854. He trained as an engineer at Trinity College Dublin but found fame as a composer and performer of comic songs, mainly about life in rural Ireland, and many of which are still sung today. On Monday, 10 August 1896, French left the Broadstone in Dublin to travel to Kilkee in County Clare to fulfil an engagement that evening at Moore's Concert Hall. He made the connection off the broad gauge at Ennis on to the 12.40 pm train to Kilkee. All went well as far as Miltown Malbay where the locomotive, No. 8 *Lisdoonvarna*, was declared a failure by its driver. While the railway staff acted promptly to try and get a relief engine for the Kilkee train, there was at that time a 16 mile single track section from Miltown Malbay south to Moyasta Junction with no crossing place, which slowed up the arrival of the replacement engine, No. 4 *Besborough*. On the footplate of that engine, there travelled a new guard for the delayed train, one Michael Talty, on a duty that would bring him immortality, though he was not to know it at the time. The train carrying Percy French eventually arrived at Kilkee at 8 o'clock but when he reached the hall he found his audience had largely dispersed, and while he did perform, it was to a very poor house. Matters might have rested there, but French sued the company for loss of earnings of £10. Had the directors of the company any sense, they would have settled there and then with the entertainer, but they did not and the case came to court. French, a renowned humourist, gave a fine performance in the witness box in a case which was well reported and obviously gave him more than £10's worth of free publicity. His honour the judge joined in the fun and awarded French costs and damages of £10. In a hole but apparently unable or unwilling to stop digging, the company appealed the decision and three months later lost again. At the appeal worse was to come for the directors when French rehearsed a few lines from a comic song he was writing about what he called 'The Wild West Clare', which was published later and is still performed, securing for the line and for guard Talty in particular a unique kind of fame. Were I a po-faced musicologist, I might say that the song consists of a dramatic dialogue between members of the railway staff as they cope with the vicissitudes of life on the line and the failure of machinery to ease the lot of mankind at the end of the nineteenth century, but I would rather just quote a few lines from it.

> Kilkee! Oh you never get near it
> You're in luck if the train brings you back
> For the permanent way is so queer, it
> Spends most of its time off the track.

'Are ye right there, Michael? Are ye right?
Do you think ye'll be home before its light?'
''Tis all depending whether
The ould engine howlds together.'
'And it might now, Michael, so it might!'

So was the West Clare Railway as bad as all that? It did have its moments, but it also survived long enough to have the melancholy distinction of being the last of Ireland's 3 ft gauge lines to remain open to the public.

Few parts of Ireland suffered greater devastation because of the Great Famine than County Clare. In 1841 its population was over 280,000; in the 1980s it had still only recovered to about a third of this. The first railway to penetrate the county was the Limerick & Ennis which opened in 1859. This was extended ten years later to Athenry, on the MGWR line to Galway, by a separate company, the Athenry & Ennis Junction Railway. In the south of the county there was a fair amount of coastal shipping along the Shannon Estuary and in the 1850s various schemes were mooted to link Kilkee and Kilrush with Cappa Pier, close to Kilrush, where these ships called. Then in 1873 the Ennis & West Clare Railway was approved by an Act of Parliament. This line had first been proposed as a broad gauge line but was re-presented as a narrow gauge railway and as such was the first in Ireland to receive parliamentary authorisation. Its route from Ennis to Miltown Malbay was similar to that later followed by the West Clare Railway. The usual story of difficulties in raising the capital of up to £160,000 led to its being abandoned. As elsewhere it was the Tramways Act of 1883 which provided the spark needed to get the railway under way. In May 1884 the West Clare Railway was given its Order in Council which authorised it to build a 3 ft gauge line 27 miles long from Ennis to Miltown Malbay. Interest on its capital of £163,400 was assured by baronial guarantees. That same year the South Clare Railway, with a guaranteed capital of £120,000, was authorised to extend the WCR line to the south of the county, with branches to Kilrush and Kilkee. While the SCR was officially a separate concern, it was always worked by the WCR and the name West Clare Railway is usually, if to the pedant slightly inaccurately, applied to the whole concern.

The contractor for both lines was one William Martin Murphy, a self-made man and Nationalist politician, later to gain notoriety because of his clash with James Larkin in the lock-out of workers in Dublin in 1913. The first sod was turned by Charles Stewart Parnell at Miltown Malbay on 26 January 1885, and the line from Ennis to Miltown Malbay opened for traffic in July 1887. The SCR section was delayed as the Grand Jury dithered over the plans for the line linking Kilrush and Kilkee, with some of its members favouring a broad gauge line built on an embankment across Poulnasherry Bay to reclaim land in the vicinity. Eventually the issue was resolved and the narrow gauge scheme prevailed. The line from Miltown Malbay to Moyasta Junction, where it divided to serve Kilrush and Kilkee, was opened for all traffic in August 1892. The line extended beyond Kilrush for about half a mile to Cappa Pier on the Shannon Estuary, and there was a through line which enabled trains to run directly between Kilkee to Kilrush, creating a triangular junction at Moyasta, the only one on the Irish narrow gauge.

The West Clare was a lengthy affair. It was 48 miles from Ennis to Kilkee and a mile less to Kilrush. The passenger service usually consisted of about three trains a day which took around three hours to travel from Kilkee to Ennis which was operated as the main line with a connecting service from Kilrush meeting the Ennis trains at Moyasta Junction. Like so many of the Irish narrow gauge lines, the West Clare was built as cheaply as possible with a resulting proliferation of severe curves and steep gradients. One particular hazard which affected trains on the exposed section of track between Quilty and Kilmurry in 1897 and again in 1899 was the full force of Atlantic gales which blew trains off the track in both those years. Subsequently an anemometer was installed near Quilty station and when winds reached a speed of over 60 mph, only specially ballasted stock was allowed out on the line; all services were suspended if the wind speed reached 80 mph. Again, as with so many Irish lines on both gauges, level crossings proliferated, affording many opportunities for accidents with road traffic or through trains not braking in time and crashing through the gates. One false economy which affected the railway for the first years of its existence was the failure to provide proper facilities for maintaining locomotives and rolling stock, which meant that boilers and other major items for repair had to be shipped off the railway to outside contractors. It was not until 1902, with the help of a Treasury loan, that proper workshops were built at Ennis. These eventually employed over seventy people and the first new wagons emerged from the shops in the year they were opened. Between 1904 and 1910 the company built some handsome six-wheeled saloons with large observation windows and clerestory roofs at its Ennis workshops to cater for the line's growing tourist traffic. Passenger levels on the WCR were always much higher in summer than during the rest of the year as it served a coastal area, with Kilkee and Lahinch being popular seaside resorts. Efforts were made to attract visitors to the scenic area the railway served. For example, up to 1916, some trains to Kilrush continued on to Cappa Pier to connect with the steamers to Limerick. The efforts of the railway to attract summer visitors to the area were largely successful in the years before the First World War, with the line carrying a record number of passengers, 236,266 in 1908.

Relations between those who paid for the line through their rates and the directors of the company were less fraught in Clare than they were in the kingdom of Kerry, but the county council did take an interest in the management of the line which its ratepayers continued to subsidise until the 1930s. The county council made several efforts to take over the line from the controlling directors on the grounds that they could run it more efficiently, but in 1925 the line was taken over, not by Clare County Council, but by the GSR. This had been preceded by several years of disruption to services and damage to infrastructure during the troubles of the early 1920s. In GSR days, it must be said, not a lot happened. Locomotives were now overhauled at Inchicore, a petrol-engined Drewry railcar was introduced on the Kilrush branch to reduce operating costs, and during the Emergency, as the greatest conflict the world had ever known was coyly referred to in the Irish Free State, services were maintained by using locally produced peat to fire the engines. Ownership again changed in 1945 with the formation of CIÉ.

CIÉ had many detractors during its years in charge of public transport in the twenty-six counties. While it never drew the vilification rightly reserved for the similarly structured transport monolith north of the border, the UTA, it never attracted much praise either and could rarely be accused of radical thinking. However, in its treatment of the West Clare, it did behave in a remarkably progressive way and brought about nothing less than the complete modernisation of the railway. In the early 1950s it ordered four diesel railcars from an English firm which had been making such vehicles for the County Donegal Railways since the 1930s. New light trailer coaches were built at Inchicore to run with the railcars. In 1955 the same firm, Walker Brothers of Wigan, supplied three bogie diesel locomotives with many mechanical parts identical to those of the railcars, to replace the steam locomotives on the railway's goods trains. The West Clare was thus completely renewed. Even though additional stopping places were added to the timetable to be served by the railcars, journey times between Ennis and Kilkee were reduced by nearly an hour. From being the butt of that famous song, the West Clare was given a fighting chance of survival, thanks to CIÉ. If the Irish narrow gauge had a future, this was it and the ghost of Percy French was trumped at last. However, despite the modernisation, the line continued to lose money, so in that respect nothing had changed. Faced with an operating deficit of £20,000 in 1960, CIÉ made the decision to close the line. The last trains ran on 31 January 1961. By that time the West Clare section of CIÉ was the last 3 ft gauge line operating in Ireland. One of the steam locomotives, No. 5 *Slieve Callan*, was preserved on a plinth at Ennis station for many years after the closure and then, as at Tralee, a minor miracle began to unfold, this time at Moyasta Junction. A group of local business people got together to rebuild part of the line north from the junction and started running trains for the benefit of visitors. The restoration of *Slieve Callan* is under way and in time the sight of a West Clare steam locomotive at work on its native heath may yet again occur.

If the West Clare Railway was the modern face of the Irish narrow gauge in the mid-1950s, this was the last thing that could be said about our next line, for the Cavan & Leitrim section of CIÉ remained a 100 per cent steam-operated Victorian railway throughout its entire life right up to its closure in 1959. The county of Leitrim has one of the lowest population densities in Ireland and in a country which for most of its recorded existence has depended on the produce of its fields for the survival of its people, Leitrim's poor land, often inundated by its over-abundance of lakes and streams, is a prime reason for this. The first railway to penetrate the county was the MGWR's line from Mullingar to Sligo which opened in 1862 with stations at Dromod and Carrick-on-Shannon. To bring the benefit of a railway to the hinterland of south Leitrim, in 1883 the Cavan, Leitrim & Roscommon Light Railway and Tramway Company was formed, another product of the Tramways Act of that year. The intention was to build a main line from Dromod through Ballinamore to Belturbet, which from 1885 was the terminus of a GNR branch from Ballyhaise on its Clones to Cavan line. From Ballinamore there was to be a branch to Arigna and on to Boyle, both in County Roscommon. Arigna, close to the shores of Lough Allen, was one of the few places in Ireland where there were significant workable deposits of both coal and iron ore, the DNA of the nineteenth-century industrial economy. Though Sliabh an Iarainn (the Iron Mountain) lay across the lough to the east, there were enough workable deposits of coal around Arigna to provide the incentive of mineral wealth to encourage the promotion of the branch, which was always known as the tramway. Perhaps wisely as things turned out, the Grand Jury of County Roscommon refused to back the scheme. The line to Boyle was never built, and though Arigna was just inside that county, the burden of guaranteeing the interest of 5 per cent on the line's capital of £190,585 fell mainly on the ratepayers of Leitrim, with a much lesser contribution coming from those in the small part of County Cavan through which the northern part of the line passed. The firm of Collen Brothers began building the railway in 1885 and in October the main line from Dromod to Belturbet was opened, followed in

May 1888 by the tramway from Ballinamore to Arigna.

Though traffic was healthy at the start, it was not until 1893 that there was an operating surplus, though this was never enough to cover the guaranteed interest on the line's substantial capital, a situation which continued throughout its independent existence. It was in connection with the management of the Cavan & Leitrim that some of the most magnificent, pointless and self-destructive rows caused by these errant children of the Tramways Act exploded. There was always the potential for tension between the promoters of such a scheme and the representatives of those who paid for it through the rates. The Grand Juries and their successors, the county councils, had the right to appoint directors to look after the ratepayers' interests. While the original promoters were often landowners of the same social class and background as those who sat on the Grand Juries, with the arrival of the elected county councils in 1898, this cosy cartel was disrupted. On the c&l the board was quickly divided into two opposing camps with distinct political and even religious differences. In 1902 the original directors managed to rig the composition of the board to leave the ratepayers' representatives in a permanent minority. One regular source of friction was the role of some of the railway's directors in the management of the Arigna Mining Company which had been set up in 1888. Several directors of the railway were also directors of the mining company which led to suggestions that they spent more time on the affairs of the mining company than on the railway, where the return on their investment was always guaranteed.

In the early years of the last century several schemes to extend the railway were considered at various times. Most of these were directed towards taking the line from Arigna via Ballyfarnon and Riverstown to Collooney in County Sligo, which at the end of the nineteenth century was already an important railway crossroads with three stations served by three different broad gauge companies. Another plan which surfaced several times but came to naught was for a line down to the Shannon at Rooskey. The grandest of all the extensions was promoted under the aegis of a great, mad, megalomaniac of a scheme, the Ulster & Connaught

Light Railways Company, which was authorised in 1900. This provided for a link from Bawnboy Road station on the C&L to the Maguiresbridge terminus of the Clogher Valley Railway, the next 3 ft gauge line to the north, which we will come to soon in its own right. Even in 1900 the U&CLR must have looked like a fantasy railway as its backers were at various times planning a 3 ft gauge line across Ireland from Newry on the east coast via the CVR and C&L to Woodlawn in County Galway, and even beyond that into Connemara. One practical and blindingly obvious minor extension to the existing C&L system fell foul of the poisonous relations between the railway and the ratepayers and was only eventually built as a consequence of the Great War. The tramway terminated several miles from the coal mines at Arigna and the coal had to be carted to the railhead for onward shipment. When the line was promoted, the company had hoped that the mining companies would build tramways down to Arigna station, but this never happened. There was a great need for this extension and even the long-disused formation of a tramway built as long ago as 1830 in connection with an ill-fated attempt to establish an iron works at Derreenavoggy, close to the coal workings, which could have been used for the line. In 1901 the Board of Works approved the scheme, as did Leitrim County Council, but the plan got subsumed in the U&CLR scheme which also had sights on the Arigna Valley. The extension was revived again in 1905, and this time the Treasury promised a grant of £24,000 to build the lines to the mines and to Rooskey. However, the old enmity between the railway and the ratepayers raised its head again and even though the railway directors agreed to indemnify the ratepayers against any losses on the lines for a period of five years, at a rowdy public meeting of the county council in February 1906, the £24,000 grant from the government was rejected and the extension was again not built.

In 1917, when all the railways in Ireland came under the control of the government's Irish Railways Executive Committee, in order to increase the output of much-needed coal from Ireland's few mines, several lines to collieries were built, including the one up the Arigna Valley. The line finally opened in 1920, having cost

£60,000 to build. It ran 4 miles beyond Arigna station to the Arigna Mining Company's pits at Aughabehy. By 1930 the seams there were exhausted and the upper part of the line fell into disuse. Of the remaining section, from Derreenavoggy down to Arigna, it could be said that it kept the C&L alive for another thirty years. For a line which depended so much on coal traffic, one astonishing feature of the C&L was that there was never any attempt to mechanise the trans-shipment of coal from narrow to broad gauge wagons at either Dromod or Belturbet, which was always done by men with shovels.

For the opening of the C&L eight 4-4-0 tank locomotives were supplied by Robert Stephenson and Company of Newcastle-upon-Tyne. Four of these lasted until the closure of the line and two have been preserved, one in the United States; the other is now at the Ulster Folk & Transport Museum at Cultra, just outside Belfast. The C&L's only other engine bought in 1904, an 0-6-4 tank No. 9 *King Edward*, proved too heavy for the track and was rarely used. The coal traffic not only kept the line busy, it made it a repository for locomotives and wagons from other lines as these closed down. The first visitors were a pair of 0-4-2 tank engines, among Ireland's first ever 3 ft gauge engines, built for the Ballymena, Cushendall & Red Bay Company in 1874/75, which were sent by the Railway Executive Committee to assist in the construction of the extension. These were the first of a number of locomotives moved to Ballinamore in the GSR and CIÉ eras. All four locomotives used on the CB&P moved north when that line closed in the 1930s, as did another four engines from the T&D. The first of these came in 1941 and the last as late as 1957 at a time when there was a final surge in the coal traffic. During the Emergency when there was a dire shortage of fuel in the Free State, up to six coal trains per day were operated over the tramway. By the 1950s the main customers were the cement factories at Limerick and Drogheda. By then there were three trains between Ballinamore and Dromod to connect with the main line services, but only one daily working on the northern section to Belturbet. Trains were generally mixed and often passengers were left drumming their fingers as the locomotive headed off to shunt goods wagons at stations along the way. In some ways the C&L, and especially the tramway, running alongside the public road with ungated crossings and stopping places indicated by nothing more than a nameboard on the roadside, was the very essence of the Irish narrow gauge. The line's fate was finally decided when plans were announced for the building of a coal-fired power station on the shore of Lough Allen which would absorb most of the output of the mines. By 1958 CIÉ reckoned that the line was losing some £40,000 per year. Resolutely steam operated to the end, the final trains ran on 31 March 1959.

The last twelve or so miles of the C&L were in County Cavan, thus bringing us back to the province of Ulster where the narrow gauge was first used and where it had its most splendid manifestation, as we will see, when we turn our attention to County Donegal. However, before heading there we have a few other Ulster lines to consider beginning with the line which, if the grand plans of the U&CLR had come to fruition, might have been linked to the C&L. The Clogher Valley Tramway (the name was changed to Railway in 1894) was yet another product of the Tramways Act of 1883. The line which found favour with the Tyrone Grand Jury was the survivor of two competing schemes, both of which had as their starting point Tynan in County Armagh on the GNR Portadown to Clones line. The route was agreed as far as Ballygawley, from where one faction wanted the line to head north-east to meet the GNR's Portadown to Derry route at Dungannon, while the other, the one which prevailed, had the line going south-west through Augher and Fivemiletown to Maguiresbridge on the GNR line from Clones to Enniskillen. As far as I am aware, the railway defined the area it served rather than taking its name from an existing geographical feature. Clogher is a small diocesan town, one of many served by the line which ambled through a predominantly agricultural district. The CVR filled a gap on the railway map of Ireland, but would almost certainly never have been built without the benefit of baronial guarantees. The capital needed to construct the 37 mile long line was £150,000, which the Grand Juries of Tyrone and Fermanagh agreed to guarantee in March 1884, the last 8 miles of the line running through the latter county. Construction began in 1885, but the CVR almost immediately came to grief when a banker who had agreed to take £70,000 worth of stock reneged on the deal. An appeal to the Board of Works resulted in a loan of £44,000 which enabled the line to be completed, traffic commencing in May 1887, following an inspection the previous month by the ubiquitous Major General Hutchinson of the Board of Trade, who must have been sick of the sight of Irish tramways by this time.

The CVR was a roadside tramway for most of its length, though for a bit of variety when it got to Fivemiletown, to reach its station trains had to run down the middle of the town's Main Street. Most of the towns and villages it served had elaborate and impressive red brick-built stations which perhaps anticipated a level of traffic the line was never likely to generate. In addition to the main stations there were over twenty roadside stopping places with the minimum of facilities, usually a nameboard, a seat and a noticeboard to which the timetable was pasted. The service in the summer of 1900 was typical of the pattern which prevailed for many years. There were two through workings along the whole length of the line which took nearly three hours to cover the 37 miles. In addition there were several short workings such as Fivemiletown to Maguiresbridge or Aughnacloy to Tynan. There were also additional short workings which ran only on fair days or market days. As with all the Irish 3 ft gauge lines, it had to have its own workshops which were at Aughnacloy, where the company's offices were also located.

The line was far from a financial success. It failed to show an operating profit in its first seven years, a pattern which was followed throughout almost its entire existence. Even in its most prosperous year, 1904, receipts were only £791 more than its working expenses. In that year alone the guaranteed dividends paid to shareholders cost the ratepayers £5,375, enough to provoke a riot or two further south! As the internal combustion engine made its mark in the 1920s, the CVR's yearly deficit in that decade was never less than £4,000. Despite its appalling balance sheet, the CVR was at the centre of some of the insanely optimistic narrow gauge megalomania mentioned in connection with the c&L at the beginning of the last century. The Newry, Keady & Tynan Railway was authorised in 1900 with a capital of £173,000 to build a 3 ft gauge line from a junction with the CVR at Tynan to Newry, while the UC&L would have taken the narrow gauge in the other direction from Maguiresbridge to join the c&L and on to Clifden in Connemara, if all had gone according to plan. Nothing I suppose was impossible, as long as you got some mug to guarantee the interest on your capital at up to 5 per cent! At partition, the CVR found itself in Northern Ireland. The line remained independent with the ratepayers of Tyrone and Fermanagh still paying the dividends of the shareholders. A government commission in 1927 recommended that the shareholders be bought out and that the management of the line should be transferred to the county councils. This duly happened and the new management made efforts to modernise the line, introducing a diesel railcar to cut costs. Despite this the losses continued and in a first showing of their true colours towards the railways of Northern Ireland, the government effectively refused to support the line any longer and it closed on 31 December 1941. Perhaps the custodianship of the GSR wasn't so bad a fate for a narrow gauge line after all.

County Tyrone had another steam tramway, less grand and ambitious than the CVR and one which slightly pre-dated it, in the form of the Castlederg & Victoria Bridge Tramway, whose engineer James Barton was poached by the CVR when it was incorporated. After the Londonderry & Enniskillen Railway reached the small hamlet of Victoria Bridge, named after the adjacent bridge over the river Mourne, in 1852, thoughts began to turn to a connection to the market town of Castlederg some 7 miles distant. Nothing happened until 1881 when plans were made for a tramway linking Castlederg to the, by now, GNR station at Victoria Bridge. Though the line was authorised before the Tramways Act became law, the Tyrone Grand Jury agreed to guarantee the interest of 5 per cent on £13,000 of the line's £20,000 capital for a period of thirty-five years. The c&VBT's Act allowed for the repayment of guarantees made in poor years if there was later a sufficient surplus in good trading conditions. This was a sensible idea in theory and though the C&VBT was moderately prosperous in its early decades, it never generated enough profit to enable this to happen. The line was inspected and approved by the Board of Trade in 1883 and carried 16,000 passengers in its first half-year. The tramway ran from a platform at the GNR station at Victoria Bridge, mostly along the side of the road, with several modest halts along the way. One of these was named Crew, without the 'e', and I have often mused whether a parcel or, heaven forfend, even a passenger finished up there rather than at the mega junction in Cheshire which had the final 'e' in its name.

Because of the gradient leading down towards Victoria Bridge station and the possibility of tramway vehicles breaking away and fouling the broad gauge line, the Board of Trade insisted that the C&VBT installed the automatic Westinghouse brake, probably the most efficient railway brake in the world at the time, and its first application in Ireland. The Board of Trade might have been better employed investigating the braking systems used on the adjacent GNR at the time, as events at Armagh in 1889 were shortly to demonstrate. The service on the tramway usually consisted of three trains a day connecting with GNR services, with extras run in conjunction with fairs. As was normal tramway practice, the locomotives' motions had to be boxed in to protect road users from coming into contact with flailing pistons and connecting rods. As they were never turned, only the side facing the road needed this treatment, giving them a slightly odd appearance. The fate of the C&VBT in the twentieth century is an all too familiar one. It performed reasonably well, generating modest surpluses up to the time of the First World War. The easy availability of cheap, often army surplus, vehicles in the 1920s on the roads of Ireland made a line such as this very vulnerable and it began to show deficits in its accounts from the mid-1920s onwards, and even the introduction of one of Ireland's first railcars, built in the workshops at Castlederg by the line's locomotive superintendent, George Pollard, could not stem the tide. In 1932, which turned out to be its last year of operation, expenditure was £1,026 ahead of receipts and accumulated debts of £4,662 rendered the C&VBT virtually insolvent. Its fate was finally determined by the railway strike in Northern Ireland in 1933. The line operated on 30 January 1933, the day before the strike commenced, but never ran again, and the company was wound up in September of that year, another addition to the growing list of Irish 3 ft gauge lines which had fallen victim to the internal combustion engine.

For most of those with an interest in railways, the Irish narrow gauge is associated with ancient steam engines bouncing along roadside tramways, the very essence of the late nineteenth-century steam railway. Before heading to Donegal to explore the two biggest 3 ft gauge systems, which were far removed from that picture, we have two final short 3 ft gauge lines in Ulster to consider, both of which were at the very forefront of technology when they were opened in the 1880s as they were powered by the new force of electricity. From the middle of the nineteenth century the spinning of flax and the production of linen became a major industry in Ulster. Some of the first mills were built at Bessbrook in County Armagh and in 1846 these were taken over and expanded by the Richardson family who created a model village at Bessbrook for their workers. As the mills grew, more and more workers were drawn from the nearby town (now city) of Newry. The need to provide transport for them and to carry coal and flax from the port up to Bessbrook led to the building of a 3 mile long 3 ft gauge tramway which opened on 1 October 1885. What was different about this line was the decision made at the outset to work it by electricity provided by hydroelectric generation from a power station located at Millvale, near Bessbrook. The line was constructed by Dr Edward Hopkinson, a pioneer of electric traction, who worked the line for the first six months to prove the technology was effective.

Power, at 245 volts DC, was supplied from a third rail between the tracks except for one short stretch where the line crossed over the Newry to Bessbrook road. Here overhead wires were used from which the trams drew their power using bow collectors on their roofs. The line ran from outside the GNR station at Newry Edward Street at average gradients of 1 in 86, steepening to 1 in 50 in places, terminating outside the mill at Bessbrook, where the tram shed was also located. The line passed under the Craigmore viaduct on the GNR's Dublin to Belfast main line, and part of its trackbed, which is used as a path by the locals, can still be seen from expresses passing overhead. Conventional looking single deck tramcars were used and they often hauled a couple of goods wagons. Apart from the novelty of its propulsion system, the tramway's other interesting innovation was in how it handled its goods traffic. The goods wagons had flangeless wheels. The wagons were kept on track literally by having a third rail at a slightly lower level than the running rail. The flangeless wheels meant they could be used as road vehicles when they were off the tramway, thus overcoming one of the great drawbacks of rail freight, the need to trans-ship goods from the railway wagon to a road vehicle for onward conveyance to a final destination. Admittedly speeds on the tramway were very moderate, but if a modern version of this technology could be made to work, it would revolutionise the carriage of goods on railways today. This very early electric tramway quietly carried on about its business for over sixty years, finally falling victim to competition from the roads in 1948, the last trams running on 10 January of that year.

Ulster's other electric railway missed, by about a month, the distinction of being the first electrically powered line in these islands to open for public service, to the Volks Electric Railway which ran along the foreshore at Brighton for about a quarter of a mile and started operations in August 1883. But because the Irish line was far longer and more complex, and ran occasional unofficial trips earlier, the moral right to the title surely lies with the Giant's Causeway Tramway, or to give it its proper title, the Giant's Causeway, Portrush & Bush Valley Railway and Tramway Company Limited. The origins of the scheme were not untypical of many other lines built to both gauges in different parts of Ireland, the desire of sections of the population in a district not served by a railway, to get one. In this case the area concerned was that to the east of the seaside resort of Portrush, which had been rapidly growing since the railway to the town from Coleraine had opened in April 1855. At a meeting in Bushmills in 1879 two schemes were considered. One was for a connection from Bushmills into the Ballycastle Railway, which was then under construction, at Dervock, with a possible extension cross country to join the BC&RB line. Nothing ever came of this, but the other line discussed was adopted and pursued, that of a tramway along the coast from Bushmills to Portrush. The meeting had been chaired by Dr Anthony Traill and he and his brother William, who came from the area, were to play a significant role in what followed. Dr Traill was later provost of Trinity College in Dublin and his bother had gained an engineering degree there. The Traills were clearly driving the scheme in a particular direction which was made clear when the Act for the tramway, passed in August 1880, permitted the working of the line by electricity. The brothers —I am desperately trying to avoid describing them as trailblazers, but can restrain myself no longer—had connections with some of the leading pioneers in the application of electricity such as Lord Kelvin and Dr William Siemens. Some of these men invested in the company and Siemens became a director. This little tramway less than 10 miles long and passing along one of the most beautiful stretches of coastline in the whole of Ireland, was at the cutting edge of science in the 1880s.

Different methods of delivering the current to the line were explored. The original idea was to use a two-rail system, the rails insulated from each other, which will be familiar to railway modellers, but a lot of current leaked away especially in wet weather. The directors settled on running the current through a third or conductor rail located on the coastal side of the line, away from the public road, similar to that used today on commuter lines south of the Thames in London. Power was eventually provided by a hydroelectric generating station at Walkmills near Bushmills. The tramway cost £21,000 to build. Construction began in 1881 from the Bushmills end and the line was inspected and approved by the Board of Trade in January 1883. The theoretical voltage was 250 and during the Board of Trade inspection, William Traill removed his trousers and sat on the third rail to prove how safe it was. Some sources suggested that the staff at the power station had been forewarned to greatly reduce the voltage while this stunt was taking place. However, the use of the third rail was not permitted at the extremities of the line where it ran through the streets of Bushmills and Portrush to reach its termini. Steam tramway locomotives hauled the trams on these sections and were also used for goods traffic. The line was extended to one of Ireland's premier tourist attractions, then as now, the Giant's Causeway, in July 1887. There were many problems with the technology in the early years, particularly due to current leakage to the extent that, in 1888 the steam locomotives ran twice the mileage of the electric tramcars. Then in 1895 an accident, when a cyclist came off his machine and came into contact with the third rail with fatal consequences, caused a major change to the way the line was worked. The Board of Trade inspector who investigated the accident discovered that the voltage in the third rail fluctuated as high as 310 and averaged 290 and he insisted that electric haulage be suspended until the system was made safe. Overhead wires were put up to replace the third rail and the electric working resumed in July 1899.

The tramway was totally dependent on the summer tourist traffic; indeed winter services were suspended in the 1920s though briefly revived during and just after the Second World War. Though a mixed gauge siding was shared with the B&NCR down to Portrush Harbour, goods traffic on the line never amounted to anything. It was never terribly successful and a wet summer could affect its balance sheet. In 1903 the directors offered the line for sale to the English Midland Railway, who had bought the B&NCR in July of that year, but the offer was declined. A similar proposal was put to the LMS in the 1920s, but again without success. Obviously vulnerable to buses and charabancs after the end of the Great War and with very limited funds to renew the track and overhead, a familiar tale is being told. After the Second World War the directors offered the line to the UTA, who also declined. Faced with falling receipts, an increasingly worn out tramway, and a predictable lack of interest from the government of Northern Ireland in a line which could have become a tourist attraction in its own right, the directors reached the end of their resources and the last trams ran to the Causeway on 30 September 1949. In the

1990s a section of the line from the outskirts of Bushmills to the Causeway was reopened as a 3 ft gauge steam tourist railway, and while it is pleasant to see narrow gauge steam engines at work in any circumstances these days, what is there today is a far cry from the Giant's Causeway Tramway in its heyday.

And so to Donegal, the home of the two largest Irish narrow gauge systems, where the 3 ft gauge reigned supreme and yet where the two dominant companies scarcely seemed to notice each other to the extent that most of the rolling stock of the two concerns could not be coupled together. Both the Donegal railways began life as broad gauge lines. The first to get under way was the Londonderry & Lough Swilly Railway which was incorporated in the early 1850s to build a line from the city of Derry to a pier on the shores of Lough Swilly. Construction did not start until 1860 and it was not until 1863 that the first train ran to the pier at Farland Point from where boats served the small communities around the shores of the lough. In 1861 an Act authorised the L&LSR to extend their line along the eastern shore of Lough Swilly to Buncrana. The route left the existing line at a remote spot that eventually (in the 1920s) became known as Tooban Junction and there was another short branch, more of a siding, to another pier, that at Fahan, on the new line, which opened in September 1864. The line from the junction to Farland Point closed in 1866 after one of the shortest innings in the entire history of Ireland's railways. The final development in the 1860s was an Act authorising the Letterkenny Railway to build a line from that town to Tooban Junction from whence they would use the existing L&LSR track to reach Derry. This route had triumphed over another proposal to build a line to the shores of the Foyle, near Saint Johnstown, where it would make a junction with the existing Londonderry & Enniskillen line. Lack of finance put an end to this scheme and it would be over twenty years before this part of the system was actually built.

At almost exactly the same time, in another part of the county, the first component of the system which was eventually to be known as the County Donegal Railways, got under way. In 1860 the Finn Valley Railway was authorised to build a line the 14 miles from Strabane, on the former Londonderry & Enniskillen line which from 1862 became part of the Irish North Western Railway, to the twin towns of Ballybofey and Stranorlar. The capital required to build the line was £60,000, but this proved difficult to raise and it was only completed with the help of a loan of £20,000 from the Public Works Loan Commissioners. When it opened in August 1863, the line was worked on behalf of the FVR by the recently constituted INWR. These two short broad gauge branches were apparently all that could be delivered to County Donegal by the conventional methods of financing railways. Though the FVR posted dividends of around 2 per cent in the 1870s, its traffic never lived up to the levels anticipated in its prospectus, and the solution to this problem for some lay in an extension from Stranorlar to Donegal town. A separate company, the West Donegal Railway, was formed with the backing of the FVR board and in 1879 was authorised to raise £150,000 to build this line with a gauge of 3 ft through the Barnsmore Gap in the Blue Stack Mountains. The almost inevitable difficulties in raising the capital soon emerged and by 1881 it was clear there was not enough money to complete the line to Donegal town. The WDR line stalled at Druminin, near Lough Eske, 4 miles from its intended destination, and when services began in 1882 the trains went no further for another seven years. However, Donegal had got its first narrow gauge line which was worked for the WDR by the FVR, whose broad gauge line was still being worked by the GNR, the successor of the INWR, and for the next twelve years Stranorlar station would play host to two gauges. The gap was eventually closed in 1889 when the line from Druminin to Donegal town was completed. Even then, not enough money could be raised to build a station and a separate company, the Donegal Railway Station Company, was formed to build it. This company then rented the station back to the WDR at £200 per annum. The line was inspected by our old friend, Major General Hutchinson, in September 1889 and opened for traffic on the 16th of that month.

Meanwhile attempts had been going on since 1860 to build a railway to Letterkenny. Some construction work had been done in the wake of the LR's Act of that year, but capital could not be raised partly because of the major national economic crisis which followed the collapse of the great London financial house of Overend and Gurney in 1866 and a stock market crash and high interest rates which then ensued. Several more Acts of Parliament followed, but the line remained derelict and unfinished until a proposal came from the Derry firm of contractors, McCrea & McFarland, that the line should be built to the 3 ft gauge to save money. The LR obtained a new Act in 1880 authorising a narrow gauge railway which also gave the L&LSR the power to regauge their existing line. With the aid of a loan of £85,000 from the Board of Works, the line from Letterkenny to Tooban Junction opened in June 1883. The LR was worked from the outset by the L&LSR which converted its existing line from Derry to Buncrana to the 3 ft gauge in the spring of 1885. The first two Swilly narrow gauge engines had been built for the ill-fated Glenariff line in County Antrim and were bought cheaply when the GIO&HC's assets were sold off to pay its chief creditor, the Earl of Antrim.

The time-honoured methods of railway promotion had clearly not been a success in delivering a railway network to County Donegal. The great expansion of the 3 ft gauge in the county which was about to take off was due to very different circumstances. In 1885, the government appointed a royal commission under Sir James Allport to investigate the conduct of public works in Ireland. Allport was one of the most respected and enlightened railway managers in Britain. In 1853 he had been appointed general manager of the Midland Railway, an office which he held continuously, with the exception of a few years between 1857 and 1860, until his retirement in 1880, when he became a director of the company. During these twenty-three years the Midland grew to be one of the most important railway companies in England. In railway circles Allport is remembered as a pioneer of cheap and comfortable railway travel for the less well-off. He saw the Third-Class passenger as an important source of revenue and, accordingly, in 1872 he inaugurated a policy, later copied by most other companies, of carrying Third-Class passengers in decent carriages at a fare of one penny a mile. When he retired in 1880 he was given an honorary directorship of the

Midland, and was knighted in 1884.

With such a figure at its helm, the Allport Commission's brief inevitably included railways, their promotion, organisation and management, and whether they needed financial support from the Treasury. The Commission's report in 1888 stopped short of advocating nationalisation, which would probably not have been acceptable in political terms at the time, but it recognised the shortcomings of the existing methods of finance when it came to extending railways into poorer and more remote districts. The report also made specific recommendations for the construction of some eleven light railways, including two in County Donegal. The findings of the Allport Commission led directly to the Light Railways (Ireland) Act of 1889, sometimes called the Balfour Act after Arthur Balfour, Chief Secretary of Ireland at the time and a driving force behind the policy of constructive unionism. For the first time this Act allowed direct state aid in the form of grants, rather than loans or guarantees, in an attempt to encourage the existing railway companies to build and work light railways in unpromising parts of Ireland. The grants could apply to lines on either gauge and, as we will see in the next chapter, led to the construction of a number of broad gauge routes mainly in Mayo and Kerry.

However, both the railway companies operating in County Donegal benefited from the Act. In 1892 parliament sanctioned the merger of the FVR and the WDR to form the Donegal Railway Company, and in 1893 it approved the conversion of the original Finn Valley line from Stranorlar to Strabane to the 3 ft gauge. A new approach into Strabane by a separate bridge over the river Mourne, leading to a new narrow gauge station adjacent to the GNR one, was also built and narrow gauge trains ran into Strabane for the first time in July 1894. The Balfour Act provided funding for two extensions to the DR system in lines from Donegal town west to the fishing village of Killybegs on which services commenced in August 1893, and a branch from Stranorlar to Glenties which opened in June 1895. This brought the route mileage of the DR up to 75 miles. Let us now complete the story of the DR's expansion and ownership before returning to the north

27 An early view of Ireland's first railway, the Dublin & Kingstown. A train leaves Westland Row station and is seen on the bridge which carried the line over South Cumberland Street. The locomotive is 2-2-0 *Kingstown*, one of three similar machines built by George Forrester and Company in Liverpool for the opening of the line. (*National Library of Ireland*)

28 There is little left today to remind us that for a brief few years in the mid 1840s, the extension of the Dublin & Kingstown Railway up to Dalkey was at the cutting edge of contemporary railway technology (see page 18–20), apart from the name of this road in Dalkey, which was photographed in 2008. (*Brian Hughes*)

29 From the middle of the nineteenth century, the major Irish railway companies did their best to promote tourist traffic and they produced much material extolling the scenic virtues of the districts they served. The smiling colleen on the cover of *Magic Miles in Ireland* was a late entry into the field. This 56-page booklet, complete with a map of the north of the country which only went as far south as Dublin, was published by the Great Northern Railway in 1939. (*Courtesy of Dr Paul Collins*)

30 If there was a more attractive livery in which to turn out a steam locomotive than the sky blue of the GNR, I have yet to see it. In August 1957, 1948 built U class 4-4-0 No. 204 *Antrim* is seen in all its glory at Bundoran Junction. (*Author's collection*)

31 The Cavan & Leitrim section of CIÉ had become a reliquary of the Irish 3ft gauge by the 1950s as CIÉ and the GSR before it had transferred wagons, carriages and engines from other narrow gauge lines as they had closed over the years. Among the more remarkable survivors were the four 2-4-2 tank locomotives which constituted the entire fleet of the Cork, Blackrock & Passage line, which had closed as long ago as 1932. One of these engines was recorded at the narrow gauge platform at Dromod in July 1957. (*Richard Kehm*)

32 It was the output of the coal mines at Arigna which enabled the C&L to remain in business for so long. As late as 1957, an additional steam locomotive had to be sent to the line to cope with the traffic. It all ended when a coal-fired power station was opened near Arigna which absorbed the output of the local mines. This is a view dating from August 1957, looking back over the bucking coal wagons as a coal train rolls along the roadside tramway not far from Arigna. (*Author's collection*)

33 The narrow gauge in County Donegal survived until 1959. While most passenger workings had been in the hands of railcars for many years, the CDR continued to use steam locomotives on its goods services and excursion trains. No. 5 *Drumboe* built in 1907 is shunting some goods wagons at Stranorlar in July 1957. It is one of a number of CDR steam locomotives which managed to escape the scrap man and is still in existence. (*Richard Kehm*)

34 CDR railcar No. 10, recorded at Stranorlar in July 1957, was the prototype for the long line of articulated diesel CDR railcars built by Walkers which provided most of the passenger services on this system from the 1930s onwards. Originally supplied to the Clogher Valley Railway in 1932, its performance there so impressed the CDR general manager Henry Forbes that the first similar railcar for the CDR was delivered two years later. On the closure of the CVR in 1941, the railcar was bought by the CDR and is now on display at the Ulster Folk & Transport Museum. (*Richard Kehm*)

35 From being the butt of Percy French's humour, the narrow gauge in West Clare survived to become, in the 1950s, the only 3 ft gauge line in Ireland to be completely modernised thanks to CIÉ. One of the new railcars paired with a trailer coach built at Inchicore is seen here at Kilrush. (*Richard Kehm*)

36 Even though passenger services on the lines serving west Cork were provided by diesel locomotives and railcars from the mid 1950s, a steam presence lingered on until the whole system was closed in 1961. One unusual feature of the former CB&SCR Albert Quay terminus in Cork was its elevated signal box which had a track running beneath it. This July 1957 view shows the signal box with 0-6-0 tank No. 552 in attendance, acting as the station pilot. This loco was built in 1891 for the MGWR; its original number was 107 and it was named *Robin*. It remained in service with CIÉ until 1963. (*Richard Kehm*)

37 The Sligo, Leitrim & Northern Counties Railway could be described in modern parlance as the victim of collateral damage in the mass closures of the GNR lines in 1957. There was no outlet for its traffic once the GNR routes though Enniskillen had gone. One of its distinctive 0-6-4 tanks *Sir Henry* was recorded shunting at Enniskillen in July 1957, a few weeks before the axe fell on these lines. (*Richard Kehm*)

38 *Sir Henry* is seen again, this time at Belcoo, where the train has been stopped for customs examination. This heavy cattle train of the type which was the lifeblood of the SLNCR for so many years was being run on 15 August 1957, just before the line was forced to close. Known only by name, SLNCR locomotives charmingly were never given numbers. *Sir Henry*, built in 1904 and still looking in excellent external condition, was reduced to scrap after the line closed. (*Author's collection*)

39 Though steam traction ended on CIÉ in 1963, steam locomotives operated by the UTA continued to appear on the GNR main line south of the border. Former NCC W class 2-6-0 No. 104 leaves Dundalk to tackle the stiff climb up to the border with a long goods train for Portadown and Belfast in June 1963. (*Richard Kehm*)

40 Ireland's last steam locomotive, Oliver Bulleid's extraordinary CC1, known universally as the Turf Burner, takes its place in the line-up at Inchicore. It was unreliable, and while it worked some test trains and a few goods trains to and from the North Wall, it was never entrusted with a revenue-earning passenger service. Its creator's retirement from the service of CIÉ sealed its fate. (*John Click/Courtesy of the National Railway Museum*)

41 Regular passenger services on the light railway from Ballinascarthy on the Clonakilty branch, to Timoleague and Courtmacsherry in west Cork, were suspended due to the fuel shortages of 1947 and never resumed. However, the line remained open for goods and sugar beet traffic until 1961, and during the summer, regular excursions were run to enable Corkonians to enjoy the sea air at Courtmacsherry. C class diesel C232 has just arrived there with one of these workings in May 1958. The locomotive had only been delivered in January of that year and its silver livery still looks very clean and attractive. (*John Edgington*)

42 CIÉ's interim livery between the ill-starred silver and the later black and orange, was the attractive shade of light green displayed here on a set of the 1952 built AEC railcars arriving at Kildare in June 1963 forming a service to Waterford. (*Richard Kehm*)

43 The silver livery which initially adorned CIÉ's diesel locomotives, was woefully inadequate to cope with the ravages of the Irish climate. This view of a goods train at Kildare in June 1963 illustrates the condition to which it was quickly reduced in normal service. The locomotive here is one of a small class of 12 Sulzer engined locos built by the Birmingham Railway Carriage & Wagon Company and delivered to CIÉ in 1956/57. Such is the state of the loco, it is impossible to identify which one it is! (*Richard Kehm*)

44 The CIÉ railcars delivered in 1952 were based on the vehicles built by AEC for the GNR in the late 1940s. The GNR railcars were painted in a most attractive blue and cream livery which was also used on the company's buses and on most of the tramcars running on its Hill of Howth Tramway. This was the GNR's vision of the future, but sadly it never had the resources to fully modernise its services. These railcars are seen at Tynan station on the old Ulster Railway main line between Portadown and Clones which was swept away, along with so much else, in September 1957. (*Author's collection*)

45 The first General Motors diesels, the 121 class, were painted in an unusual and short-lived silver/grey livery trimmed with yellow. One of them, B133 is seen at Amiens Street station probably on a train for Sligo on 16 August 1961. The through platforms at Amiens Street were added when the line across the Liffey was built at the end of the nineteenth century. (*Author's collection*)

46 After a spell in green livery, CIÉ's diesel fleet were repainted in a new black and amber livery from the mid 1960s onwards. Variations of this livery continue to be used well into the Iarnród Éireann era in the new millennium. C224 is seen at Dundalk in June 1964 on a goods train. (*Richard Kehm*)

47 The final use of some of the GNR and CIÉ railcars of the 1940s and 1950s was on the suburban service between Howth and Bray before the advent of the DART. With their engines removed, pushed and pulled by 1950s vintage C class diesel locomotives which had at least been rebuilt with GM diesel engines which were more reliable than their original Crossley power units, the old railcars fitted with plastic seats provided a service of sorts. The sight of the overhead wires above this set entering Connolly in the early 1980s is at least a sign that this ordeal for the unfortunate commuters on this vital corridor was nearing its end. (*Author*)

48 It is probably true to say that the resurgence in the fortunes of Ireland's railways began with the electrification of the Howth to Bray line in the 1980s. The acronym DART (Dublin Area Rapid Transit) has become a part of the everyday language of Dubliners and original fleet of German-built two-car electric units, two of which are seen here arriving at Dun Laoghaire in June 1986, has since been added to as the passenger numbers carried have continued to soar. (*Author*)

49 One of the most scenic routes still open for traffic in Ireland is surely the south Wexford line from Rosslare to Waterford, built as part of the grand scheme hatched by the Great Western Railway and the GSWR to open a new sea route across the Irish Sea in the first decade of the last century. In October 1983, a General Motors diesel brings a passenger train from Waterford to Rosslare off the great engineering feature of the line, the longest railway bridge in Ireland, the 2,131 ft long 13-span Barrow Bridge. The disused platform in the foreground was built in the 1960s to facilitate workers building the nearby Great Island power station. (*Author*)

50 The great viaduct over the river Boyne at Drogheda was the last link in the Dublin to Belfast line to be put in place. The first passenger trains used a temporary wooden viaduct opened in June 1853 to enable visitors from the north to visit the great exhibition in Dublin which had been promoted by William Dargan. Countless other special excursions have crossed the bridge since then, including this one formed of NIR 80 class railcars which was bringing Down GAA supporters to Croke Park to see the All Ireland Football semi final in August 1991. Down beat Kerry that day and went on to win the All Ireland title that year. (*Author*)

51 Until the arrival of the first of the new generation of diesel railcars, branded the Arrows, in the mid 1990s, virtually all passenger trains operated by CIÉ and latterly Iarnród Éireann consisted of diesel locomotives hauling sets of unpowered carriages. Typical of the early IÉ era is this view of a 071 class General Motors diesel locomotive at the head of a set of air-conditioned coaches seen on the quayside line at Wexford on the last leg of its journey from Connolly station in Dublin to Rosslare. (*Iarnród Éireann*)

52 In the last decade, Iarnród Éireann's emphasis in acquiring new passenger rolling stock has shifted from locomotives and carriages to railcars. Typical of the change are these four-car units built in Spain, seen on a test run from the new railcar servicing depot at Drogheda, passing through Gormanston station on the former GNR main line. A relic of 'auld dacency' can be glimpsed on the right of the picture in the shape of the GNR wooden waiting shelter on the up platform. Examples of this standard GNR shelter could once be seen at stations all over the north of Ireland. (*Iarnród Éireann*)

53 The Hill of Howth tramway was held in great affection by generations of Dubliners and there was much regret at its closure in 1959. This was the last electric tramway in all of Ireland and it would not be until the next century, with the advent of the Luas, that this form of transport returned to the country. Here tramcar No. 7 built for the opening of the tramway in 1901 waits for passengers at Sutton station on the GNR Howth branch. (*Richard Kehm*)

54 One of the problems with Heuston (as Kingsbridge was renamed in 1966), designed by the architect Sancton Wood for the opening of the GSWR line in the 1840s, is that it is some distance from the city centre. Whilst Dublin's first generation electric trams linked the station to the city centre and a variety of bus services have also fulfilled the same function over the years, rail passengers arriving in the capital now have the option of taking a tram on the Red Line of the new Luas system, another magnificent embellishment to the city, to the heart of Dublin or to the city's other great railway terminus, the former GNR citadel in Amiens Street, Connolly station. (*Iarnród Éireann*)

55 Luas line A, from St Stephen's Green to Sandyford and beyond—when planned extensions are opened—follows the course of the old railway line from Dundrum to Harcourt Street for most of the way. One advantage the tram has over the train is that it is able to continue down Harcourt Street past the site of the old station and get much closer to the heart of the city. The trams are quiet, clean and unobtrusive, elegant twenty-first-century technology blending in with the splendid Georgian architecture of Harcourt Street itself. (*Alamy*)

56 Since the turn of the millennium, Iarnród Éireann's passenger figures have been increasing in percentage terms at one of the consistently highest rates in Europe. This is partly a reflection of the Republic's economic success but is also a response to the increasing levels of investment which are at last being made in the country's railways. (*Iarnród Éireann*)

57 In 2005 delivery began of a fleet of 67 new carriages for Iarnród Éireann's InterCity services. The order, worth €117 million, given to CAF (Construcciones Y Auxiliar De Ferrocarriles) of Spain was both the first new order for InterCity carriages in almost twenty years and the largest ever fleet investment in the history of Ireland's railways. The new stock normally runs in eight-coach rakes and operate in push-pull fashion with a 201 class loco at one end and a driving trailer at the other. This method of operation means that the locomotive does not have to run round the train at termini and allows a quicker turn round. Here driving trailer No. 4001 heads a service on the Cork line. (*Iarnród Éireann*)

of the county. Much of the traffic on the DR, such as coal, originated from Derry and it was inconvenient to have to trans-ship this at Strabane between the two gauges. Despite opposition from the GNR, naturally, the DR was authorised to build a narrow gauge line to Londonderry in 1896. This line, which opened in August 1900, reached the city by running on the opposite side of Lough Foyle from the Donegal shore, which was already occupied by the GNR route. The 14½ mile long line via Donemana and New Buildings ended at the city's fourth terminus at Victoria Road, beside the only bridge over the Foyle. A mixed gauge siding was later built to the nearby Waterside station of the BNCR. Also authorised in 1896 was an extension from Donegal town to Ballyshannon. Because neither the Derry nor Ballyshannon lines served impoverished or congested districts, there was no financial assistance for either, which helps explain why the Ballyshannon line did not open until September 1905.

By this time the ownership of the DR had changed. In 1903 one of England's biggest railways, the Midland, whose main lines ran from St Pancras station in London to Carlisle, bought the B&NCR. To run its new Irish acquisition, the MR established a management structure based in Belfast called the Northern Counties Committee consisting of locally based management and colleagues from across the Irish Sea. When the MR lost its independence in the 1923 grouping of Britain's railways this structure was perpetuated and continued to manage these lines, the name changing from MR/NCC to LMS/NCC. Probably because there was little or no room left for an expansion of its empire in Britain, and seeing Ireland as the only place left to extend its interests, the MR approached the DR with a view to purchasing it. The arrival of a powerful new neighbour on its doorstep alarmed the GNR who objected to the deal. Eventually the two companies bought the DR jointly. A similar structure to that which managed the MR's other interests in Ireland was set up to run the narrow gauge lines in County Donegal, in conjunction with the GNR. To manage their acquisition, a joint committee was set up, made up of three members from each company. This body, the County Donegal Railways Joint Committee, remained in existence up to

1971. One effect of the acquisition was that ownership of the Derry branch of the CDR passed to the MR to create the illusion of competition with the GNR-owned line on the other side of the Foyle. It was after the CDR had been created that the final part of its network was built. The original plan of the Letterkenny Railway back in the 1860s had been for a line from that town towards the River Foyle and not the route which was eventually built and worked by the L&LSR, towards Derry. Over forty years later this idea was revived by the nominally independent Strabane & Letterkenny Railway which was authorised in 1904 to build a line linking those two towns, Lifford and Raphoe. Financed mainly by the new joint owners, this line opened in January 1909 and brought the CDR network up to a route mileage of 124½, making it by some distance the biggest narrow gauge railway company not just in Ireland but in the whole of the British Isles.

Turning back to north Donegal, we embark on the great epic of the Irish narrow gauge, which was officially known as the Letterkenny & Burtonport Extension Railway. This was one of two extensions to the L&LSR system which were the direct result of the Balfour Act of 1889. The first was a relatively straightforward addition of the existing line to Buncrana to bring it to Carndonagh, a small town near the head of the Inishowen Peninsula whose tip, Malin Head, is the most northerly point on the map of Ireland. The 18½ mile long line which opened on 1 July 1901, with a service of three trains daily in each direction, was paid for by a grant of £98,527 from the Treasury. This was but small change compared to the other extension which was approved in 1898. There had been discussions about extending the L&LSR towards the Atlantic coast of County Donegal earlier in the decade but lack of finance had scuppered these ideas. By 1898 the Congested Districts Board had built a new harbour at Burtonport and thoughts turned to a railway to transport the fish landed there. The route as the crow flies from Letterkenny, from where such a line would start, to Burtonport, is less than 30 miles, but the crow would have to fly over high mountain peaks to get there, so the route by rail, as built, was just shy of 50 miles.

The line traversed some of the bleakest and most remote

landscapes in the whole of Ireland and served scarcely a sizeable village on the way. The railway was planned by the L&LSR who would work it, and by the Board of Works who would pay for it to the tune of some £300,000. It was a difficult line to construct with stretches of bogland into which the contractor, the English firm of Pauling & Company, reported that whole sections of completed track sank without trace, alternating with rocky outcrops through which a line had to be blasted. The main engineering feature of the line, the Owencarrow viaduct 380 yards in length, carried the track over a valley through which flowed the Owencarrow river and down which were funnelled Atlantic gales in winter, leading to trains being blown off the track on two occasions. The first in 1906 did not cause any fatalities, but on 30 January 1925 a train was blown off the viaduct again, this time resulting in the death of four passengers. An ominous feature of the line, which seasoned travellers would have noted from a study of their copy of Bradshaw or another railway timetable compendium, was the use of the word 'Road' after several stations on the L&BER, such as Dungloe Road and Dunfanaghy Road. Translated into the reality on the ground, this meant that the station concerned was a considerable distance from the place it purported to serve and a further journey in a horse-drawn car would be required to reach one's destination.

The distance from the L&LSR's Graving Dock station in Derry to Burtonport was 74½ miles and those proposing to embark on this epic, the longest through run on the Irish 3 ft gauge, would have needed to set aside about five hours for it. When the line opened there were two trains only on weekdays and one on Sunday. The Board of Works insisted that an additional service be provided, but by 1916 the L&LSR had cut the service back to two trains a day. At times we all tend to look at the past through the eyes of a romantic rather than wish to have our view of it disturbed by the intrusion of reality, and when something as emotive as a steam locomotive is involved, many of us react in the dewy-eyed sort of way which is evoked in others by Labrador puppies. To temper the romance of the thought of a steam locomotive battling the gradients up to Barnes Gap and then screeching round the curves and on to the Owencarrow viaduct, perhaps we should bear in mind that we would probably be sitting on wooden slatted seats bereft of upholstery, in a carriage lit by a dim oil lamp, at least in the early years of the L&BER, and without heating apart from maybe a footwarmer, some of which the L&LSR acquired second hand from the MGWR. Steam heating was never provided by the company. By the time you were well out on the extension, whatever relief the hot water supplied in Derry provided would have long gone and you would be huddled in your coat to try and keep warm.

There were many disputes between the Board of Works and the L&LSR over the line. Despite the vast amount of money spent on it, the line seems to have been poorly made, as later reports into its condition suggested. The L&BER was a separate organisation and the board insisted that the locomotives supplied for the opening of the line, a quartet of 4-6-0 tanks which the Swilly claimed were anyway inadequate for a line of this length, carried the letters 'L&BER' on their tanks and in theory they were not to be used elsewhere on the L&LSR system, which of course was far from the case. There were many exchanges of angry correspondence provoked when a Board of Works official found one of their locomotives at work away from the Burtonport line. The Swilly took matters into their own hands and in 1905 acquired two magnificent 4-8-0 tender engines, by far the largest machines ever to run on the Irish 3 ft gauge and indeed the only tender engines of this wheel arrangement to run anywhere in these islands. Built by Hudswell Clarke in Leeds, these were followed in 1912 by two massive 4-8-4 tank engines from the same manufacturer. At last there was now adequate motive power to get to Burtonport. These rows dragged on for years until finally, in 1908, the matter was brought before the Vice-Regal Commission on Irish Railways which arbitrated between the warring parties and ordered the Board of Works to pay for improvements to the line and provide £7,000 to buy additional rolling stock for the Burtonport line.

With the opening of the government-funded extensions to Carndonagh and Burtonport, the total route mileage worked by the L&LSR was 99. The two Donegal companies between them now operated over 220 miles of 3 ft gauge track. From 1909 they were neighbours at Letterkenny, where the CDR line from Strabane terminated at a separate station beside the Swilly one. Up to that time the only link between the two was a tenuous one. Wagons could be hauled from the Swilly station at Graving Dock along the mixed gauge tracks owned by the Londonderry Port and Harbour Commissioners on the west side of the River Foyle, past the GNR station at Foyle Road, put on a wagon turntable at the Carlisle Bridge and hauled by capstans along the bottom deck of the bridge to reach the CDR line on the other side of the river, again by means of a wagon turntable. This performance was hardly likely to encourage much through traffic. There was virtually no co-operation between the two companies. Swilly wagons had brake pipes, couplings and buffers which were incompatible with CDR vehicles. It was only with the opening of the S&L line that the CDR acquired a couple of batches of covered wagons which had couplers which could be adjusted to run with L&LSR stock. Through ticketing was unheard of, and when in 1922 the Swilly wanted to test one of the CDR's successful 2-6-4 tank engines on its line with a view to buying similar machines, the request was turned down by the CDR's feisty general manager, Henry Forbes.

As the twentieth century progressed, the two railways took very different courses. The partition of Ireland left nearly all of both companies' lines in the Free State, but with their main stations in Northern Ireland at Strabane and Derry. Because they crossed into Northern Ireland they escaped the clutches of the GSR, but the border imposed different tariff regimes. Customs examinations delayed the carriage of goods, and passengers were subjected to having their luggage searched by officials, many of whom would later have been considered unsuitable for the Gestapo because of their lack of charm. Derry was cut off from its natural economic hinterland in County Donegal and in time traditional patterns of commercial activity were realigned to cope with the political reality on the ground. This was on top of the nationwide problem besetting the minor railways which we have discussed elsewhere, the rapid growth of road transport in the wake of the Great War. As early as 1925, the L&LSR was losing money and needed subventions from both jurisdictions to stay afloat. In 1927 the Swilly directors approached the CDR to take over the working of their system but were rebuffed. A deputation from the CDR toured the system in one of their railcars but declined to become involved. While, as we will see, the CDR had been experimenting with railcars as far back as 1906, the L&LSR doggedly, and with mounting financial problems, continued to work its lines with steam.

Then in 1927 separate pieces of legislation passed in both the Free State and Northern Ireland allowed railway companies to operate bus services and starting in 1929, the L&LSR began to buy out existing operators. By the end of 1931 it owned 37 buses and 2 lorries and was on a course that was to turn it from a railway operator into a bus company. By 1931 the road services were already making money while the railway continued to lose it. The railway also suffered from the 1933 strike which was a great boon to lorries waiting to pounce on the railways' goods traffic. The first blow fell in 1935 when the Carndonagh extension was closed completely on 30 November of that year, after only thirty-four years in existence. An attenuated passenger service was maintained on the remaining part of the original Swilly line from Tooban Junction to Buncrana, with the company's bus services carrying most of the passenger traffic on the route. Services on the Burtonport line continued until 1940 when, on 3 June, the whole of the L&BER section was closed and passenger trains to Letterkenny were withdrawn. In August a firm of contractors began to lift the line from the Burtonport end. This led to much local protest in the area and Donegal County Council asserted that as the line was the property of the Free State, as the successor to the British government which paid for it to be built in the first place, the L&LSR had no right to dismantle it. As fuel shortages began to affect bus services, the line was reopened as far as Gweedore for goods traffic in February 1941. Passengers were also conveyed on these trains. This stay of execution ended in 1947 when the L&BER closed for the second time, this time for good.

The war had a dramatic effect on the Buncrana line on which a full passenger service was restored in 1942. With the threat and reality (in April 1941) of German attacks on Derry, which was a major port and a base from which the Battle of the Atlantic was waged, many Derry citizens began to commute from across the border in neutral County Donegal. Passenger numbers increased from just over 50,000 in 1940 to nearly 450,000 in 1945. After the war ended, the Swilly's more profitable bus services began to take over from the passenger trains. The last trains ran on the Letterkenny line in July 1953 and to Buncrana the month afterwards. But that was not the end of the Swilly. The company was to continue to operate bus services for many decades after its last trains had run. It has passed through several changes of ownership but is still active on fare stage and schools work in Donegal. Right up to the present day, the legal notice of ownership on the sides of its buses and on the road fund licence discs on the buses' windscreens clearly states that the vehicle is owned by the Londonderry & Lough Swilly Railway Company!

When we left the CDR, it was secure in the ownership of two powerful railway companies and had just opened its last extension, the Strabane & Letterkenny line. Its history through the first half of the twentieth century was very different from that of its neighbour. In 1910 Henry Forbes, who deserves a book in his own right, was appointed secretary to the joint committee. Forbes came from the GNR, and though he was an accountant and not an engineer, he became traffic manager in 1916 and then general manager from 1928. From driving off armed attackers on a train in which he was travelling as a passenger in 1920 to his legendary passion for economy and his realisation that the railway needed to be modernised, Forbes dominated the affairs of the CDR until his sudden death in 1943. While there is a view that his parsimonious attitude was counter-productive and he did not extract as much funding from the relatively prosperous joint owners (in 1923 the Midland's share was inherited by the LMS) to renew the system as might have been obtained, it was through his advocacy of the use of railcars that his reputation is assured. Forbes was followed by Bernard L. Curran who had joined the railway from the LMS/NCC five years before. Curran was another superb leader though with a much more conciliatory management style than his predecessor, and he steered the railway through its declining years in the face of economies and cutbacks while always maintaining the high standards of service to the public which was a hallmark of this undertaking.

The first railcar was a modest inspection car built by the Birmingham firm of Allday & Onions, which arrived in 1907. This was nothing more than a road vehicle on railway wheels and survives to this day in the Railway Gallery at the Ulster Folk & Transport Museum at Cultra. In 1926, during the General Strike in Britain when coal was in short supply, this was used to convey mail on the Glenties branch. Its effectiveness in this role impressed Forbes who realised that in the face of mounting road competition, vehicles such as this could operate services much more economically than a steam locomotive. In the same year he bought two 17-seat railcars from the Derwent Valley Railway in Yorkshire and had them regauged for use on the CDR. The pair gave good service until their withdrawal in 1934. Between 1930 and 1931 several new railcars and trailers were then built with the chassis and running gear supplied by the GNR from Dundalk works and the body work built by a local firm in Strabane. In 1933 two GNR buses were converted to run on rails and in 1934 another second-hand vehicle was acquired and regauged, this time from the broad gauge Dublin & Blessington Steam Tramway which had closed the previous year. In historical terms, the most significant vehicle among these early railcars was No. 7, a nondescript, actually downright ugly 32-seater railcar, the joint product of Dundalk works and O'Doherty's, the Strabane coachbuilders. No. 7, which entered service in 1930, was the first railcar in the British Isles to be powered by a diesel engine and as such is the Neanderthal ancestor to the thousands of such vehicles which have been built from that day on.

Henry Forbes was involved in the management committee which ran the Clogher Valley Railway in the neighbouring counties of Tyrone and Fermanagh, and in 1933 the CVR ordered a railcar which was to be the prototype for all the CDR railcars which followed. This was a 28-seater vehicle built by Walker Brothers of Wigan. It was powered by a Gardner diesel engine which was located in a cab at the front of the railcar and drove the front bogie, whose wheels were also connected by coupling rods for greater traction. This cab was articulated from the passenger saloon behind, which helped to keep some of the noise and the diesel fumes away from the passengers. When the CVR closed in 1941, this railcar was bought by the CDR, becoming its No. 10, and is now on display at the Ulster Folk & Transport Museum. Between 1933 and 1951 a further ten railcars were built jointly by Walker Brothers and the GNR. The last pair, Nos 19 and 20, built in 1950/51, which were bought by the Isle of Man Railway when the CDR finally closed, were replicated by CIÉ in the four railcars supplied to the West Clare section in 1952. All these railcars could only be driven from one end and had to be turned at termini, but as there were turntables already there for the steam engines, this was no major impediment to their successful operation. The CDR railcars formed the vast majority of passenger services from the 1930s onwards, except on the Derry branch which remained steam worked to the end. In relative terms, the CDR had a modern and impressive steam fleet which from the 1930s onwards was made up mostly of 4-6-4 and 2-6-4 tank locomotives built between 1904 and 1912. These were kept in good repair for goods services and excursion trains, but it is fair to say that the railcars gave the CDR a real chance to compete with road transport and prolonged the life of most of the system.

There is so much to admire about the CDR and the way it conducted its affairs that many more pages than are available here would be required to even start to tell its story. From the 1930s onwards, it provided that which is often aspired to these days, an integrated public transport service. It had a fleet of road freight vehicles which delivered goods and parcels brought by rail to outlying districts. Bus services, run in conjunction with the GNR, fed passengers on to the railway rather than competed with it. The flexibility of the railcars meant they could stop to pick up passengers at level crossings or virtually anywhere along the line, and they usually hauled a van or two for luggage, light goods and parcels. To overcome some of the delays caused by customs examinations, sealed containers were used to bring goods from the south through Northern Ireland to destinations in County Donegal. Some flat wagons were fitted with rollers which enabled loads such as stone and coal, in detachable wagon bodies, to be trans-shipped from one gauge to another at Strabane without the need for cranes or shovels. Perhaps because the roads in County Donegal were so poor and because of its progressive and innovative management, the dedication of its staff and the financial security and modest investment which its relatively prosperous joint owners provided, the CDR survived the first onslaught of road transport after the Great War virtually unscathed. During the Second World War traffic greatly increased, as was the case throughout Ireland, north and south, as oil shortages drove passengers and goods off the roads and back to the railways. On the CDR, passenger numbers virtually doubled between 1939 and 1945. However, as things got back to normal after the war, the great increase in competition from the roads began to impact on the railway. The first section to close was the Glenties branch which lost its regular goods and passenger services in December 1947, though occasional special goods workings continued sporadically into 1949.

In 1948 Britain's railways were nationalised and the LMS's stake in the CDR passed to the London Midland Region of the newly formed British Railways, which found itself now running a railway which was mostly located in a foreign country. From 1953 the Railway Executive which had been set up at nationalisation was replaced by the British Transport Commission, which continued to appoint three members to the joint committee, as had been done by the British partner since its formation in 1903. In August 1948 the Derry branch, which it will be recalled was in the sole ownership of the MR and latterly the LMS, was passed to the UTA, thus sealing its fate. The CDR continued to work the line, but it was closed by the UTA at the end of 1954. By the early 1950s the once powerful GNR was also in financial difficulties. In a rare act of cross-border co-operation for the time, the two governments took over the GNR in September 1953, forming the

GNR Board to manage its affairs. The GNR's interest in the CDR thus passed to the two governments. In 1955 the joint committee began to run its own bus services, a sign of things to come, for the losses on the narrow gauge lines continued to mount and it was almost inevitable that the end was not far off. Right through the 1950s the CDR continued to be run properly. Initiatives included the excursions which were jointly promoted with the GNR, known as the 'Hills of Donegal', which culminated in passengers being escorted on foot the 2 miles or so between the CDR and GNR stations in Ballyshannon. There were special trains for Orangemen and Hibernians, and a flow of container traffic between Dublin and Letterkenny was developed. However, these only postponed the inevitable and in 1959 the joint committee made an application to abandon its rail services. The last regular services on the remaining lines from Strabane to Letterkenny and Ballyshannon ran on the last day of 1959. The joint committee remained in existence to run the replacement road services until 1971.

So ends this brief journey along the highways and byways of the Irish narrow gauge which was part of the country's transport infrastructure from the 1880s up to the start of the 1960s. Apart from the unquestionably romantic nature of some of the lines and the nostalgia which they still evoke to this day, the question has to be asked as to whether this alternative network actually made any significant economic contribution to the areas they served and whether the large amount of money which was poured into these lines, both from the Treasury and from the pockets of the unfortunate ratepayers who happened to live in the areas they passed through, was money well spent. As with many such questions there is no clear definitive answer. As the nineteenth century progressed, the presence of a railway running through a district was certainly perceived to be essential for its prosperity. Conventional methods of raising the money to build railways, which in their pre-operational phase demanded a lot of capital, had not delivered railway communication to many parts of Ireland by the 1880s. The narrow gauge was used solely on the grounds that it would take less capital to build a 3 ft gauge line than a broad gauge one, and the initial restriction of baronial guarantees to the narrow gauge was a powerful incentive to encourage its use. Despite the rows between the directors and the ratepayers, there can be no doubting that those who promoted the various narrow gauge companies were well intentioned. There were no outright scams among them, though a fair degree of incompetence did emerge over the years. The later schemes, those built with Treasury grants following the Balfour Act, can be viewed as genuine attempts to help disadvantaged areas of the country and bring their infrastructure and in turn their economic prospects into line with the rest of the country in the same sort of way that EU money flooded into the Irish Republic for road building and other such projects at the end of the last century.

A frequent part of the promoters' pitch was that the building of a railway would make the transportation of agricultural and other produce from a district much easier. I doubt if any of them realised at the time that this was in some ways an argument against such a line. The census of 1841 determined that just under one million people were engaged in manufacturing. By the census of 1881 this had fallen to 379,000. Even allowing for the Famine and mass emigration, this was a substantial drop. Outside north-east Ulster the manufacturing revolution which had transformed the cities and towns of Victorian Britain into the workshop of the world was nowhere to be seen in Ireland. Whereas before the Famine most industrial requirements of the rural Irish economy such as ploughs and hand tools would have been made locally in small workshops and forges, with the coming of the railways these local businesses had to compete with the output of large factories in places like Birmingham and Sheffield which produced better equipment more cheaply and could transport it via the railways to every corner of the country. Small local manufacturing enterprises such as mills, tanneries, even distilleries and breweries, were now vulnerable to this sort of competition, and many succumbed. The result was that the Irish economy was probably more squarely based on agriculture at the end of the nineteenth century than it had been at the beginning. The one thing which the spread of the railways into the remoter parts of the country did help was depopulation. They made both emigration and migration for seasonal work much easier and there must have been many thousands in Cork, Kerry, Clare and Donegal who had the last glimpse of their home parish through the window of a narrow gauge carriage as it took them on the first part of their journey to a new life far from the land of their birth.

Perhaps distasteful as it is to admit it, market forces triumphed in the end. Most of the Irish narrow gauge lines were built with subsidies of varying types, because without them they would never have been built at all. Even when the only competition they had was the horse and cart, they were still only on the fringes of viability. They never generated enough profit to renew themselves, and while this made them a delight for the railway enthusiast as they operated increasingly obsolete equipment on battered tracks, once an alternative appeared in the form of the bus and lorry, they were terribly vulnerable. Only the CDR and the West Clare in CIÉ days attempted to modernise, and it is significant that these were among the last survivors of these lines to remain open. They also had patrons to help them do this; left to their own devices, there would not have been enough cash in the kitty to buy railcars.

And so with the last trains on the West Clare section of CIÉ on 31 January 1961, the era of the 3 ft gauge in Ireland came to an end. Or, not quite, as it happens. It is a little known fact that there is probably two to three times as much narrow gauge track in use in Ireland at the start of the twenty-first century as there was before the first 3 ft gauge lines closed in the 1920s and 30s. Many know nothing of this narrow gauge empire, which is located mostly in the midlands, though there are even a few offshoots in Northern Ireland. The bulk of these lines are run by Bord na Móna and are used to convey peat for use in both power stations and for horticultural purposes. Bogs are particularly suited to narrow gauge railways as they are light and can be laid, and relaid, across the unstable land without the major work which would be required to make roads to bring lorries to the areas where the peat is being harvested. Many of these lines are permanent. The Bord na Móna system has lofty bridges over the River Shannon, bridges under existing roads and railways and level crossings. Other lines consist of temporary track which can be lifted and relaid elsewhere when a bog is exhausted. The next time you scatter a bit of moss peat on your flower beds, if it was produced in Ireland you can be reasonably sure it began the journey from the bog to your garden bumping along in a wagon on an Irish narrow gauge railway.

Chapter 6

THE GOLDEN AGE OF IRELAND'S RAILWAYS (1880–1914)

T he three and a half decades from 1880 until the declaration of war in August 1914 can be viewed as the golden age of the Irish railway network. These years saw the last major expansion of the system, bringing it close to its greatest extent in terms of route mileage. The growth of the narrow gauge, which was covered in the last chapter, was an important element in this, but there was a significant expansion of broad gauge mileage in this period as well. Beyond the lines which were built, these were to be the last decades when the railway had a virtual monopoly of the traffic on offer. In a country such as Ireland, where the traffic potential of many lines was barely enough to cover their running costs, this was significant and many lines had been built, and were still being built, which would not have been in existence if left to the market. To illustrate this point, in 1893 the balance of outstanding loans owed to the Public Works Loan Commissioners by railway companies was £734,695.

The 5 ft 3 in. gauge lines built from 1880 onwards fall into three broad categories, branches off existing lines, lines built to complete earlier schemes and those which would not have been built without active government intervention. Typical of the first of the categories were lines like the short branch off the BNCR main line to Ballyclare which opened in 1884. Also on the BNCR system, in 1883 the Limavady branch was extended 10 miles to

Dungiven by the independent Limavady & Dungiven Railway. Worked by the BNCR and later taken over by the bigger company, a similar story is that of the line built by the Draperstown Railway to reach that small County Tyrone town with a branch off the Derry Central line at Magherafelt, which was absorbed by the BNCR in 1895. On the GNR the town of Ardee in County Louth was linked to the main line in 1896 by a branch from Dromin Junction, and a branch off the Dundalk to Clones line at Inniskeen reached Carrickmacross in 1886. One other GNR branch opened in the 1880s was built with the support of baronial guarantees. This was the line from Ballyhaise, on the Clones to Cavan line, to Belturbet, where it was to make a junction with the Cavan & Leitrim narrow gauge line.

Elsewhere in Ulster, a railway which had been struggling in the previous two decades began to recover its strength from the 1880s onwards. This was the Belfast & County Down which in 1865 had to lease its most profitable line, that to Holywood, to the Belfast, Holywood & Bangor company to keep afloat. In 1884 the BCDR's financial health was such that it was able to take over the BH&B and move on to complete its compact network of lines in County Down. The first part of this process was a line which was backed by a baronial guarantee, one of only two such 5 ft 3 in. gauge lines in Ulster. This was the Downpatrick, Killough & Ardglass Railway which was authorised in September 1890. The line, which opened in 1892, was 9 miles long and ran from Downpatrick to the fishing village of Ardglass where there was a short extension from the station through the streets down to the harbour. Joseph Tatlow, who was general manager of the BCDR at the time of the opening of the Ardglass branch, had a wry comment about this line in his memoirs: 'Primarily it was intended for the development of the herring traffic which for years had abounded on the coast, but no sooner was the line opened, than that perverse migratory fish sought other seas, and did not return to Ardglass for I don't know how long.' Figures, collated by the Board of Trade, showing how much fish was moved by rail from Irish ports seem to bear Tatlow out. In 1894, 406 tons of fish were transported from Ardglass; in 1899 this was down to 195 tons.

In conjunction with the opening of the new line, the BCDR built a loop line at Downpatrick which enabled trains to run direct from Belfast to Newcastle without having to reverse at Downpatrick, which had remained a terminal station when the main line was extended to Newcastle in 1869. This created a rare, for Ireland at any rate, triangular junction. In theory, trains to and from Ardglass could act as connecting services to Downpatrick from through main line trains. In practice, many services to Newcastle continued to reverse at Downpatrick. Those visiting Ireland's only operating preserved broad gauge railway, the Downpatrick & County Down Railway, can still today roll into the loop platform, as it was called. The final part of the BCDR was a line north from Newcastle to Castlewellan. The GNR's line through County Down to Banbridge was extended to Ballyroney in 1880, with that company's eyes firmly fixed on Newcastle. Strangely, the GNR did not make its move for over twenty years, and when it did, the BCDR countered with a proposal for a line of its own from Newcastle to Ballyroney and a demand for running powers to Scarva on the GNR main line. Common sense prevailed and the line was built jointly, the 7 miles from Ballyroney to Castlewellan by the GNR, and the remainder to Newcastle by the BCDR. When both lines opened in March 1906, the GNR had access to the popular seaside resort and this allowed Newcastle to become one of the few provincial towns in Ireland to be served by two railway companies.

The GSWR continued to add to its empire in its preferred way, which was noted in a previous chapter, mainly by taking over lines which others had built. The first such acquisition was a line which had been promoted originally in 1861 as the Midland Counties & Shannon Junction Railway, which planned a line from Clara on the GSWR Athlone branch to Banagher, an important port on the Shannon, and then across the river and into County Galway. Construction began and then stopped in 1864 when the money ran out. Nothing happened for many years until the company was re-formed as the Clara & Banagher Railway, which, with the help of a loan from the Board of Works, opened the 17 mile long branch in 1884. The GSWR entered into an agreement to work the line for ten years and at the end of this, bought the line from the board for a bargain price of £5,000. One line which the GSWR did at least partly fund was the branch from Sallins to Naas and Tullow, which opened in 1886. The GSWR financed the line as far as Baltinglass, but the final 10 miles to Tullow were underwritten with a baronial guarantee. These are usually associated with lines far from the capital and it is even odder to have them in place for a route which, for a time before 1914, had a through service from Kingsbridge provided by a coach which was slipped or uncoupled, while the train was in motion, off the rear of a main line express on the approach to Sallins. Under the control of its own guard, the slip carriage rolled into Sallins and was then added to the branch train and hauled on to Tullow. Commuting from Naas is therefore not a recent phenomenon.

Even though County Wicklow is very close to Dublin, because of the high ground and mountains which make up so much of its land mass, it had very few railways. Apart from the line down the coast from Bray, the Shillelagh branch and part of the GSWR's Tullow line, only one other passenger line was built in the county, the Dublin & Blessington Steam Tramway, which opened in 1888. This was a classic urban roadside steam tramway, which in this case strayed quite a distance into the Wicklow countryside. The 5 ft 3 in. gauge line which opened in 1888, backed by baronial guarantees, ran from Terenure via Templeogue, Tallaght, Jobstown and Brittas the 15½ miles to Blessington. A short extension, a further 5 miles to Poulaphouca, was opened by the separate Blessington & Poulaphouca Tramway in 1895. Steam tramway locomotives hauled double-deck tramcars which had the luxury of roofs at a time when trams in the city were mostly open topped. At Terenure the D&BST made a connection with the Dublin United Tramway Company's tracks, which were also 5 ft 3 in. gauge. There was no through running, but through tickets to the Blessington line were available and mail was picked up at the GPO, brought to Terenure on DUTC cars and then transferred to the D&BST. The DUTC conveyed parcels and some freight on its tracks, and wagons brought down on the steam tramway were hauled at night to various locations around the city. These included wagons of livestock which were taken close to Smithfield Market on DUTC tracks, from where the beasts were driven through the streets the rest of the way to the market. There is a business opportunity which those operating the Luas seem to have overlooked. Proposals to electrify at least part of the line were never followed through and an operation such as this was very vulnerable to competition from buses and lorries in the 1920s, which led to the complete closure of what was by then the final roadside steam tramway in the British Isles on the last day of 1932. There was another steam tramway on the western outskirts of the city. This was the Dublin & Lucan, a 3 ft gauge line which opened from Conyngham Road to Chapelizod in 1881, Lucan in 1883 and was extended to Leixlip in 1890. In 1896 the company was reconstituted as the Dublin & Lucan Electric Tramway. The gauge was changed to 3 ft 6 in. and it commenced operations as an electric line in March 1900. Why it did not convert to 5 ft 3 in. gauge to allow through running over the DUTC tracks it met at the Phoenix Park is something of a mystery. Bus competition led to its closure in 1925, but the DUTC bought the line, regauged it as far as Lucan and it continued as part of the city's tramway system until it closed in 1940. One type of traffic which the Lucan trams catered for was due to a quirk in the licensing laws which allowed bona-fide travellers, who could prove with their tram tickets that they were going more than 3 miles out of the city, to drink in pubs a lot longer than was permitted within the city limits. Special cars were run on Sundays on the Lucan line to convey such bona-fides, as they were called, to various hostelries the required distance out of the city.

Some of the actions of the GSWR had the effect of tidying up loose ends which had been left behind when other companies got into trouble. One such was the branch line from Maryborough to Mountmellick which opened in 1885, the only part of a planned line to Mullingar which the grandly named Waterford & Central Ireland Railway had managed to open. This name was adopted by the Waterford & Kilkenny in 1868 after the company had reached Maryborough from Kilkenny in 1867. The GSWR bought the W&CIR in 1900, its none too generous offer of £17. 10s. for each £100's worth of W&CIR stock being accepted. This may have been a relief to its shareholders, for in over forty years of its independent existence the company had never managed to pay a dividend on its ordinary shares. The GSWR also gobbled up two branches in County Cork built by local companies. The first of these was a 9 mile long line from Banteer, on the line from Mallow to Tralee, to Kanturk and Newmarket. The Kanturk & Newmarket Railway was worked by the GSWR, but after a few years the company sold out to the GSWR. The other Cork line was the branch from Fermoy to Mitchelstown which opened in 1891 and was taken over by the GSWR in 1900. The last branch line built by the GSWR was to the small town of Cashel, which might have been served by the original line to Cork in the 1840s, had the plans not been altered. Cashel, an ancient episcopal town, was finally added to the railway map of Ireland in 1904 by a branch 6 miles long from a junction at Goold's Cross on the Cork main line. The line terminated in the shadow of the famous Rock of Cashel with its round tower and ruins.

The existing railways in the south and west of County Cork were much extended from 1880 onwards. In 1879 the Ilen Valley Railway obtained powers to extend its existing line from Drimoleague to Bantry. However, before construction began, the powers were transferred to the Cork & Bandon company which also took over the West Cork Railway and the Kinsale line at the same time. The new line was ready for Board of Trade inspection in June 1881 and services commenced the following month. The terminus was graphically called 'Hilltop', some distance from and above the town and its pier. In August 1880 the Clonakilty Extension Railway received royal assent. This was the culmination of several attempts to bring a railway to the town. The company was assisted with a £20,000 Treasury loan which enabled the 9 mile long branch from Clonakilty Junction to be opened in August 1886. There was just one intermediate station, Ballinascarthy. In 1887 a short tramway was built off this line to serve a flour mill at Shannonvale. This was to be Ireland's second long-lived horse-powered line though as it did not carry passengers, it never achieved the fame of the Fintona branch in

County Tyrone. In its later years the motive power carried a white livery and answered to the name of Paddy.

In 1888 the Cork & Bandon changed its name to the Cork, Bandon & South Coast Railway, which reflected the larger area it now served and which was shortly to get even bigger. The first of these lines was a branch which left the Clonakilty line at Ballinascarthy, a 5 ft 3 in. gauge tramway built under the terms of the Tramways Act of 1883. This was the Ballinascarthy & Timoleague Junction Light Railway which was authorised by an Order in Council, not by an Act of Parliament, and was underwritten by baronial guarantees. Robert Worthington began to construct the 6 mile line in 1887. Then in 1889 the Cork Grand Jury backed a 3 mile long extension to the fishing village of Courtmacsherry which was promoted by a separate company, the Timoleague & Courtmacsherry Extension Light Railway. The line, part of which was a roadside tramway, opened to Timoleague in 1890 and Courtmacsherry the year after. A short extension to the pier at Courtmacsherry was added in 1893. For many years summer excursions to the coast at Courtmacsherry were well patronised by the citizens of Cork city. The next new line was a short but important one and the first broad gauge line we have encountered built with the financial assistance made available under the Light Railways (Ireland) Act of 1889, the Balfour Act. This was a 1½ mile extension of the Bantry line from its existing station down to the town and the harbour. The line, promoted by William Martin Murphy who hailed from Bantry, was made possible with the help of a Treasury grant of £15,000 and opened in 1892. The final part of the CB&SCR system was also a Balfour line. This was an 8 mile extension from Skibbereen to Baltimore. Another new company was set up, the Baltimore Extension Railway, and of its nominal capital of £60,000, £56,700 was supplied in the form of a Treasury grant. The line which was worked by the CB&SCR opened in 1893. Attempts were made almost immediately to fund the improvement of the pier at Baltimore to develop the fishing industry there and extend the railway to the shore for the fish traffic. This dragged on for many years and it was not until 1917 that the pier was extended and a line was built to serve it. The rails on Baltimore pier were the most southerly in the whole of Ireland. The CB&SCR at its greatest extent, including the lines it worked, amounted to 94 route miles of track.

The unplanned way in which the Irish railway system evolved had provided the three major cities, Dublin, Belfast and Cork, with termini not linked to each other. We saw in the last chapter how this was resolved in Belfast. The major difficulty in Cork was that the broad gauge lines which terminated on the north and south sides of the River Lee were isolated from each other. This created many problems. For example, fish landed at the ports served by the CB&SCR had to be carted through the city if they were to find a market in the rest of Ireland, and goods consigned from other parts of the country destined for stations on the Bandon or Macroom lines had to go the opposite way, by road. The number of stations in Cork was reduced by one in 1893 when the present-day Kent station at Glanmire Road replaced the original 1856 GSWR terminus at Penrose Quay. Trains from Queenstown and Youghal were diverted from Summerhill when the new station opened, using bay platforms at its eastern end. Agitation for a link across the river seems to have come mainly from the GSWR and the GWR as they developed their lines to Rosslare, though it had been recommended earlier by the Allport Commission. At last in 1906 an Act was passed which authorised the Cork City Railways to build a line which ran through the streets between Glanmire Road and the CB&SCR station at Albert Quay, crossing the branches of the River Lee on two lifting bridges. Largely financed by the GWR, the line was worked by the GSWR and a speed limit of 5 mph was imposed. No regular passenger service ran over the line, though the occasional excursion snaked through the streets of the city at the very low speed allowed.

Connecting the main Dublin stations was an altogether bigger problem than that faced in Cork. All the companies sought a connection to the port of Dublin at the North Wall and the first to achieve this was the MGWR, whose Liffey branch was opened in 1864. This ran from Liffey Junction, a mile out from the

Broadstone, and then followed the Midland-owned Royal Canal at the back of the present Croke Park to the North Wall. The GSWR was even more distant from the North Wall than the Midland with its terminus and goods yards at Kingsbridge to the west of the city. It reached an agreement with the Midland to use the Liffey branch which it accessed with a new line, opened in 1877. This ran from Islandbridge Junction, just outside the terminus, and almost immediately crossed the river and plunged into a tunnel under the Phoenix Park. At Cabra, close to the Dublin cattle market, sidings were laid for this important traffic. GSWR trains joined the Liffey branch at Glasnevin Junction and used this to reach Church Road Junction in East Wall, where the GSWR had cattle pens and a goods yard by the river. A driving force behind the GSWR line was the London & North Western Railway which had been heavily involved with trade on the Irish Sea since the 1840s with their *Irish Mail* from Euston to Holyhead having the distinction of being the oldest named train in the world. In 1877 the LNWR opened its own station at the North Wall beside its steamer berth, where a hotel was also provided. The same year, the GNR got its connection to the North Wall with a short branch from East Wall Junction to Church Road Junction which was partly funded by the LNWR again. The GSWR, GNR and MGWR all provided regular connecting services off the LNWR steamers from its North Wall station until 1922.

The only one of the main companies still isolated from the others was the DW&W, though at least it had some sort of circuitous link to the rest of the national network with the opening of the line from Macmine Junction to Palace East in the 1870s. However, what was really required was a link in Dublin. Despite running the *Irish Mail* and dominating the cross-channel trade for most of the nineteenth century, the LNWR did not hold the Post Office contract to carry the mail to Dublin. This was in the hands of the City of Dublin Steam Packet Company, which operated out of Kingstown, but mail from the other stations had to be brought to Westland Row by road. Various proposals had been made over the years for a connection between the DW&W line and the rest of the city's railways. A couple of schemes were for lines along the banks of the Grand Canal; others had tunnels under the Liffey or under the quays. There were also at least two proposals for a central station for the city, which would have been located near College Green. It is a pity this was never followed through, for the GSWR terminus has always been inconveniently situated at a considerable distance from the city centre. The obvious line, from Westland Row across the river to Amiens Street, which had been authorised in the 1860s but not built, was revived in an Act of 1884 for the City of Dublin Junction Railway, which was backed by the four main Irish railway companies and the CoDSPC. Even for an important line like this in the heart of the capital, the old Irish problem of raising the finances cropped up again. Eventually the line was opened in 1891. There was one station at Tara Street and new through platforms were built beside the GNR's terminal platforms at Amiens Street. An additional connection was added in 1892, the short steep line from Amiens Street down to the MGWR's Liffey branch at Newcomen Bridge Junction, which allowed through running to both the GSWR and MGWR systems. The final piece to the Dublin railway jigsaw was added in 1901. The GSWR had to pay the Midland for the use of the Liffey branch, so it took over a failing company which was trying to build a suburban line from Kingsbridge to the North Wall. When the line opened there were stations at Glasnevin and Drumcondra, but they attracted little patronage and could not compete with the DUTC's frequent electric trams. The passenger service ended in 1907, but the year before, a new short line was built from North Strand Road Junction allowing trains from the Drumcondra line to run through Amiens Street to Westland Row and Kingstown as well as down to the North Wall. This did not save the passenger service on the line but has proved invaluable ever since.

The Waterford & Limerick added many miles of track to its existing network in the 1880s and 90s which was to leave the company as the fourth biggest in Ireland in terms of route miles owned or worked. The first new line was a short branch off the North Kerry route. The town of Tralee was some distance from the coast, but between 1828 and 1846 a ship canal was built from deeper waters at Fenit to the town. The canal was prone to silting and could only be entered at high water, and thoughts turned to a railway from the pier at Fenit as a more satisfactory alternative. In 1880 steps were taken to improve the pier and build a railway from Fenit to join the existing line from Tralee to Limerick. The short 7 mile branch, with intermediate stations at Spa and Kilfenora, was not opened until 1887 and was worked by the w&L.

However, the main thrust of the expansion of the w&L was northwards. In 1869 the Athenry & Ennis at last reached Athenry where it made a junction with the MGWR line from Dublin. North of Athenry, a line to Tuam had been opened since 1860. The Athenry & Tuam company had initially made an agreement with the MGWR to work the line for ten years. Soon after this expired, the working of the line passed to the w&L. Then in 1890 a company with the ungainly name of the Athenry & Tuam Extension to Claremorris Light Railway Company was authorised by the Privy Council to build a 17 mile long line from Tuam to Claremorris which, since 1862, had been served by trains on the line from Athlone to Castlebar and Westport. The A&TEC was offered a baronial guarantee from the Mayo Grand Jury, on condition that it arranged for the line to be worked by the w&L for a period of at least twenty years. In January 1891 the contract to build the line was awarded to William Martin Murphy, though services did not commence until April 1894. The MGWR was clearly unenthusiastic about the newcomer and set numerous conditions surrounding the use of its station at Claremorris. For over a year trains from Tuam terminated at a temporary station called Claremorris South. Another complication was the promotion, at this time, of the branch from Claremorris to Ballinrobe which the Midland supported, was to work and wished to accommodate at Claremorris station. This line and another not far away in County Galway, from Attymon Junction to Loughrea which was opened in 1890 and was also worked by the MGWR, were two 5 ft 3 in. gauge lines promoted under the terms of the Tramways Act of 1883 with the assistance of baronial guarantees. The last conventionally financed addition to the MGWR system had been the short 7 mile long branch from Crossdoney Junction, on the Cavan line, to Killeshandra, opened in June 1886.

Returning to County Mayo, the other issue which had emerged was a plan to extend the line from Tuam northwards towards Sligo. The idea of a line north from Claremorris was first mooted in the early 1880s and efforts were made to interest the nearby Sligo, Leitrim & Northern Counties Railway in working such a line if it were built. However, the SLNCR had its own financial problems at that time and did not become involved. The catalyst for the building of the line from Claremorris through Swinford and Charlestown to Collooney, where it would make a junction with the MGWR line to Sligo, was the Light Railways (Ireland) Act of 1889. The Treasury effectively gave the W&L a grant of close to £150,000 to enable the line to be constructed. The line was supported by the Mayo and Sligo Grand Juries and in 1892 two Orders in Council were granted authorising the line to be built. These divided it into two sections, from Swinford to Collooney and from Swinford south to Claremorris. Both were to be opened by 31 December 1894 when the powers for compulsory purchase of land were to expire. The Board of Works had actually contracted Robert Worthington and William Martin Murphy to begin preliminary earthworks in January 1891, long before the formal authorisation was given by the Privy Council. There was inevitably some jousting with the Midland for the use of its facilities at Sligo and over Claremorris station. In the end the W&L agreed to pay £500 per year for ten years for access to Claremorris station and from the opening of the line in October 1895, trains to both Tuam and Sligo used the Midland station. The new line, from Claremorris North Junction to Collooney Junction, where it joined the MGWR line to Sligo, was 46 miles long. It was a typical light railway, constructed as cheaply as possible with sharp curves, steep gradients and many level crossings. After the Second World War it came to be graphically described by railwaymen as the 'Burma Road'. At Collooney a junction was made with the SLNCR which allowed through running in the direction of Enniskillen. This link, which was about half a mile in length, passed under the MGWR, which was at a greater height than the W&L line on the approach to Collooney. The positioning of the existing stations meant that none of these could be used by the new line and resulted in the W&L building its own station at Collooney, thus endowing this tiny County Sligo village with three stations served by three different companies—as many as Belfast!

The W&L now had a through line running from Waterford to Sligo, a distance of about 145 miles. A journey along the length of its main line was an epic, in some ways more daunting than that from Derry to Burtonport, discussed in the last chapter. The timetable for the summer of 1900 shows three trains leaving Sligo at 8.50 and 11.50 am and 5.10 pm. The 8.50 am, stopping at virtually all stations, reached Limerick at 3.40 pm, left an hour and five minutes later and finally arrived in Waterford at ten minutes past eight in the evening. Assuming that through passengers used the break at Limerick to stretch their legs, the amount of time spent in the railway carriage for the journey was 10 hours and 15 minutes, which works out at an average speed of just over 14 mph. The Waterford & Limerick was now the fourth largest railway company in Ireland after the GSWR, the GNR and the MGWR, and had outgrown its original title. From 1 January 1896 it changed its name to the Waterford, Limerick & Western, a label which reflected its far-flung interests. However, the company did not have long to enjoy this status, for in 1898 it entered into discussions with the GSWR with a view to an amalgamation. The proposal came before parliament in 1899 and there was much opposition to it, especially from the MGWR who did not want the GSWR in its territory north of Athlone. However, the WW&L chairman Percy Bernard gave evidence of how much the company had depended on subsidies and rebates from the English GWR in relation to cross-channel traffic and the concern which was now felt that these might wither away, given the new warm relationship between the GWR and the GSWR as they worked closely to develop the new route from Rosslare to Fishguard. The Act allowing the amalgamation received royal assent in August 1900 and took effect from 1 January 1901. The 1900s was a decade of changing identities on Ireland's railways. In addition to the CB&SCR and the WL&W, the Dublin, Wicklow & Wexford adopted the rather grander name of the Dublin & South Eastern Railway from 1 January 1907 and of course, as mentioned in the previous chapter, the BNCR had been taken over by the English Midland Railway in 1903.

We saw in the last chapter how government funding in the wake of the Balfour Act had delivered many miles of 3 ft gauge tracks in Donegal. The Act also produced some spectacular broad gauge lines in remote districts of Mayo and Kerry, and these lines, funded by the government for the MGWR and the GSWR, are the focus of the next part of our story. The genesis of all these lines lay in the report of the Allport Commission. In the case of Mayo, among the lines advocated by local interests was an extension of the Ballina branch towards the coast to Killala and beyond that to Ballycastle, from Ballina via Crossmolina towards Belmullet at the head of Blacksod Bay or another variant of this starting from Castlebar rather than Ballina. In the end, two lines were agreed: one was the line north from Ballina to the coast but going no further than Killala; the second line was an extension of the existing Westport branch towards Mallaranny and Achill Sound to serve Achill Island. The MGWR was slightly aloof at first from the promoters, but eventually agreed to work these lines if they were built for the company without their having to make a financial commitment and if they were built to the 5 ft 3 in. gauge. The Killala line was the first off the blocks. Its course was agreed in 1890 and in the following year the contract, worth £29,000 for the 8 mile line, was awarded to T. H. Falkiner. The work progressed quickly and the whole line was ready for inspection by Major General Hutchinson of the Board of Trade at the end of 1892. Services to Killala commenced on 2 January 1893.

The Achill line, 27 miles long, was a much bigger undertaking. Initially the line was only to go as far as Mallaranny, but following a visit by Arthur Balfour himself to the area in the autumn of 1890, it was said that local interests convinced him of the necessity of taking the line through to Achill Sound. With the decision to extend the line to Achill having been made at a late stage, it was decided to divide the construction into two separate sections. The MGWR was deemed responsible for the first section from Westport to Mallaranny, the Board of Works looking after the rest of the line which was promoted by a separate entity, the Achill Extension Railway Company. The contracts for both parts, worth £110,000, were awarded to Robert Worthington and this included some heavy engineering works, including two short tunnels and a seven-arch viaduct near Newport. The line opened in three phases: Westport to Newport in February 1894; Newport to Mallaranny in July of that year; and the AER section in May of the following year. The MGWR was keen to exploit the tourist potential of the area it was now serving and in 1895 bought a county house called Ennell Lodge near Mallaranny, and twenty acres of surrounding land to convert into a hotel. The hotel opened in 1896 and the company began to offer travel and accommodation packages there. A golf course was built in the grounds in 1900.

To strike a more sombre note, this fine hotel was situated in an area where many ordinary people lived in desperate poverty, still largely dependent on the potato for subsistence half a century after the Great Famine. The railway was used at times to bring meal and other foodstuffs to those affected by crop failures. One old and faded photograph survives of Achill people crowding round a goods wagon to collect supplies of meal, a scene similar to that which we see all too often today in the Third World on our TV screens. This was happening in the west of Ireland almost within living memory. There is one final and equally mournful footnote to the Achill line. At the beginning and at the end of its life, trains ran over the line bringing home to Achill the bodies of local people who had died in tragic accidents, both associated with the poverty of their area which forced them to migrate to seek work elsewhere. In 1894, a boat packed with migrant workers from Achill and heading to Westport Quay where the passengers would have joined a steamer to take them to Scotland to work on the potato harvest, capsized, drowning thirty people. Their bodies were brought home on a special train before the line officially opened. Then in September 1937, the month the line was scheduled to close, ten young men from Achill, migrant workers on a farm in Scotland, were burned to death when their locked dormitory caught fire. Once again a special train was used to bring their bodies home. Some of the young men who died in 1937 were related to those who had perished in 1894.

The third addition to the MGWR network as a result of the Balfour Act was the line from Clifden to Galway. As with the other Balfour lines, a railway into the heart of Connemara had been talked about for years, but these proposals had foundered on the difficulty of raising the finance. This part of west Galway had suffered terribly during the Famine and the decades that followed. The land in the interior was generally poor, much of it bogland, so the population was concentrated on the coast. The most important town was Clifden. However, to build a line to serve the coastal communities would have made the journey from Galway to Clifden a long one, as the railway would have had to skirt round the bays and inlets on the coast. Most came to favour an inland route serving Oughterard, Maam Cross and Recess on the way. The Balfour Act resolved the problem of finance and shortly after the Chief Secretary's fact-finding visit to the west in the autumn of 1890, the Midland was given a grant of £264,000 to build a line from Galway the 47 miles to Clifden. In 1891 the contract to construct the line was awarded to Charles Braddock of Wigan, but he ran into financial difficulties in 1892 and was replaced by Falkiner, who was nearing the end of his work on the Killala line at the time. There was some heavy engineering work, especially at the Galway end, where after passing through a short tunnel the line had to cross the Corrib on a bridge which had three 150 ft long spans and a short lifting span to allow the passage of shipping. The line opened in two sections, from Galway to Oughterard in January 1895 and through to Clifden on 1 July of that year. Clifden was 174 miles from the MGWR terminus in Dublin. The line from Clifden made a junction facing towards Dublin, so all passenger trains on the line had to reverse in and out of Galway station. The service was usually three passenger trains per day in each direction, taking around two hours for the journey. In keeping with their desire to promote the new lines in the west as tourist destinations, the Midland expanded their hotel business. The company had taken an interest in a hotel in Eyre Square in Galway beside its station in the 1850s, and in 1895 it took over and extended an existing establishment at Recess. In 1903 a new tourist express was added to the timetable, leaving the Broadstone at midday, reaching Galway at 3 pm with connections to both the Achill and Clifden lines.

The other beneficiary of the largesse of the Balfour Act was County Kerry and the GSWR. As far back as the 1830s, Valentia was one of many locations that had featured as a possible site for a packet station for the Americas. The promotion of a grand trunk line across Ireland to a packet station on the south or west coast, as advocated by the Irish Railway Commissioners back in 1838, was a sort of Irish railways version of 'El Dorado', which absorbed the time of many men over many decades yet never came even close to realisation. By the 1890s this dream had been finally abandoned and the reality on the ground was that there was little chance of railways being built to serve the south-west of County Kerry if their financing was left to the market. In 1885, with the help of baronial guarantees, the GSWR had opened a 12 mile long branch from Farranfore, on the Killarney to Tralee line, to Killorglin, and there matters rested until the extension of this line to Valentia was suggested by the Allport Commission in 1888. The government agreed to fund the line with a grant of £85,000 for the 27 miles and the GSWR set to work in 1890. The line had to climb through the mountains beyond Killorglin on gradients as steep as 1 in 59. There were several short tunnels and near Kells station the line crossed the graceful curving 70 ft high Gleensk viaduct over the river of the same name. From Kells the line descended for 6 miles to reach sea level at Cahirciveen before crossing the Valentia river on a long girder bridge to terminate at Valentia Harbour, close to the pier used by the ferry to Valentia Island. The line, which opened in 1893, must have been a leading candidate in a strong field for the most scenic railway line in Ireland. The second Balfour line in Kerry was that from Headford Junction, 7 miles east of Killarney, to Kenmare. This route which received a grant of £50,000 from the Treasury and ran for 22 miles through mountainous and thinly populated country to reach the little town of Kenmare at the end of a long inlet from the Atlantic opened in September 1893.

Before leaving Kerry, one other addition to its railway network which opened at this time deserves a mention. If the Valentia branch was possibly the most scenic railway line in Ireland, that which ran from Listowel to Ballybunion from 1888 to 1924 was, unquestionably, the weirdest. Ballybunion is an agreeable small seaside town in the north of the county. Similar towns around the coast of Ireland, from Portrush to Tramore, had prospered with the coming of the railway. Several schemes for both broad gauge lines and narrow gauge tramways linking the town to the North Kerry line were promoted in the 1880s, seeking baronial guarantees, but none of them was approved. Unknown to its citizens, the solution to Ballybunion's transport problems had already been found, by one Charles Francois Marie-Thérèse Lartigue, a French engineer working in his country's colonies in North Africa, who had been thinking about ways of designing a cheap and light method of constructing railways in remote locations. Lartigue had observed the heavy loads which camels could carry through the desert on pallets hung from their humps and this inspired him to think about a monorail. Lartigue's system involved a running rail which was carried at the top of 'A' shaped metal trestles whose legs were fixed at the bottom on to wood or metal sleepers. There were light rails about a foot above the sleepers fixed to the outside of the uprights of the 'A' frames to stabilise the rolling stock. The trains ran on vertical double flanged rails which bore all the weight. Rolling stock also had horizontal double flanged wheels which ran on the outside rails. The Lartigue system was first used in North Africa in connection with the production of esparto grass, which was used in paper-making, with the wagons hauled by mules. The track was light and could easily be dismantled and erected elsewhere, and Lartigue believed that his system would be particularly useful in parts of the British Empire.

It is a long way from the deserts of North Africa to the coast of north Kerry, and the monorail's journey there was via the centre of London. In the 1880s, in what today is one of the most expensive parts of the city, between Victoria Street and Birdcage Walk, was a piece of waste ground called Tothill Fields. In 1886 a demonstration line was built there to show off the Lartigue monorail. This showed all the advantages of the system, steep grades, sharp curves and turntables to enable stock to switch tracks. The Lartigue Company wanted a permanent line to demonstrate the system and the people of Ballybunion wanted a railway. In some way these two aspirations came to be interwoven and a company was formed to build a monorail from Ballybunion to meet the North Kerry line at Listowel. The line was built by the company at a cost of £33,000. No baronial guarantees were sought. Construction began in late 1887 and the line was opened in March of the following year. Three 0-3-0 tender engines were supplied by the Hunslet Engine Company of Leeds to work the line, which offered what was virtually the standard Irish minor line service of three trains a day with additional services in summer. The Lartigue had so many differences from any other railway in Ireland, or anywhere else for that matter, that it would take many pages to describe them all. To highlight just a few, the passenger coaches, slung from the monorail, had longitudinal seats which meant that the passengers' heads were next to the running rail. This must have made travel on the trains incredibly noisy. Loadings on either side of the train had to be equalised: not so much a problem with passengers, but if livestock were being transported, a cow on one side of the wagon would have to be balanced by a couple of sheep or pigs on the other. But perhaps the maddest thing of all about the monorail was the thinking in the Lartigue Company that decision-makers, captains of industry and military men from the European colonial empires, would make their way to County Kerry to view this wonderful new advance in light railway technology. Nobody came of course, and though the company was in receivership in 1897, the railway struggled on. It hoped to make enough from visitors during the summer months to sustain it through the winter when traffic was sparse. Its best year was 1913, when it made a surplus of £875. The line suffered some malicious damage during the Civil War, but the end came in 1924 when it finally closed.

None of the lines discussed to date in the chapter was of major significance in the context of the national network. They were important to the areas they served and, indeed, both for the government and their local promoters, the Balfour lines were viewed as providing a great opportunity for economic regeneration. There was really only one project built in the period between 1880 and 1914 which was of national significance. This involved the opening of a new route across the Irish Sea and led to a flurry of activity in the south-east of the country. The Dublin, Wicklow & Wexford Railway extended its line from Palace East to New Ross in 1887. This was a difficult line to build, with a 748 yard long tunnel at Mount Elliot followed by a 596 ft bridge with five spans, one of which opened, over the River Barrow near New Ross. The intention had been to extend this line into Waterford, but before this could be achieved, a bigger player entered the stage.

It will be recalled that back in the 1840s Brunel's Great Western Railway had been closely involved in schemes to establish ports in Pembrokeshire and in Wexford to grab a share of commerce across the Irish Sea. The depression caused by the Famine in Ireland and the failure of the GWR's South Wales Railway to reach Fishguard had put paid to these plans, leaving much of the Irish traffic in the hands of the London & North Western Railway and its Irish partner, the GSWR. The GWR had to satisfy itself with subsidies and rebates to the W&L and steamer services from south Wales to Waterford. This did not put the GWR in a position to effectively compete with the main routes further north. Towards the end of the nineteenth century GWR interest in the south-east of Ireland revived. In 1893 an Act was obtained by the Fishguard Bay Railway & Pier Company to build a pier and a short stretch of railway at Fishguard. The GWR then built a line from its existing route to Haverfordwest to connect with this line. An Act of 1894 allowed the FBR&P to acquire Rosslare Pier and the connecting line to Wexford and change its name to the Fishguard & Rosslare Railways & Harbours Company. Finally, in 1898 the GWR entered into an agreement with the GSWR and the F&RR&HC to establish a new short sea route between the two islands with appropriate railway links. This was a very ambitious project. The F&RR&HC was to build a railway from Rosslare to Waterford, a bridge across the River Suir to link up with the existing Waterford, Dungarvan & Lismore line and its continuation, the Fermoy & Lismore. It was also authorised to buy these two companies. There was to be a cut-off line from near Fermoy to Dunkettle on the Youghal branch to shorten the journey to Cork, though this was dropped in 1901, and trains continued to run via Mallow. There was also a short link at the Rosslare end from Killinick Junction on the new line to Felthouse Junction, which allowed local services from Waterford to Wexford to avoid Rosslare. In conjunction with these new lines, the DW&W extended its line from New Ross to Waterford in 1904, joining the Rosslare route at Abbey Junction outside Waterford station.

Work began in 1900 on the line from Rosslare to Waterford, which was built by the Scottish firm of Robert McAlpine & Son. The route includes the longest railway bridge in Ireland, over the River Barrow, near Campile. The Barrow Bridge is 2,131 ft long and has thirteen fixed spans with an electrically operated opening centre span. Equally impressive was the bridge over the Suir at Waterford, 1,205 ft in length with a lifting span in its centre. Both bridges were built by the Glasgow firm of Sir William Arrol & Company. The South Wexford line offers one of the great scenic railway journeys in Ireland with its spectacular river crossing and the line snaking along the north bank of the Suir to reach Waterford. To cope with the additional traffic, Waterford station had to be rebuilt. The completed station's eight platforms was the greatest number in Ireland and the main through platform, at 1,210 ft in length, was the longest in the country. This meant blasting into Mount Misery which towers above the site and rebuilding the road to Kilkenny on concrete piles over the river. It is believed that this was the first extensive use of ferroconcrete in all of Ireland. The new line opened and steamer services began in August 1906, with expresses from Cork running through to Rosslare to connect with the steamers.

In contrast to events in the south-east, the last lengthy broad gauge line to be built in Ireland proved to be an almost complete waste of time. This was the Great Northern line from Castleblayney to Keady and Armagh, which was opened as late as

1909/10. When the Navan & Kingscourt Railway was building its line in the 1870s, various proposals were put forward for extensions further northwards to Carrickmacross or Castleblayney. Nothing came of these, but their later revival led to the eventual building of the Keady line. In 1893, against the expressed wishes of the GNR, the Midland announced plans not just for a short extension of the Kingscourt line but for a major trunk route from there through Armagh and Dungannon to a junction with the Belfast & Northern Counties at Cookstown. In the face of opposition from the GNR and reservations on the part of some of its own shareholders, the MGWR scheme was withdrawn. However, in 1900 an independent company backed by the MGWR, the Kingscourt, Keady & Armagh Railway, was authorised by parliament to build this line. The GNR was forced to treat with the KK&A and in return for them dropping the line to Kingscourt, the GNR agreed to assist the scheme and work the line. Their financial involvement was initially a subscription of £50,000, though it later had to cough up a further £300,000. The company changed its name to the Castleblayney, Keady & Armagh Railway and construction of the 18 mile long line, which proved difficult to build through hilly and boggy land, began in 1903. There were two viaducts on the line made from the new material concrete, the longest of which, Tassagh viaduct near Keady, had eleven arches and was 570 ft in length. The summit of the line at Carnagh, south of Keady, at 613 ft, was the highest point on the Great Northern and the second highest reached by a broad gauge line in Ireland. The 8 miles from Armagh to Keady opened in May 1909; the remaining 10 miles to Castleblayney followed in November 1910. The CK&A was taken over by the GNR in 1911, but the line was a commercial disaster and was worked at a loss until 1924 when the section south of Keady was closed, partition finally putting an end to its already very modest prospects. The GNR had paid a heavy price to keep the Midland out of its territory.

Railways have always been seen as a very safe form of transport and from the 1840s onwards, when an accident did occur, it was investigated by officers from the Board of Trade whose reports usually contained recommendations for improvements to prevent something similar happening again. One of the first recorded fatalities on an Irish railway was that of one William Thompson who, somewhat the worse from drink, leapt or fell from a D&K train near Blackrock on Sunday, 22 February 1835. A similar fate in similar circumstances occurred to a drunken racegoer who fell from a UR train near the Maze in July 1841. There are many incidents of railway staff being killed or injured, especially in the early years, which were caused by inexperience with the new technology, and many more were killed in accidents when lines were being built. One frequent cause of accidents in the early years was due to a lack of understanding of metallurgy, which led to the failure of axles and in some cases boilers. In October 1842 one of the original D&K engines, *Hibernia*, dating from 1834, blew up at Kingstown when its firebox imploded. Fortunately the crew were not present on the footplate at the time or they would have been killed instantly. The worst fatal accident up to that time in the British Isles happened near Sallins in October 1853 when the engine of a passenger train failed and a following goods train ploughed into its rear, killing sixteen people. As speeds increased as the century progressed, sometimes the maintenance of the track did not always keep up and several instances of trains derailing on poor track were recorded, such as one near Ballinasloe in October 1864 which led to the death of two passengers. Colonel Rich of the Board of Trade cited excessive speed on poorly maintained worn-out track and bad drainage as the main causes of the incident. By and large Irish railways in the nineteenth century had a safety record comparable with those in the rest of the kingdom, which made what happened near Armagh on a June morning in 1889 all the more shocking. What the Armagh disaster highlighted were methods of operating railways, not just in Ireland but across the kingdom, which were inherently hazardous. In fairness to the Board of Trade, their inspectors had been drawing attention to many of these practices for years, but they had been ignored. An accident as catastrophic and avoidable as that at Armagh was almost certainly bound to happen sometime, somewhere; it was unfortunate for the reputation of Ireland's railways that the disaster took place on the tracks of the GNR.

The line from Armagh to Newry was a difficult one to work with steep banks in both directions. For most of the first 3 miles out of Armagh, trains to Newry faced a severe climb. Starting at 1 in 82, this steepened to 1 in 75 for a further 2 miles before the first summit on the line at a place called Dobbin's Bridge was reached, after which it was downhill to the first station at Hamiltonsbawn just under 5 miles from Armagh. On 12 June a special train had been arranged to take a large party, consisting mostly of children who were attending Sunday schools in Armagh, to enjoy a day at the seaside at Warrenpoint. The engine driver booked to work the train, Thomas McGrath, was not that familiar with the line from Newry to Armagh, having only worked over it before as a fireman and not as a driver. The locomotive allocated, an 1880-built 2-4-0 tender engine, was of a type normally used on the Belfast to Dublin line. While this line had steep gradients, they were not as severe as those on the erstwhile Newry & Armagh company's route. The empty stock for the excursion, consisting of thirteen vehicles including two brake vans, duly arrived at Armagh via Portadown well before the advertised departure time of 10 am. However, the numbers booked for the excursion were such that the Armagh station-master, John Foster, proposed to add two additional carriages to the train. What happened next is unclear, but it seems there was some sort of altercation between McGrath and Foster. McGrath at first refused to take the fifteen coaches on the grounds that his engine was unsuitable for such a load over a steeply graded line, which led to Foster taunting him that other drivers had taken such loads without complaint. James Elliot, a chief clerk in the general manager's office, who was in charge of the train and was to travel on the engine, made the sensible suggestion that the excursion be assisted up the bank to Hamiltonsbawn by the engine of the scheduled 10.35 passenger train, but this offer was refused by McGrath, who seemed to have been stung by Foster's remarks.

The excursion left 15 minutes late at 10.15 am, its locked carriages containing about 940 passengers, around 600 of whom were children. At first all went well with the engine steaming strongly, but as the incline bit, it began to lose speed and eventually stalled about 120 yards from the summit and safety, at around 10.33 am. In a subsequent test run made under the supervision of Major General Hutchinson, the Board of Trade inspector who conducted the inquiry into the accident, the same locomotive driven by an experienced man brought a train of the same weight as the excursion to the summit without difficulty. Because the excursion was so heavily laden and passengers were being carried in the brake vans, it was suggested but never proven that the hand brakes might have been accidentally tampered with, inadvertently causing the train to stall. At this point there was an operating problem for the railway but no danger to the passengers. Then James Elliot, the man in charge of the train, intervened. The logical thing to do was to send someone down the bank to attract the attention of the driver of the following lightly loaded 10.35 am train, which could have pushed the stalled excursion over the summit. However, Elliot suggested to the driver, who agreed though he should have known better, to divide the train, take the first section to a siding at Hamiltonsbawn and then come back for the rest. This was an act of folly for two reasons: firstly because it would have been impossible to complete this manoeuvre without delaying the following scheduled passenger train anyway; but mainly because the excursion was fitted throughout with Smith's simple vacuum brake. This worked in the following way. A pipe ran through the train connected to the engine which had a pump to expel the air and create a vacuum in this pipe. When the air was expelled, the brakes on the wheels of the carriages could be applied. However, the act of dividing the train meant that the vacuum brakes on the ten carriages packed with excursionists left on an incline of 1 in 75 were rendered inoperable and were being held by only the handbrake in the rear van. In the act of setting the engine back to uncouple the first five coaches, it may have nudged the remaining carriages and set them off down the incline, slowly at first but by the time of the impact at a speed estimated to be over 40 mph. Even if there had been no train following, a disaster was now bound to occur as the runaway carriages would certainly have derailed on the curve where the Newry line diverged from that to

Portadown. The 10.35 train left Armagh and was making good progress up the bank when its driver Murphy saw the runaway carriages hurtling towards him. He managed to stop his train lessening the impact slightly, but could do little else as the flimsy wooden carriages disintegrated on impact. In all, seventy-eight were killed and around 250 injured in the crash.

Public opinion across the country was so shocked by the events at Armagh that fine June morning that parliament acted with uncharacteristic speed and passed, later that year, the Regulation of Railways Act which gave the Board of Trade sweeping powers to impose on railway companies operating practices which are still at the core of the safe operation of passenger trains in these islands to this day. The Act addressed two main areas which events at Armagh had highlighted. Prior to the Act trains were generally dispatched on the time interval principle. This meant, for example, that a slow moving goods train could not be followed along the same line by a passenger train for perhaps twenty minutes, while a goods train might be sent out ten minutes after a faster passenger train. Using this procedure, there was no way of ensuring that the train in front was clear of a section of track before another train followed. If the first train broke down or stalled, as happened at Armagh, it was only the eyes of the crew of the train following which could prevent a collision. In bad weather or at night this was an inherently risky way of working a railway, yet before Armagh it was widely used. This system was replaced by what was called block working. A line was divided up into sections or blocks usually defined by the location of signal boxes. Now, no train was permitted into a section or block of track until the signalman in the box in front had communicated with his colleague in the rear, usually by means of bell codes, that lovely tinkling sound which many will recall hearing from mechanical signal boxes, that the previous train was out of that section. He even had to observe that there was a tail lamp on the last vehicle to make sure that part of the train had not become uncoupled and left behind in the section to obstruct a following train.

The other revolution post-Armagh came in the way passenger

trains were braked. The type of vacuum brake used at Armagh meant that once carriages were uncoupled from the engine, their brakes could not work. This practice was turned on its head. Passenger trains would henceforth be fitted with an automatic vacuum brake which worked in exactly the opposite way to the brakes on the Armagh excursion. Under this system the brakes were applied once air was allowed into the brake pipe to destroy the vacuum. Had this been in use at Armagh, when the carriages had been uncoupled and the flexible hoses carrying the vacuum between them had been disconnected, the brakes on the ten carriages left on the incline would have been applied automatically. This also meant that if carriages became detached from a train through a failure of a coupling, the fragile rubber vacuum hoses would tear apart, air would be admitted to the pipe on the detached carriages and their brakes would be applied. This was also what happened when a passenger pulled the communication cord, though this only admitted a small amount of air to the brake pipes and the effect was much less dramatic than that usually portrayed in the cinema. The great majority of trains in Ireland today use air brakes rather than vacuum brakes, but exactly the same principle applies. They are fail safe mechanisms: if the pipe fractures for any reason or air pressure falls, the brakes come on. The modernisation of signalling in recent decades has all but banished the traditional signal box and its semaphore signals from Ireland. Much of the signalling on the Iarnród Éireann network is controlled electronically from rooms in Connolly station in Dublin. However, even though the technology has changed, the fundamental principles of this system are still those introduced after Armagh, with the lines divided into blocks, now protected by remotely operated colour light signals. The events of 12 June 1889, with the sudden and violent deaths of so many children in particular, must have been the greatest imaginable trauma for the people of Armagh. It is rare in history to be able to say with absolute certainty that something good came out of a catastrophe. In the case of the Armagh disaster, it did.

With the completion of the Keady and south Wexford lines, the

Irish railway network, apart from a couple of short lines to coalfields built during and after the Great War, had reached its greatest extent. The system grew from around 840 miles in 1853 to 2,092 in 1872, 3,044 in 1894, and to a maximum of 3,442 in 1920, of which about 500 miles were 3 ft gauge. The railways seemed to be performing well against the demographic trend. In the 1890s, while the population of England and Scotland increased by 9.13% and 4.69% respectively, that of Ireland declined by 4.29%, yet railway traffic, as measured by receipts, increased by 22% compared with 31% in England and 36% in Scotland, with Irish passenger numbers increasing by 29%. In England, minerals, mostly coal, bulk loads were ideally suited for rail transport, and accounted for about 49% of the goods traffic in the first decade of the last century, but in Ireland this figure was less than 2%. One traffic flow which had always been important for the Irish companies was the carriage of livestock. All over the country, the major fairs led to the running of special trains. One of the biggest of these was the October fair at Ballinasloe. In 1891 there were 25,000 sheep, 10,000 cattle and 1,500 horses at the fair, and the Midland Great Western had to run forty-three special trains loaded with stock in conjunction with the event. Of the 5,580 goods trains operated by the MGWR in 1891, 1,723 of these were livestock specials which had served over a thousand fairs. The Dublin cattle market was held on a Thursday and this brought a mid-week surge of special trains from all over the GSWR system to the cattle sidings at Cabra close to the market. In Ulster the carriage of livestock from the west of Ireland to the east coast ports was a major source of traffic for the Sligo, Leitrim & Northern Counties throughout its existence, and in 1914 the GNR opened a new cattle yard close to the docks at Maysfield, today the site of Belfast Central station, to handle this traffic.

At the network's peak there were about 1,400 railway stations throughout the country. Traffic as measured in terms of the amount of passengers and goods carried increased steadily throughout the nineteenth century. For example, the GSWR in 1850 had annual passenger figures of about 2,100 per mile. By 1913 this had increased to 5,400. To cope with the increasing traffic, many miles of single track were doubled. Much of the Midland main line from Dublin as far west as Ballinasloe was double track by the end of the nineteenth century, as was the Sligo line as far as Longford. The BCDR had double track on its main line out to Comber and the Bangor branch had been doubled by the end of the century. On the GNR, substantial portions of the Derry Road were doubled at the turn of the last century including the sections from Portadown Junction to Trew and Moy, Dungannon to Donaghmore and St Johnstown to Derry. At Belfast, in 1907 a new engine shed which had an allocation of over fifty locomotives and a goods yard was built at a cost of over £40,000 at Adelaide, along with a third road linking the shed to the Great Victoria Street terminus. Plans to extend this third line as far as Lisburn were halted by the war. At the other end of its main line, the GNR opened an electric tramway in 1901 from Sutton to Howth over the Hill of Howth, which became an attraction for generations of Dubliners and tourists.

One element largely missing from the Irish network, which was an important source of revenue in Britain, was commuter traffic. The lines with recognisable commuter services in Ireland were few and far between. Using the timetables of 1900 as a guide, these included the lines into Belfast from Carrickfergus on the BNCR, from Bangor and Dundonald on the BCDR, and Lisburn on the GNR main line. The Howth branch at the southern end of the GNR main line had a service of sorts, but only two trains arrived in Amiens Street from Howth before 9 am. The lines from Bray to both Amiens Street and Harcourt Street stations in Dublin had a similar level of service, but the MGWR and GSWR routes into the city had nothing to speak of in the way of suburban services. South of Dublin, only the line from Queenstown into Cork had commuter trains. Within all the three major cities, any local trains had to compete with electric trams which provided a much quicker and more frequent service. At this time long distance commuting, of the sort which is common today, was unheard of.

We have mentioned the MGWR's hotels earlier, but in an effort to encourage tourism, other companies built them as well. The GSWR's Great Southern in Killarney, opened in 1854, was one of the first railway hotels in the world. A subsidiary of the GSWR opened several others in Kerry at Caragh Lake, Kenmare, Waterville and Parknasilla. In addition, the company operated more modest commercial establishments at Limerick Junction and close to its stations in Dublin and Cork. In 1899 the GNR bought hotels in resorts which it served at Bundoran, Warrenpoint and Rostrevor calling them Great Northern Hotels. The site of the hotel at Bundoran, high above the beach and reached by a long drive through its surrounding golf course, was particularly impressive and featured in almost every postcard of the resort which was published. The BNCR, whose activities in attracting tourists to Glenariff we saw in the previous chapter, also built a 2 mile long coastal path which incorporated tunnels and bridges over the sea near Whitehead, around great basalt cliffs known as the Gobbins. It was also in the hotel business, having run the 100 bedroom Northern Counties Hotel in Portrush from the 1880s. Its other hotel, the Laharna in Larne, ideally placed to exploit the scenic delights of the Antrim coast road, was claimed to be the biggest in Ireland. In 1898 the BCDR joined the club with the opening of the opulent Slieve Donard Hotel in Newcastle adjacent to its station. It also built a club house for what became the Royal County Down Golf Club to encourage golfers to travel down to Newcastle to play on its links. The BCDR, like many other railways, was at the peak of its prosperity in 1914, paying a dividend of 6½ per cent in that year.

There had been a gradual improvement in the standard of passenger comfort over the years. Travel was usually available in three classes, First, Second and Third, with the standard of comfort dictated by how much the passenger was prepared to pay. Even though the English Midland Railway, under the guidance of James Allport, the man whose report had done so much to stimulate the final phase of railway building in Ireland, had abolished Second Class in the 1870s, it took a while for the Irish railways to follow. In fact the otherwise progressive GNR only got rid of Second Class in 1951! In its very early years the MGWR had even offered a Fourth Class, which speaks volumes about the amount of disposable income of many of its prospective passengers. The great majority of passenger carriages in use at the turn of the century were still six-wheeled vehicles, many without lavatories or corridor connections to the rest of the train. The MGWR was still building these in the 1900s. These were gradually replaced by longer carriages running on four-wheel bogies. The first GSWR bogie coach was built in 1885 and gradually the bogie carriage, which offered a much smoother ride, began to prevail. The GNR introduced their first bogie vehicles in 1889, but MGWR passengers had to wait until 1902 when a new set of carriages was built for the Limited Mail. Sometimes a carriage would have compartments for all three classes; these were called tricomposites, and provision also had to be made for both smokers and non-smokers. As late as the 1950s the SLNCR had a tricomposite coach in regular use which had just one First-Class compartment. This was divided in the middle with a wooden partition. Smokers sat on one side; non-smokers on the other.

Dining cars were another innovation. The GNR was running a breakfast car in 1895 on its Kingstown to Belfast service which connected with the overnight boat from Holyhead; on the return journey it was advertised as a tea car. The GSWR introduced dining cars on the Day Mail trains between Dublin and Cork in 1898. Generally innovations such as these were introduced on the prestige services, the mail trains and boat expresses, and gradually filtered down to more mundane workings as additional new carriages were added to the fleets. For the opening of the Cork to Rosslare route, the GSWR built some of the finest carriages of the Edwardian era. These were 66 ft long bogie vehicles with corridor connections, with the dining cars in these sets running on six-wheel bogies. For most of the nineteenth century Irish trains were unheated except for foot warmers—brass hot water bottles, in effect, which must have provided little comfort for a long journey. Only in the last century did the practice of using steam from the locomotive to heat the carriages become prevalent; indeed, steam heating of older coaches continued to be used by IE until 2006. In Ireland the inevitable leaks from the flexible steam heating pipes between the carriages continued to create a most atmospheric effect in winter, long after most of Europe had abandoned it.

Lighting from the earliest times to the late nineteenth century, if it was provided, was by means of oil lamps in the roof of the carriage. Various forms of gas lighting were later used, notably in Ireland on the GSWR, but the combination of gas lights and wooden carriages had some horrendous consequences after crashes in England, turning a smash into a pyre. This led some companies, including the WL&W, to begin using electric lighting as early as the late 1890s. The GNR went straight from oil lamps to electricity from the 1890s onwards.

The improvements enforced by the Regulation of Railways Act in the wake of the events at Armagh in 1889, in relation to braking and signalling, were gradually extended across the country. The use of the automatic vacuum brake was only applicable to vehicles which were used on passenger services. The great majority of goods trains continued to run with wagons which only had handbrakes, but as their speeds were slow this did not present much of a hazard, though surprisingly a large proportion of the goods wagons used on the 3 ft gauge lines did have vacuum brakes. If only in this respect, they were decades in advance of the broad gauge railways. As late as the 1980s CIÉ was using unbraked wagons with the traditional guard's van bringing up the rear for the carriage of sugar beet. There was an unusual type of goods wagon which survived in Ireland for a long time called the convertible. This was a conventional wooden van which did not have a full roof but had a canvas cover in the middle. This could be used for either goods or livestock. When carrying the latter, the canvas was rolled back to give the beasts some ventilation. The Board of Trade had campaigned for many years to have cattle wagons fully roofed to afford the animals some protection from the weather and from the sparks thrown out by the engine. While most livestock wagons had been fitted with roofs before 1914, some of the open-topped models were still in use on the Tralee & Dingle right up to its final closure in 1953.

There is always the temptation, when dealing with something as emotive as the steam locomotive and a mode of travel in the form of the railways to which most people today are well disposed for all the right environmental reasons, to allow romantic notions of the past to colour our perception of the reality of what rail travel in the nineteenth century was really like. The innovations and improvements outlined above in heating, lighting and carriage construction would have taken a long time to be cascaded from the prestige services down to everyday passenger workings throughout the country. Partly, this was because railway vehicles were built to last. Carriages would normally be expected to remain in service for at least thirty years, and if money for investment in new rolling stock was tight, as it invariably was in Ireland, it was much easier to patch up older vehicles in the existing railway workshops and run them for much longer than their anticipated life span, than to try and raise the capital for replacements. As an example of this, there were many six-wheeled carriages dating from the turn of the century or before still running on CIÉ trains in the 1950s and 60s.

Therefore, it is easy to forget that the realities of travel for many ordinary people squeezed into Third-Class carriages was often a far from agreeable experience. Surviving accounts of travel in such trains in the nineteenth century present a far from romantic picture. An Irish Canadian writer, Margaret Dixon McDougall, who journeyed around Ireland in the 1880s, has left a graphic account of part of a journey on a Great Northern service from Derry to Omagh.

> This train, like all third-class trains, which I have yet seen, including one second-class train, by which I travelled a little way, was extremely filthy. One would think a little paint or even soap and water were contraband of war as far as these cars are concerned. After steaming a short distance the solitary lamp went out for want of oil. When the cars were stopped at the next station we were told to go into another compartment that had a lamp—they never seemed to think for a moment of replenishing with oil the lamp in the compartment where we were. The compartment into which we were moved was pretty full already. A good many were smoking strong tobacco, some were far gone in the tipsy direction, one of whom was indulging very liberally in

profanity. I was the only woman in the compartment; but my countrymen, as always, were polite, inconveniencing themselves for my accommodation. Even the profane person made a violent effort to curb his profanity when he noticed me.

Another theme which emerges from writers who recorded their journeys by rail around Ireland towards the end of the nineteenth century is the all-pervading presence of emigration, with seemingly every train on which they travelled witnessing heart-rending scenes as children left their parents for maybe the last time to seek some sort of a life away from the economic wasteland which was post-famine Ireland. J. M. Synge records one such scene which he witnessed on a journey from Tralee to Mallow as some young people began their journey to Queenstown and the emigrant ship:

> At several stations girls and boys thronged in to get places for Queenstown, leaving parties of old men and women wailing with anguish on the platform. At one place an old woman was seized with such a passion of regret, when she saw her daughters moving away from her for ever, that she made a wild rush after the train and when I looked out for a moment I could see her writhing and struggling on the platform, with her hair over her face, and two men holding her by the arms.

A similar scene was recorded by Margaret Dixon McDougall at Castlebar:

> The day on which I had to return to Sligo from Castlebar an immense crowd was gathered at the station, and I wondered what was the matter. It was a gathering to see emigrants start for America. The emigrants took the parting hard. If they had been going to instant execution they could not have felt worse. Three young girls of the party had cried until their faces were swollen out of shape. The crowd outside wept and

wailed; some clasped their hands over their heads with an upward look to heaven, some pressed them on their hearts, some rocked and moaned, some prayed aloud—not set prayers, but impromptu utterances wrung out by grief. The agony was so infectious that before I knew what I was about I was crying for sympathy.

This was a land still racked by sporadic local famines, where evictions were commonplace; indeed other writers have recorded how detachments of police used the trains to move around the countryside to enforce these. Apart from those who emigrated permanently, there was the great mass of itinerant farm labourers (one estimate puts their number at over 100,000 annually in the 1860s) who travelled round Britain in the spring and summer following the harvest in the hope of earning enough money to send back home to pay the rents on their small holdings to which they returned in the autumn and winter.

As well as the farm labourers, there were the navvies, the thousands of Irish labourers who helped to build the railway network in Britain from the 1840s onwards, living in appalling conditions in shanty towns close to the workings and often attacked by their English and Scottish counterparts who felt they had taken work which was rightly theirs. This was a far cry from what the development of a railway network throughout Ireland had been supposed to achieve, and from the aspirations of the many who had tirelessly promoted and invested in lines across the country since the 1830s.

Chapter 7

ǀ ALL CHANGE (1914–1950)

By 1914 the Irish railway network was at its most profitable and confident. There was no alternative to the train for journeys of any distance. There was no competition from the few unreliable buses and lorries on the road, and private car ownership was in its infancy and restricted to the very rich or the very enthusiastic. For the railways across the Irish Sea, things began to change almost immediately after war was declared when they were placed under government control. In Ireland, the semblance of normality was to last a futher two years before the old world was turned on its head, when events began to unfold from which the country's railways never really recovered. In 1914, with the Irish railway network close to its greatest extent in terms of route mileage, all of Ireland was an integral part of Great Britain and the British Empire, sharing the same customs and tariff regimes, postal and phone systems. The railways were subject to the same regulatory system as the rest of the kingdom enforced by the Board of Trade and its officers. This world was about to change radically. The events of the period between 1914 and the partition of Ireland in 1921 have been researched and written about by many eminent historians and do not need to be repeated here. What does concern this narrative is how the political developments of these years affected the Irish railway network, both in terms of events which took place at the time, and in the longer term, the consequences which they brought in their wake.

At the start of the Great War there were military garrisons the length and breadth of Ireland and one of the Royal Navy's most important bases was located in Cork Harbour. After decades of agitation, there was at last a Home Rule Act in place, given royal assent by King George V in September 1914, though with the agreement of both Nationalist and Unionist politicians, its enforcement was suspended for the duration of the war. At first there was general cross-party support for the war and horror at the German violation of Belgian neutrality, and many Irishmen from both sides of the great divide joined the British Army. The military connection with the GSWR was strong. One of the platforms at Kingsbridge was known as the military platform and the GSWR main line served the Curragh camp, the largest army base in Ireland. Newbridge, closer to Dublin, was a military town and after war was declared, traffic to these and many other garrison towns in the south and west greatly increased as the army was expanded from peacetime levels to that needed to fight a major European war. In the period of mobilisation at the start of hostilities, between 5 and 21 August 1914, the GSWR ran 172 special trains for the forces which conveyed 60,000 men, 10,000 horses and 200 wagons containing guns and baggage. On the BCDR, the camp at Ballykinlar between Downpatrick and Castlewellan, one of several opened in County Down, was served by a halt which was opened in 1914, though this was not advertised in the public timetables. Several of the companies including the GNR and the GSWR converted existing stock to form ambulance trains.

While conscription was never imposed in Ireland, the railways suffered some staff shortages as men enrolled in the forces from 1914 onwards. In 1915 the *Railway Magazine* contacted railway managers to access this and some of the Irish responses are of interest. Frederic Pim of the DSER reported that fifty employees had joined the army; ninety-eight from the MGWR also signed up. Thomas Andrews, a director of the BCDR, wrote that 10 per cent of its staff had left the railway for the forces. The major railway workshops were involved in the production of munitions. In 1916, Inchicore works was turning out 3,000 fuse bodies per week. However, in the early years of the war it is difficult to find much evidence of it making a profound impact on Ireland. As late as the summer of 1916, a piece appeared in the *Railway Magazine*, obviously produced by the MGWR, extolling the joys of a holiday in the west of Ireland as if nothing had happened. The pitch was to those who might normally have gone to the continent and mentioned the fact that during the summer, MGWR road motor coaches ran the 50 miles between the railheads of Clifden and Achill.

In 1914 the railway companies in Britain were brought under government control under the terms of the Defence of the Realm Act. This was a course of action that many in Ireland had been advocating for some time. Some politicians believed that the Irish railway companies were inefficient and were holding back the development of the country's economy through high charges and the provision of inadequate services. An extreme version of these anti-railway sentiments was articulated by James Connolly writing in June 1915:

> The land of Ireland is well intersected with canals which in other countries provide the very cheapest kind of carriage for goods, but the railway companies of Ireland have bought up the canals to prevent them serving the Irish public. Thus the public lose the facilities which the canals would give, and the railways, secure in their monopoly, settle down into a state of slovenly inefficiency which makes them a national scandal. Irish railway companies make no attempt to develop Irish industry, or to develop Irish districts. Rather, they seem to regard themselves as alien enemies, holding a position over a conquered people which enables them to compel that people to go on for ever paying a War Indemnity for the mere right to live.

Connolly, being Connolly, would not be naturally sympathetic to large capitalistic organisations such as the railway companies and his view of the role of the canals is perhaps a bit naive, but his comments echoed a widely held view which in 1906 had led to the appointment of a Vice-Regal Commission to inquire into the condition of Ireland's railways. After four years of deliberations the Commission issued two reports. The majority report advocated that the Irish railways should be taken into public ownership, while a minority report came out against nationalisation but in favour of the formation of larger companies through amalgamation. As often happened with such reports, they were shelved.

Then in 1916, the events of Easter week unfolded. The railways were left largely unscathed by the fighting. The worst damage was wrought on the DSER in Dublin. Its works at Grand Canal Street was occupied by rebels for the duration of the rising and Westland Row and Harcourt Street stations were also seized. Shells fired from the British gunboat, *Helga*, moored in the Liffey, damaged the Loop Line Bridge. In military terms the Easter Rising was a failure, but the effects of the retribution meted out by the British authorities against the leaders completely changed the political landscape. The reality of the war finally hit the Irish railway companies when, from 1 January 1917, they were placed under government control. The instrument of this was the Irish Railways Executive Committee, which was in charge until 1919 when the Ministry of Transport took over, government control continuing until 1921. The government agreed to compensate the railways on the basis of their net receipts for the year 1913. However, this did not take into account the great hike in inflation and costs which the war had produced. In this period expenditure rose by some 250 per cent and the wage bill by 300 per cent, while income only rose by about 100 per cent. One of the causes of the increase in the wage bill was, from the point of view of the staff, welcome restrictions on the number of hours they could work. In the end the government paid the Irish railway companies £3 million in compensation, but this was nowhere near enough to cover the arrears of maintenance which had built up. As the First World War ground on, the government tried to maximise the output of Ireland's few coal mining areas and the Irish Railway Executive Committee organised the building of two broad gauge branches to serve collieries at Wolfhill, near Athy, and Castlecomer in County Kilkenny, which opened, ironically, just after the ending of hostilities. The extension of the C&L line from

Arigna to the nearby mines was also the result of this initiative.

The railways escaped relatively lightly during the war against British rule in Ireland, which ended with the partition of Ireland and the establishment of the Irish Free State and Northern Ireland. However, the Civil War wrought enormous destruction on the railway infrastructure in the Free State as anti-treaty forces waged a guerrilla campaign against the newly formed government. Railways were a soft target and difficult to defend. Trains were deliberately wrecked, signal boxes were burned down and bridges and sections of track were blown up. In 1922/23 there were over thirty serious incidents on the DSER lines alone, and on the GSWR over a hundred signal cabins were damaged or destroyed. The single most destructive act was the demolition by anti-treaty forces of Mallow viaduct in 1922 which took the Dublin to Cork line over the River Blackwater. A temporary station called Mallow South was opened on the south side of the viaduct to which passengers had to be taken by road until the viaduct was rebuilt in 1923. The effects of escalating costs and the years of civil discord had brought the railways of the Free State to their knees and the new government had to act quickly to keep the railways running. There was still great political uncertainty at this time as to where the final border would be drawn. The Boundary Commission, which was to undertake this task under Article 12 of the Treaty establishing the two states, had yet to meet, let alone report.

There had already been discussions about a possible amalgamation between the GSWR and the CBSCR, but these were put on hold pending a government decision on what to do with the railways. The Free State's options were amalgamation or nationalisation. A similar debate had been taking place in Britain at this time, which led in 1923 to the grouping of the railways of England, Scotland and Wales into four large companies, and what followed in the Free State was along these lines. When it became clear that the Boundary Commission was not going to change the interim border established under the Government of Ireland Act of 1920, an amalgamation of the GSWR, the MGWR and the CB&SCR to form the Great Southern Railway went ahead in 1924.

The DSER and a further twenty-two minor lines, mostly narrow gauge, were incorporated into the group from 1 January 1925 to form the Great Southern Railways.

The GSR incorporated only companies whose lines were wholly located within the twenty-six counties. This meant that any railways whose lines entered Northern Ireland were excluded. The broad gauge companies affected were the GNR, the Sligo, Leitrim & Northern Counties, and the Dundalk, Newry & Greenore. This also created anomalies in that the CDR and the L&LSR, whose lines were mainly in the Free State, were not part of the new state's main transport company because their tracks crossed the border. In the case of the Swilly, only the last few miles into Derry were in Northern Ireland; the rest of its route mileage was in County Donegal. A small number of minor lines, notably the Listowel & Ballybunion, the Dublin & Lucan and the Dublin & Blessington, were also excluded. This had the immediate effect of bringing about the closure of the Lartigue monorail in Kerry and the Dublin & Lucan, though part of the latter was saved by the DUTC. The new company was responsible for just over 2,000 route miles of railway which served twenty-three of the twenty-six counties, the exceptions being Monaghan, Louth and Donegal.

The GSR was a private company with shareholders, but its task was to run a railway system which the government saw as vital for the economic well-being of the state. It was almost *de facto* the first of that singularly Irish of institutions, the semi-state company. Had the management of the GSR decided to close down hundreds of miles of uneconomic lines for commercial reasons, the government would have blocked the move. The GSR took over a railway system which was very run down with a big backlog of maintenance dating back to the war years and which was greatly exacerbated by the destruction which had taken place during the Civil War. In addition to all of these problems, for the first time the railways had serious competition from road transport as a flood of buses and lorries, many of them British forces surplus, began to operate passenger and freight services throughout the state.

North of the border there was no change to the structures or ownership of the railways following partition, except that the former BNCR system, owned by the Midland Railway since 1903, had passed to the London, Midland & Scottish Railway, one of the 'big four' companies formed by the amalgamation of the railways of Britain in 1923. The BCDR and the Clogher Valley and Castlederg 3 ft gauge lines remained independent. None of those companies crossed the border, but for the two which did, the GNR and the SLNCR, the new political order presented major challenges. The GNR main line now passed through an international frontier and in all, GNR tracks crossed the border in seventeen places. Because the two parts of Ireland were operating different regimes of tariffs and duties, room had to be found for customs officials of both jurisdictions at stations close to the border. Trains were delayed as passengers and goods were cleared by these officials. The inconvenience for passengers however was minor compared to the damage partition did to the economies of both parts of Ireland. Long-established patterns of trade, many of which the railways had been built to reflect, were disrupted. The city of Derry in particular was cut off from its natural economic hinterland, County Donegal.

All of this took place at a time when competition from the roads was getting into full swing. In what was now Northern Ireland, the railway companies themselves had been operating buses since before the war. In 1902 the BNCR became the first railway in the British Isles to run buses, two steam-powered vehicles which connected with the trains at Greenisland station, and the BCDR was operating its first buses by 1916. However, unregulated, private operators flourished in the 1920s with around 180 providing services in 1927, often competing directly with the railways. By this time most towns and villages had a bus service, often provided by small locally based operators. In 1926 the Northern Ireland parliament passed an Act to license vehicles, crews and bus routes, and in the following year, in response to this regulation, several of the larger operators formed the Belfast Omnibus Company which by 1935 was carrying as many passengers as the province's railways. Another Act in 1927 empowered the railway companies to operate bus services on the same terms as the private operators such as the BOC. The NCC took up the challenge, rapidly building a large network of bus services and buying up local operators. In 1930 it opened an enclosed modern bus station at Smithfield in the centre of Belfast and by 1934, over 500 route miles, about twice the mileage of its railways, were being served by NCC buses. The GNR also got involved in buying competing bus operators and by the early 1930s it had a fleet of over 170 buses operating on both sides of the border. Those railway companies also built up fleets of lorries to bring goods to and from railheads. These measures had the effect of curbing some of the wasteful competition between road and rail, both for goods and passenger traffic. However, there were still many private operators on the road who had the minimum of costs and overheads and their unrestricted activities were badly affecting the railway companies.

The Northern Ireland government asked the respected and recently retired general manager of the English Great Western Railway, Sir Felix Pole, to investigate these issues on its behalf. Pole recommended that the government take over all road transport operations by bringing the operators under the control of one public body. Legislation based on Pole's report led to the establishment in 1935 of the Northern Ireland Road Transport Board. The effect of this legislation was to prevent the railway companies from carrying on with their road transport operations. They were forced to trade their vehicles for shares in the NIRTB which, in theory, was supposed to co-ordinate road and rail transport in the province and use its buses and lorries to feed traffic on to the railways. Very quickly it became clear that this was not going to happen, and the NIRTB became a government-sponsored competitor to the railways, and thus a more serious threat than the many unco-ordinated private operators, which it replaced, could ever be. Often NIRTB vehicles, sometimes the same buses and lorries which the railways had previously owned, were based on railway property, green liveried cuckoos in the railways' nests.

A similar situation had developed south of the border where the biggest bus company was the Irish Omnibus Company, founded in 1926. In the Free State, the Railways (Road Motors) Act of 1927 allowed the GSR to run buses. The railway company reached an agreement with the IOC and eventually took it over in 1934. The IOC in turn took over many of the private operators or priced them off the road with low fares. Thus by the mid-1930s the GSR had a firm grip on bus services in the Free State. A further Act of 1932 put curbs on the activity of private bus operators, forcing them to be licensed and to publish timetables, and an Act of 1933 gave the GSR the power to compulsorily purchase competitors who were operating both passenger and freight services. While these measures may seem a bit Stalinist from the perspective of the twenty-first century, they were an attempt to create some sort of co-ordinated public transport system in the Free State. Bus services were now often run to connect with trains rather than compete with them, and while these measures did not solve the worsening financial position of the railways, at least they prevented destructive all-out competition between road and rail. The GSR's road fleet was operating 92 passenger and parcel services in 1929. By 1934 its road vehicles were generating a profit of £80,394, and in 1936 its fleet comprised 308 buses and 647 lorries and vans. Under Northern Ireland legislation, the GNR was prevented from running bus services there, but it continued to expand its road transport services in the parts of the Free State its railways served and, as we saw in Chapter 5, by the early 1930s the L&LSR was well on the way to reinventing itself as a bus company.

While these measures were sensible, they could do nothing to improve the general deterioration in the GSR's financial performance. Most of the interventions by assorted administrations from the 1920s through to the end of the century were aimed at making the railways once again profitable. With hindsight, this was an exercise in futility, akin to that of King Canute, because it failed to take on board the changed world in which the railways were now operating.

A snapshot of the receipts earned by the GSR in the 1920s and 30s confirms this.

GSR Receipts

1922	£6,788,829 (combined receipts of the companies which formed the GSR in 1925)
1925	£4,294,382
1929	£3,986,034
1930	£3,812,747
1931	£3,485,609
1934	£3,033,166
1938	£3,166,128

The graph was heading steadily downwards for a variety of reasons. Between 1923 and 1938 there was a five-fold increase in the number of private cars registered in the Free State. The international trade depression which followed the Wall Street Crash in 1929 had the effect of curtailing all kinds of economic activity across the western world, and in the Free State these effects were exaggerated by the so-called Economic War with Britain. When Eamon de Valera's government, in 1932, withheld the payment of land annuities due to the British government under the various schemes dating back to the late nineteenth century, by which tenants bought their farms from the landlords and became proprietors, the British retaliated with tariffs on imports of Irish agricultural goods which dropped in value from £35 million in 1929 to around £18 million in 1935. De Valera retaliated with duties on British imports, including coal, which was a big help to the GSR.

The amalgamation of the independent railway companies to form the GSR was supposed to address their underlying financial difficulties. Some savings were made by concentrating maintenance work at Inchicore, where major repairs to both broad and narrow gauge locomotives were now undertaken. The former DSER works at Grand Canal Street in Dublin and that of the MGWR at the Broadstone were run down. The latter was given a new role as the maintenance depot for the GSR's growing road fleet. The Broadstone, which was located some distance from the city centre, ceased to be a passenger station in 1937 when Midland line services were diverted to Westland Row. The 1930s saw the first significant reduction in both track and route mileage. Most of the former MGWR main line was reduced to single track in the 1920s and line closures followed. The narrow gauge closures in these years were mentioned in Chapter 5. Now broad gauge lines began to follow. The Kinsale branch closed completely in 1931, and other lines lost their passenger services including the Bagenalstown to Palace East line and the branches to Killaloe and Edenderry. Passenger services to Castlecomer were also withdrawn in 1931. This was one of the last lines in the country to be opened, in 1920, to serve the coal mines in the district and only saw passenger trains for eleven years. The first of the Balfour lines went in 1934, that from Ballina to Killala, to be followed by the lines to Achill and Clifden in 1935 and 1937, respectively.

The GSR years were largely ones of retrenchment. These were depressing times in the Free State and as if to reflect this, the GSR's chosen livery for its locomotives was grey. Apart from the closures, the GSR had little money available for investment. It added only fifty-nine new steam locomotives to its fleet between 1925 and 1945 and of these, twenty-six had been ordered by the MGWR before the amalgamation. It did however, against all the trends up to that time, produce in 1939/40 the three finest steam locomotives ever to run in Ireland, the 800 class. Designed for services on the Cork line, they were actually too heavy to run anywhere else. Painted green, not grey, and named *Maedhbh*, *Macha* and *Tailte*, these were the biggest 4-6-0s ever to run in these islands, though fate conspired to deny them the chance to show their full prowess before the arrival of the diesels in the 1950s. One of the trio, No. 800 *Maedhbh*, survives and is the impressive centre-piece of the railway collection at the Cultra museum. Other glimmers in the GSR gloom were the only Pullman cars ever to run in Ireland, three of which were introduced in 1926, the use of modern colour light signals between Dun Laoghaire and Amiens Street from 1938 and the Drumm battery trains, the invention of a University College Dublin don, Dr James Drumm, which provided quiet and clean electric traction at a budget price on the lines from Bray to

Amiens Street and Harcourt Street stations in Dublin in the 1930s.

In Northern Ireland the deterioration in the financial position of the railways was broadly similar to that in the south in the inter-war years and they faced the same competition from the roads, though the formation of the NIRTB probably made the situation worse. The NCC was shielded from the worst effects of generally declining revenues by being part of the LMS, which provided levels of investment which the other companies would have envied. Colour light signalling replaced traditional semaphores at York Road station in Belfast; and at Coleraine, track improvements allowed trains to run through passing loops on single track sections at speed; and in 1933 the first members of a new class of express locomotives, the W class 2-6-0s, were introduced. In 1931, work began on a new flying junction at Bleach Green near Whiteabbey. When this opened in 1934, the new junction and its associated lines allowed trains from Belfast to run direct to Portrush and Londonderry without reversal at Greenisland for the first time since the line opened in 1848. This work, which included a new 630 ft long viaduct over Valentine's Glen, near Whiteabbey, to carry the double track main line over the Larne branch, cost £65,000 and was partly funded by the government as an unemployment relief scheme. The result of all these improvements was that the NCC was able to offer some of the fastest schedules ever seen in Ireland in the age of steam. New rolling stock was built for the crack expresses to the north-west such as the *Portrush Flyer* and the *North Atlantic Express*, which the new W class locos hauled often at speeds of a mile a minute for part of their journey.

The GNR also began to struggle financially in the inter-war years, but it was also an era of improvement and innovation for the company. As mentioned earlier, the last part of its network to be built, the line from Castleblayney to Keady, was the first to close, though the remaining part of the route from Armagh to Keady retained passenger trains until 1934 and remained open for goods traffic for many years after that. The GNR was a public company with shareholders expecting dividends, and these reflected the general financial performance of the business. Before the formation of the GNR, UR shareholders had been accustomed to enjoying dividends of over 7 per cent. GNR shareholders were regularly getting a return of 5 per cent up to the war years, but by the 1920s this had declined to 3 per cent. By 1931 this dwindled to 0.5 per cent and after that no dividends were paid on ordinary shares until the 1940s. One major problem which had affected traffic on the Dublin to Belfast line was the condition of the viaduct over the Boyne at Drogheda. This had been deteriorating for many years and restrictions were imposed in the 1920s on the weight of locomotives permitted to use the bridge barring, for example, the use of the GNR's most powerful goods locos, the SG3 class, south of Dundalk. In 1930 work began on the complex and difficult task of rebuilding the bridge while keeping the line open for traffic. A new bridge was built within the existing structure. As this was inevitably narrower, it could only carry a single track. However, only one train at a time had been allowed on the old bridge for years and with improvements to the signalling and the track layout on the approaches to the rebuilt bridge, there was no effect on track capacity. The new Boyne bridge did enable the GNR to construct heavier and more powerful locomotives and with the introduction of the V class 4-4-0s in 1932, the timings of expresses between Belfast and Dublin were improved.

In the 1930s the GNR began to develop railcars for use on more lightly trafficked lines. The company had been involved in producing such vehicles for the CDR from the 1920s. The first broad gauge railcar, logically called railcar A, entered service in 1932 and was followed by a series of larger and more elaborate vehicles. The GNR also introduced the first railbus in 1934. This was literally a road bus converted to run on rails using wheels which combined a steel railway flange and a rubber tyre, the invention of two engineers at Dundalk works. The railbuses had a platform at the rear, level with the height of station platforms. They also had steps which allowed entry from rail level. This enabled the railbus to pick up passengers at level crossings and other locations which did not have platforms. These vehicles, which the GNR also supplied to the SLNCR, had operating costs, a fraction of those of a conventional steam locomotive and enabled the company to continue to operate a passenger service on many lines which might otherwise have lost them. The NCC also experimented with railcars, producing some of the ugliest vehicles ever to run in Ireland in the process, with low roofs and an elevated cab for the driver. They also introduced several diesel shunting locomotives which were produced by the Belfast shipbuilders, Harland & Wolff, who were trying to diversify their business following a slump in shipbuilding in the 1930s. The GNR and the NCC did suffer serious damage in the bitter twelve-week long railway strike in Northern Ireland in 1933 which came about when wage cuts on staff were imposed by the railway companies. BCDR staff did not join the dispute. On the GNR two malicious derailments were linked to the strike: one near Castlebellingham where rails were removed, leading to the derailment of a passenger train and the death of two railway staff; the other at Omagh Market Branch Junction occurred when the junction points were tampered with, leading to the derailment of a train from Dungannon to Derry.

Good management and the careful shepherding of scarce resources enabled the GNR to come through the difficult years of the 1920s and 30s almost intact. There were some cutbacks but relatively few. Parts of the Derry Road and the line from Armagh to Clones were reduced to single track. One addition to the company's activities came about in 1933 when it took over the working of the Dundalk, Newry & Greenore lines from the LMS. Passenger services ended on the Newry to Armagh line in 1934, as did those on the Ardee branch, though in the case of the latter, trains were replaced by GNR buses, many of which were built at Dundalk works. The company could still operate road services in the Free State and both its bus and road freight activities expanded south of the border and on a few cross-border routes. The GNR also had some services in Dublin city, notably the busy route from Eden Quay to Howth.

By 1939 the national network was still just over 3,000 miles in extent. Ireland's railways had therefore come through two very difficult decades with cuts of less than 10 per cent in the route mileage, though the financial position of all the companies north

58 The complete modernisation of the West Clare by CIÉ in the 1950s gave the line a new lease of life but ultimately did not save it from closure. On 24 June 1959, at Moyasta Junction, where the main line from Ennis divided to serve at Kilrush and Kilkee, passengers from the connecting service from Kilrush are moving over to join the railcar on the right of the picture, which has arrived from Kilkee and will run through to Ennis. (*Desmond Coakham*)

59 The grandeur and folly of much of the Irish narrow gauge is expressed in this view of a disappearing Tralee & Dingle train, seen near Dingle in CIÉ days. Close examination of the photo reveals one house in this great sweep of landscape. It is not surprising that the construction of railways in such unpromising parts of the country had to be heavily subsidised either by the ratepayer or the government. (*Author's collection*)

60 This view shows the main engine shed on the Cavan & Leitrim, that at Ballinamore, and might be captioned, 'different gauge, same mess' (see plate 65). Worth noting are the obligatory water tank on the right of the building and the small wooden coaling stage where coal was loaded into the bunkers of the engines. The three locomotives include one of the original C&L locos of 1887 to the right. Next to this is the former T&D No. 3, sent north when its own line closed in 1953, and on the left, one of the four 2-4-2T engines from the Cork, Blackrock & Passage which were sent to the C&L when the Cork line closed in the 1930s. (*John Edgington*)

61 There was always time for a yarn on the Cavan & Leitrim, a stronghold of steam to the very end. Here one of the former Tralee & Dingle line tank engines which saw out their days on the C&L section of CIÉ, calls at one of the roadside halts on the tramway to Arigna. (*Jack Patience*)

62 Because of the long climb out of Cork, many Dublin-bound trains had to be double-headed in the days of steam. In September 1951, a train from Cork to Dublin, with two Post Office vehicles at the front, pounds up the bank near Rathpeacon with J15 class 0-6-0 No. 104 piloting B2A class 4-6-0 No. 401. (*Author's collection*)

63 Commuting on the line between Bray and Amiens Street has long predated the DART. In June 1950, small tank engines and six wheeled coaches were the order of the day. F1 class 2-4-2 tank No. 438, seen here approaching Tara Street station, was built in 1909 just down the line at the D&SER's Grand Canal Street works. No. 438 was withdrawn by CIÉ in 1952. (*Author's collection*)

64 Just before the new diesel railcars took over these services, on 6 April 1953, D14 class 4-4-0 is seen on Wexford Quay with a service from Dublin to Rosslare. By 1958, the great majority of CIÉ passenger trains was in the hands of diesel traction. (*A.W. Burgess*)

65 The largest engine shed on the CIÉ network was that at Inchicore in Dublin. This 1950s view shows some of the dirt and clutter which was invariably associated with engine sheds and the steam locomotive. The engine nearest the camera, No. 612, built in 1891 by the MGWR and originally named *Hector*, was not withdrawn until 1961. (*Author's collection*)

66 This locomotive, which was built in 1914, was never allocated a running number but carried a plate indicating that its name was *Sambo*. It was the works shunter at Inchicore where it was built and spent its entire career pottering round the works with perhaps the occasional excursion down the hill to the yard at Kingsbridge for a bit of variety. Seen taking water—too much water by the looks of it—at Inchicore shed, *Sambo* was withdrawn in 1962, the year after this picture was taken, lasting almost to the end of steam on CIÉ. (*National Library of Ireland*)

67 The driver and fireman of a J15 pose for the camera as they wait for the signal to drop to give them the road, at Straffan in County Kildare on the line from Dublin to Cork. (*National Library of Ireland*)

68 By July 1961, the sight of a locomotive in steam was becoming increasingly a rarity on the CIÉ system. Acting as station pilot at Kingsbridge is J15 class No. 136, built just up the line at Inchicore works in 1888 and withdrawn from service the following year. The J15s were Ireland's most numerous type of steam locomotive with over 100 being built between 1866 and 1903. (*National Library of Ireland*)

69 The SLNCR was unique in so many ways. Most of its services were hauled by a series of 0-6-4 tanks, built between 1882 and 1951 by Beyer Peacock in Manchester. This type of wheel arrangement was hardly ever seen elsewhere in these islands. *Lissadell* was in service from 1899 until 1954 and, like other SLNCR locomotives, was known by name only; they were never given numbers.

70 In the days of steam, most of the Irish railways used 0-6-0 tender engines of various types to haul their freight traffic. GNR NQGS class No. 112 built in 1911 steams through Balbriggan with a long goods train. (*Des McGlynn collection*)

71 While the *Enterprise* was the best-known GNR named train, the *Bundoran Express* reappeared in the timetables after the Second World War to provide a service for both pilgrims in search of penitence at Lough Derg and those intent in pursuing rather less spiritual activities in the stately pleasure domes of Bundoran. The train, which originated in Dublin, had a through coach from Belfast, attached and detached at Clones, and ran non-stop on the part of the route which crossed through Northern Ireland and thus was not subject to Customs examination. Here it grinds round the sharp curve through Enniskillen station, headed by the 1948 Beyer Peacock built sky-blue liveried U class 4-4-0 No. 204 *Antrim*. (*Author's collection*)

72 One of the odder vehicles to be seen on Irish tracks was the railbus. This was literally a road vehicle converted to run on rails, the rear wheels combining a steel railway flange and a rubber tyre. Entry and exit was via the platform at the rear which was level with station platforms. The railbus provided a means of maintaining a passenger service where the traffic on offer would not have justified the expense of providing a steam locomotive and carriages. The GNR's railbus No. 1 was built at Dundalk works in 1934 and is seen here at the down main line platform at Drogheda. It was providing the passenger service on the Oldcastle branch on 3 June 1957. (*F.W. Shuttleworth*)

73 On 5 May 1960, VS class 4-4-0 UTA No. 58 (the former GNR No. 208) *Lagan*, is seen leaving Portadown with a special working run in connection with the Spring Show at the RDS in Dublin. The VS class, dating from 1948, were the last of a long line of 4-4-0 locomotives built to haul passenger trains on the GNR. (*Des Fitzgerald*)

74 This view taken on 1 July 1955 shows the first of what became CIÉ's A class diesels being craned aboard a ship at Manchester docks for the journey to Dublin. The A and C class diesels revolutionised services on CIÉ though their original Crossley diesel engines proved unreliable and were later replaced by General Motors power units. (*Author's collection*)

75 A view of the diesel shop at Inchicore works in March 1959. Several A class diesels, which had only been delivered a few years earlier, are seen stopped for repairs, an all-too-common occurrence. The reliability of CIÉ's first generation of diesel locomotives left much to be desired. (*National Library of Ireland*)

76 Nos 124 and 126, two members of the first class of General Motors diesels bought by CIÉ, are seen a[t] Inchicore works on a very murky day early in 1961 shortly after delivery. Such was the reliability of thes[e] machines and those that followed them, by the 1980s, virtually every diesel locomotive at work on the railway[s] of Ireland was either built by General Motors or powered by GM diesel engines. (*Author's collection*)

77 The modern face of CIÉ, 1960s style. The black and orange livery introduced at that time only began finally to be phased out in the new millennium, and examples of those black and white tiles which were used extensively at principal stations at that time can still be seen. (*Author's collection*)

78 Whilst there was some attempt to modernise and upgrade the railways in the Republic, this was the state to which most of Ulster's railway network was reduced by the UTA. This is Newtownstewart station in County Tyrone a few years after the closure of the erstwhile GNR's Derry Road in 1965. (*Eric Challoner*)

and south was increasingly difficult. Then, for the second time in a generation, Europe and the world was plunged into war. Once again, war had profound effects on the railways, but this time they were very different north and south of the border. Northern Ireland, as part of the United Kingdom, was in a state of war with the Axis powers while the Free State remained neutral throughout the greatest conflict the world had ever known and which was referred to, I have always felt, rather coyly, as the 'Emergency'. The GSR was faced almost immediately with a coal shortage. Coal supplies for the railways had always been imported from Britain. With the British economy fuelled almost entirely by coal, straining to produce war material, there was little coal to spare for a neutral Eire. The few active coal mines in Ireland could not make up the shortfall caused by the loss of imported supplies. The GSR had to use turf and duff, a substance made from slack and coal dust, to eke out its supplies, and services began to suffer from 1940 onwards. The fuel crisis extended to imports of oil and petrol as well as coal, and this meant that private motoring virtually ceased and public road transport was also affected. This forced traffic, both passenger and goods, which had been lost to the roads, back on to the railways. From 1942 onwards services on many branch lines had to be suspended because of the coal situation. On other routes services were confined to two or three days a week and the remaining main line trains were often subjected to long delays as crews struggled to make steam from the rubbish in their bunkers and tenders. Ironically, through all of this the GSR's finances improved as traffic poured back on to a network ill-equipped to deal with this increased volume because of the coal shortages.

The position north of the border was completely different. The lack of oil and petrol meant that private motoring was also effectively proscribed for the duration of the conflict, but the railways, seen as vital to the war effort, were given adequate supplies of coal to maintain their services. Revenues from passenger and goods traffic on the GNR rose from £1.3 million in 1938 to £3.4 million in 1944. Goods traffic increased from 750,000 tons in 1938 to 1.75 million tons in 1944. Dividends even returned to the shareholders in the 1940s. A short addition to the GNR network was opened in 1942 when a branch about 2½ miles long off the Knockmore Junction to Antrim line was built from near Crumlin to a wartime aircraft factory at Gortnagallon close to Lough Neagh. Following the entry of America into the war, Northern Ireland became one vast training camp with all the additional traffic which that brought, and the naval base at Derry played a vital role in the Battle of the Atlantic. As part of the campaign against the German U-boats, the runway at RAF Ballykelly had to be extended to allow the use of bigger aircraft with a longer range. The extended runway now crossed the NCC main line between Ballykelly and Limavady Junction. Special arrangements had to be made to link the base's control tower with the railway signal box to ensure that aircraft were not allowed to land or take off as trains were approaching. The British authorities thought that Northern Ireland was beyond the range of German bombers and Belfast and its industries had totally inadequate air defences. The Luftwaffe made two devastating attacks on the city in April and May 1941. The bombers were aiming at the docks and the Harland & Wolff shipyard, but on both occasions the nearby York Road station was also attacked. On the night of 4/5 May much of the station, the adjacent railway hotel and the goods shed were destroyed, as was a large amount of rolling stock. With the attacks on Belfast, many moved out of the city which brought additional traffic particularly to the passenger trains of the BCDR and in turn some dividends to its shareholders for the first time in many years. The company prospered to the extent that it ordered what was to be its last new locomotive in 1944, though the good times were tempered by the most serious accident in its history, a rear end collision in fog between two passenger trains at Ballymacarrett Junction in January 1945, which resulted in the deaths of twenty-three people. The SLNCR, which had depended on subsidies from the Northern Ireland government from the mid-1930s on account of the loss of much of its livestock traffic during the 'Economic War', also experienced high levels of traffic. The line returned to profit for a few years and started its own bus and road freight services in Eire.

The fundamental problem which the GSR had experienced throughout its existence was its inability to raise capital for investment in its services. Those running the company and those in the government knew that this issue would have to be addressed, and discussions to lead to some sort of restructuring of the company began in 1943. However, dealings in GSR shares were allowed to continue throughout this process and the value of this hitherto moribund stock suddenly began to appreciate. This led to allegations of what would be called today, insider trading, and suggestions that some people had been tipped off to buy GSR stock. In true Irish fashion, a tribunal was set up to investigate the matter and while this was going on, the Fianna Fáil government published its Transport Bill which proposed to replace the GSR with a new company, Córas Iompair Éireann. The bill was defeated in the Dáil and a general election resulted, probably the only time in history where a railway has brought down a government. Fianna Fáil was returned with a working majority and reintroduced the bill which led to the establishment of CIÉ on 1 January 1945. The GSR had done a good job throughout its troubled existence with the minimum of resources and its safety record had been exemplary. It is ironic therefore that in its last month a serious collision occurred at Straboe near Portlaoise when a goods and cattle train from Dublin, which had stopped because of a shortage of steam caused by poor coal, was hit in the rear by the night mail train from Dublin to Cork. The engine which was hauling that goods train, J15 class 0-6-0 No. 184, built in 1880 by the GSWR at Inchicore works, was undamaged in the crash, remained in service until 1962 and subsequently became one of that small band of Irish broad gauge steam locomotives which was saved from the scrap man.

CIÉ was the result of the merger of the GSR and the DUTC which ran Dublin's trams and buses. The stock in those two companies was exchanged for shares in CIÉ which was for its first five years a public company. CIÉ had a share capital of £13.5 million, but the Transport Act allowed it a total capital of £20 million. The additional stock, which it could issue to create the money for investment which was the main point of the restructuring, was guaranteed by the government. Though born in political controversy, the company started trading in the benign conditions of the 'Emergency' where it had virtually no competition. With the end of the war, the fuel situation eased and services on the lines which had been suspended in 1942 were resumed. CIÉ's honeymoon period was short lived. In its first year it recorded a surplus of revenue over costs on its railway operations of over £220,000, but a deficit of nearly double that in 1946. The company had inherited 475 broad gauge and 28 three ft gauge locomotives from the GSR. There were up to eighty different types of engines among this lot. The most recent were the three 800 class 4-6-0s of 1939/40 but many dated back to the previous century. The CIÉ steam fleet was a delight for the railway enthusiast but a nightmare for those who had to try and maintain a service with it. The age of the locomotive fleet made for high maintenance costs and low availability. Then in 1947 all of Europe experienced one of the hardest winters on record. British coal exports stopped as production was directed towards its own freezing population. CIÉ found itself with a coal shortage as bad as the wartime years and services had to be ruthlessly pruned back. It was well into the summer before normal coal supplies were resumed. Some branch lines lost their passenger services again in 1947, but this time for good. The 1947 balance sheet showed a loss of over £900,000—so much for the restructuring and the financial stability the new company was to bring. The railways from this point on presented politicians with a dilemma with which they grappled for the rest of the twentieth century when the issue, as we will see, was eventually more or less resolved. Put bluntly, the debate was whether the value of the railways to the state could be judged solely by its balance sheet or whether there was an economic and social dimension to its activities which had to be included in the equation.

The board of CIÉ had very clear ideas as to how to address the financial problems of the railways: modernisation using diesel traction and widespread closures of lightly trafficked lines. The politicians, knowing that closing railways was not necessarily a winner with the voters, but alarmed at the growing deficits of CIÉ, did what they usually do and bought some time for themselves by appointing a respected outside figure to report on the problem. This person was Sir James Milne, until the nationalisation of Britain's railways in 1948 the general manager of the Great Western Railway, whose brief was to examine all aspects of CIÉ's activities. In so far as the railways were concerned, the Milne report could have been written by a train buff. He was against branch line closures, seeing them as vital feeders to the main lines and did not think that an all out programme of dieselisation would make economic sense in Ireland because the high capital costs could not be justified in the light of the sparse services being operated. He did support the acquisition of diesel railcars but suggested that instead of diesel locos, CIÉ should build a new fleet of fifty steam locomotives over a six year period. Most of Milne's major conclusions such as the creation of a national highways authority were ignored, but the report did spark a debate largely because of his critique of current CIÉ management. The government's solution was to nationalise CIÉ and this came about in June 1950. At the same time CIÉ took over responsibility for the Grand Canal in pursuit of the injunction given to it by the legislation, part of which is worth quoting. The board of CIÉ was to 'promote the provision of an efficient, economical, convenient and properly integrated system of public transport for passengers and merchandise, by rail, road and water'. We will see in the next chapter how successful CIÉ was in applying these fine sentiments to the transport needs of what was now the Irish Republic.

North of the border, for a short time after the war, the railway companies continued to enjoy a measure of prosperity. The SLNCR ordered a new railcar and two new locomotives. The railcar came from Walker Brothers, the only broad gauge example built by a firm which had been making similar vehicles for the CDR for many years. The two steam locomotives were ordered from the Manchester firm of Beyer Peacock which built over 300 locomotives for the Irish railway companies throughout the age of steam, a figure only bettered by Inchicore works. By the time the new locos were ready for delivery in 1949, the good times were over and the SLNCR bought them on a sort of hire purchase arrangement funded by the Northern government. They carried plates to the effect that they were the property of Beyer Peacock and not the SLNCR. As with all the other SLNCR engines, these were named *Lough Melvin* and *Lough Erne* but were never given numbers. In a final act of generosity to its Ulster offshoot, the Northern Counties Committee, by the LMS before it was nationalised to become part of British Railways in 1948, the first of a new class of large tank locomotives were delivered to York Road. The WT class were tank engine versions of the successful W class tender engines of the 1930s. A total of eighteen of these fine machines were built between 1946 and 1950 giving the NCC's steam fleet a modernity that must have made those responsible for the CIÉ locomotive fleet most envious. The Milne report calculated that the average age of the CIÉ's steam locomotives in 1948 was 51! Some of the WTs, or 'Jeeps' as they were known to both railwaymen and enthusiasts, the name a tribute to their reliability and versatility, were to end their days as the last steam locomotives at work in these islands.

The GNR used the improvement in its revenues to invest in new rolling stock. The company ordered fifteen new steam locomotives after the war. Ten of these were additions to existing classes. Five of the versatile UG class 0-6-0s came from Beyer Peacock, who also built another five of the light U class 4-4-0s for use on secondary routes. The original batch of U class dated back to 1915 though the 1948 locos had more modern cabs and tenders. The last new GNR locomotives were also possibly the finest, the Vs class 4-4-0s of 1948, the final fruit of the long relationship between the Great Northern and Beyer Peacock. Unable to stray beyond the main line because of their weight, these beautiful machines fittingly took their place at the head of the main expresses between Ireland's two largest cities. Before the war some GNR top link locomotives had begun to appear in a new livery, a sublime shade of sky blue, lined in black and white with the frames and buffer beams picked out in red. After the war the blue livery was applied to other engines. The original U class engines were painted blue and given names, as were the 1948 additions to the class. The same livery was applied to the elegant S class 4-4-0s, originally dating from 1913/15 but completely renewed at Dundalk works in the 1930s. Named after Irish mountains, to my mind these were the most aesthetically pleasing locomotives ever to run in these islands. Sky blue locomotives steaming through the lush green Irish landscape hauling rakes of coaches in the GNR's attractive teak livery—railway heaven. Oh for a time machine!

But there was much more substance to this final GNR renaissance than the undoubted aesthetic appeal of its steam fleet. The company realised that the only hope it had of survival was modernisation. It had been successfully operating diesel railcars from the 1930s, and in 1948 the company ordered a fleet of twenty new railcars from the English firm AEC. These represented the Great Northern's vision of the future. The railcars ran in pairs with trailer coaches sandwiched in between. Various combinations were possible as long as the trailers were fitted with the appropriate control equipment. The AEC railcars, which were turned out in the attractive blue and cream livery already applied to the GNR's buses, were extremely versatile and they were seen all over the system from Howth to Bundoran. In 1951 the GNR was operating the most modern fleet of diesel trains in these islands; the tragedy for the whole country was that it never had sufficient resources to complete the modernisation programme. The other great innovation of this period was a train whose name has entered the language. One of the great problems which the partition of Ireland created for those companies whose lines crossed the border was the delay to trains which took place as they were stopped for customs examination. Trains on the GNR main line had to stop for this examination by the two jurisdictions at Goraghwood on the northern side and at Dundalk. In 1947 the company obtained the agreement of the authorities on both sides of the border to run a train non-stop from Belfast to Dublin with customs examinations conducted at the two termini. The name given to the new service, which ran for the first time on 11 August 1947, was the *Enterprise*. The new service was an immediate success and a second non-stop express was introduced in 1948. From October 1950 the *Enterprise* was extended to Cork. CIÉ and the GNR both provided a set of carriages for this working with locomotives being changed at Amiens Street. The *Enterprise* only ran through to Cork until 1953. Named trains have always been rare in Ireland, but the name *Enterprise* is still in use and is now applied to the whole service between Dublin and Belfast.

Despite the investments in new rolling stock and services, the financial position of the GNR gradually worsened as internal combustion engines across the north of Ireland began to rev up again following the ending of wartime restrictions. While the GNR's income was still healthy, working expenses began to rise inexorably, surpassing revenue by £118,000 in 1949. Both governments were aware of what was happening and had been having discussions to find a solution. The days of the GNR as a private company were clearly numbered and in December 1950 its directors announced that they had reached the end of their resources and gave notice that they would be ending their railway operations the following February. The two governments offered to buy the company for £3.9 million, but the company held out for a price of £4.5 million, which was eventually agreed. In order to run the undertaking, the governments set up the Great Northern Railway Board which had ten directors, five from each jurisdiction, and this eventually took over the running of the company's services in 1953. This was a rare example of cross-border co-operation for that time, forced on the governments by the need to keep the railways running. It was not to last, but it allowed the ethos of Ireland's finest railway to survive for a few years longer.

From the debacle of the formation of the Northern Ireland Road Transport Board in the 1930s, which deprived the railways of the ability to run buses and road freight services in the province and created a culture of competition rather than co-operation between road and rail, many railway oriented folk were rightly suspicious that the Northern government had an anti-railway bias. During the war the railways came into their own again and made a valuable contribution to the war effort, but as revenues began to fall away in the post-war years and with the impending nationalisation of Britain's railways which was going to affect the operations of the NCC with the abolition of its parent company, the LMS, some form of reorganisation was clearly going to be required in Northern Ireland. The wartime prosperity of the BCDR was short lived. Its resources were also drained by compensation payments of over £70,000 in the wake of the Ballymacarrett accident of 1945. As competition from the roads began to accelerate once again, the company reached the end of its resources and announced that it was planning to abandon rail services on all but the Bangor line. The government's solution was based on the model of the NIRTB. It bought the BCDR for £485,990 and along with the NIRTB, it became part of a new body, the Ulster Transport Authority, which was established on 1 October 1948. The theory was that the UTA would co-ordinate road and rail services in the province just as the NIRTB was supposed to do in the 1930s. The new body was also charged with being financially self reliant, to be profitable and not need subsidies from the public purse. We have heard all this before in another context—politicians engaging in this sort of wishful thinking was an exercise conducted on both sides of the border. From 1 January 1948 the LMS and the NCC had been taken over by the British Transport Commission with the nationalisation of Britain's railways. In December 1948 the BTC agreed to sell the NCC to the UTA for £2.6 million. The UTA took over the running of the NCC system from 1 April 1949. April Fools Day is perhaps a good date to associate with the UTA. At first the public were inclined to believe the spin about co-ordination and integration, but these were frankly incompatible with the UTA's other imperative, to make a profit. And to have any chance of making a profit it would have to cull much of the railway system which it had inherited. This it began to do with gusto.

All of the former BCDR system, with the exception of the branch to Bangor, was closed by April 1950, though Newcastle continued to be served by GNR trains running via Banbridge. Next on the agenda was the former NCC section. Cookstown lost its passenger trains from York Road in 1950, though goods traffic lingered on until 1955. The same fate befell the Limavady branch, passenger trains going in 1950, goods traffic lasting until 1955. Draperstown and Dungiven, which had not seen passenger trains since the 1930s, now lost their remaining goods service in 1950, and the Derry Central line also closed to passengers at this time. The busmen were triumphant as Unionist politicians sat on their hands and acquiesced in the slaughter. So much that had taken so long to build was destroyed in an instant. There was no attempt to modernise these lines and no understanding of the railway as a social or economic asset to the communities it served. Perhaps the dumbest of the closures was that of the BCDR main line through east Belfast. Already by 1950 the city was expanding out into County Down, and places like Dundonald, Comber and Newtownards were ideal candidates for a modernised commuter service. The blackest of times for the railways of Ireland had started at the hands of the assassins of the UTA.

Chapter 8 ∾

| BACK FROM THE BRINK

In 1950 most of the Irish railway network was under state ownership. Only the GNR, the SLNCR, the L&LSWR and the CDR were nominally independent. However, of these, the GNR was formally taken over by the two governments in 1953 and run by their appointees through the Great Northern Railway Board, and this affected the CDR as well, a half-share of which had been owned by the GNR since 1906. The L&LSWR abandoned the last of its railways in 1953 and became entirely a bus operator, and therefore no longer plays a part in this story. The SLNCR was dependent on subsidies from both governments to keep going, and although it had achieved the distinction of being the last independent railway company in Ireland, it could only survive as long as those subsidies continued. The future of Ireland's railway network was now in the hands of the two governments, and over the next twenty years they displayed a very different approach to the railways within their jurisdictions. Broadly speaking, the Stormont government wanted to see the back of as much of the network as it could get away with as quickly as possible, while various administrations south of the border made some effort to invest in and modernise the railways in the Republic.

The UTA had acquired about 340 route miles of railway in 1948. Its first wave of closures, discussed in the last chapter, saw the end of most of the former BCDR system and a large part of that which it had inherited from the NCC. However, there was some attempt to modernise what was left. With the example of the GNR's new AEC railcars in mind, the UTA in 1950 acquired engines and transmissions from AEC which they used to convert two NCC coaches into a pair of railcars. A further coach was converted to run as a trailer between the two. This unit became the prototype for a series of railcar sets known as multiple engined diesels (MEDs), which were built in 1952/53 using the frames and other components from other former NCC carriages. The MEDs were mainly associated with the Bangor line which, by the end of 1953, became the first complete timetabled service in the British Isles to be worked in its entirety by diesel railcars. The UTA's modern steam fleet continued to work services on the remaining former NCC lines, but between 1957 and 1962 a further series of railcars was built, again conversions from NCC carriages for use on these services. These were designated multi purpose diesels (MPDs), and in all thirty power cars were built along with a number of trailers including buffet cars for use on services to Londonderry, Portrush and Larne. Such was the output of the MPD power cars that, normally working in pairs, they were capable of hauling goods trains in addition to their normal passenger duties. The UTA was probably the only railway operator in Europe which regularly used railcars for this purpose.

The formation of the GNR Board at first made no perceptible difference to the working of the railway. It had to overcome a major setback in 1954 when heavy rains in the Dublin area on 8 December turned the River Tolka into a raging torrent which swept away the bridge carrying the Belfast line over the river and the East Wall Road, just north of Amiens Street station. Goods services were quickly diverted over the former MGWR line to Navan and passengers were bused around the break in the track. Astonishingly quickly, by today's standards, a temporary bridge was erected by the end of the month and services were resumed over this while a new permanent bridge was built. The Board was as keen as the company had been before to continue the process of modernisation and dieselisation and in 1954 issued tenders for three new types of diesel locomotives. However, those holding the purse strings allowed only one diesel locomotive to be delivered. This was an eight-wheeled German-built MAK 800 hp diesel hydraulic loco which appropriately, given its output, was numbered 800. The Board was however allowed to order some additional railcars in 1954. The twenty-four railcars were assembled at Dundalk works from parts supplied by British United Traction and entered service between June 1957 and October 1958. The BUT railcars, as they were called, had 150 hp AEC engines and were very flexible in service. Eight of the railcars had driving cabs at one end and a corridor connection at the other, but the remaining sixteen railcars had a corridor connection and a driving position at both ends. They could run in sets of up to eight vehicles composed of four power cars and four trailers. Additional trailers were converted from existing locomotive hauled stock, and soon after their introduction the BUT railcars were being employed on the *Enterprise* services. The GNR continued to offer an impressive range of services to its customers. Timetables from the early 1950s make fascinating reading. In addition to all its railway services, these contained details of the bus routes operated by the GNR Board in the Republic, of which there were about ninety, ranging from what were in effect city services in north County Dublin, through town services in Dundalk and Drogheda, to those serving remote spots in west Donegal such as Glenties and Portnoo. As one might have expected, the timetables provided full details of steamer services across the Irish Sea, but more surprisingly perhaps they contained information on flights to Britain operated by both British European Airways from Belfast, and Aer Lingus from Dublin. A note in the timetable indicated that tickets for these air services could be bought at any GNR station.

By now the *Enterprise* was firmly established with two non-stop services running daily, morning and afternoon, but another named train re-entered the timetable in these years which also managed to subvert some of the restrictions imposed by the border. This was the *Bundoran Express* which ran in the summer months to convey visitors to this popular seaside resort, created to a large extent by the GNR whose seafront was dominated by the company's hotel. The equally important purpose of this train was to provide a service to pilgrims visiting St Patrick's Purgatory on Lough Derg in County Donegal. Lough Derg was close to Pettigo on the Bundoran branch. The village of Pettigo is bisected by the border, but fortunately its station was in County Donegal and this enabled the GNR to run the *Bundoran Express* non-stop from Clones to Pettigo through the parts of the Irish North line which crossed into Northern Ireland, thus avoiding the need to stop for customs examination. This was the only passenger train which ran through Enniskillen without stopping, grinding its way around the sharp curve through the station at walking pace. The term 'express' was perhaps a little euphemistic for a service which took over five hours to cover the 160 odd miles from Dublin to Bundoran at an average speed of just over 30 mph.

The newly nationalised CIÉ in the Republic ignored the Milne report, and sadly for railway enthusiasts, no new steam locomotives with one bizarre exception were to appear from Inchicore, but the CIÉ Board did begin to pursue a policy of dieselisation. CIÉ had been operating its first diesel locomotives since 1946 when it built five 0-6-0 shunting locomotives at Inchicore. These were followed in 1950/51 by a pair of bogie diesel locos which were suitable for main line services. While Milne had not been in favour of diesel locomotives, he did encourage the CIÉ board to acquire diesel railcars, and between 1951 and 1954 sixty railcars were supplied by AEC very similar to those that company had made for the GNR a few years before. As an aside, one quirk of Irish railway terminology is the use of the word 'railcar' to describe these self-propelled diesel-engined passenger-carrying carriages. Elsewhere in these islands, such vehicles are commonly known as diesel multiple units. In Ireland, from the time these vehicles were first introduced on both the broad and narrow gauges in the 1930s up to the present day, they have always been referred to as railcars. CIÉ's new railcars soon began to appear on services all over the network and were popular with passengers. They remained in service until the 1970s when many vehicles had their engines removed and were converted to push-pull trailers for use on suburban services between Bray and Howth. Many Dublin commuters will remember, without nostalgia, these vehicles in their later years on these services, complete with orange plastic seats. Despite the success of the AEC railcars, it would be the 1990s before the next batch of railcars was delivered for use in the Republic. The two railway operators north and south of the border adopted very different solutions when it came to motive power from the mid-1950s onwards. While the UTA went entirely for railcars, CIÉ opted for diesel locomotives hauling unpowered carriages.

In 1950 CIÉ appointed a new chief mechanical engineer, O. V. S. Bulleid, who had previously held a similar position with the Southern Railway in England. Bulleid was one of the most innovative if controversial engineers of the age of steam. His final project for the Southern Region of British Railways, as the SR became after nationalisation, was a revolutionary new design of steam locomotive called the Leader class. This looked nothing like a conventional steam locomotive. It ran on six-wheeled bogies and had a driving cab at each end with the fireman consigned to a cramped and very hot compartment in the middle. A sum in the region of £500,000 was spent by BR on the project, and while the locomotives contained a wealth of innovations, many of these proved unreliable on test runs. Once Bulleid went to CIÉ, the project was abandoned. However, many of the features of the doomed Leader class were applied by Bulleid to the last steam locomotive ever built at Inchicore, which was known to all and sundry as the Turf Burner. This was an attempt to use turf, the only fuel which Ireland had in abundance, to make steam to haul trains. While this proposition was attractive on the face of it, turf has a much lower energy output than coal and it is surprising that the board of CIÉ allowed Bulleid to continue, at their expense, work which had proved very unreliable and costly in England. An existing 2-6-0 locomotive was heavily rebuilt, losing its chimney in the process, as an experimental test bed before the Turf Burner itself was built. The new locomotive was steamed for the first time at Inchicore in August 1957 and made a number of test runs on the Cork line and hauling goods trains from the North Wall, though it was never entrusted with a revenue-earning passenger train. When Bulleid retired the following year, the experimental programme was dropped and the Turf Burner never steamed again. Sadly, the last steam locomotive ever built in Ireland was reduced to scrap at Inchicore in the early 1960s.

Though Bulleid is associated with innovative steam designs, it should not be overlooked that during his time in charge at Inchicore, CIÉ's dieselisation programme really steamed ahead (to use an inappropriate metaphor). He was a realist who knew that while the concept of using an indigenous fuel such as turf was attractive for Ireland in an economic sense, the advantages of diesel traction were many and irrefutable. He actually advocated buying locomotives from the USA where diesel traction was long established and had virtually led to the end of steam by the early 1950s. However, in the unfavourable economic climate of the 1950s in the Irish Republic, the many thousands of dollars required were not available to CIÉ and the company turned to British manufacturers. Between 1955 and 1957, CIÉ bought over a hundred new diesel electric locomotives (the diesel engines generated electric power which was used for traction) from British manufacturers. The first of these were the sixty locomotives of the A class built by Metropolitan Vickers in Manchester which had 1,200 hp Crossley diesel engines. The A class was intended for main line goods and passenger work and these were followed by a smaller and less powerful version from the same manufacturer for branch line and secondary duties. These thirty-four C class locomotives had 550 hp Crossley engines. The programme was completed by the twelve locos which became the B class, built by the Birmingham Railway Carriage & Wagon Company and powered by 960 hp Sulzer engines. While there were serious problems with the reliability of the Crossley engines, the arrival of this large fleet of new diesel locomotives was a clear indication that the government of the Republic had some faith in the future of its railways. The acquisition of the low-powered C class diesels, which were designed to be used on secondary lines where traffic was light, was also a signal that CIÉ and its political masters were making a commitment to the survival of these lines too. The average age (51) of CIÉ's steam locomotives when the company was set up, as mentioned in the previous chapter, was not the only such problem facing the company. The average age of its passenger carriage fleet when it was nationalised in 1950 was 49. To at least begin addressing this issue and to run with the new diesel locomotives, 100 new carriages were ordered in 1955 from the English builder, Park Royal. These impressive vehicles had steel-clad wooden bodies on steel underframes and were built to the full width of the Irish loading gauge. Before the end of the decade some additional railcars, built to a distinctive Bulleid design, and some smaller diesel shunting locomotives were also added to the fleet to further the transformation of CIÉ's railways in less than a decade. Initially the new locos and some coaches were turned out in a silver grey livery which looked most attractive for the first week or two after they had left Inchicore works, but was woefully ill-suited to withstand the onslaught of the Irish weather. By the late 1950s this was replaced by an attractive light green colour scheme which was used until a black and orange livery was introduced in the early 1960s. Variations on this 1960s livery continued to be used into the new millennium.

With the formation of the GNR Board, the usual platitudes had been issued by the politicians, as they had done at the creation of CIÉ in 1945 and later at its nationalisation in 1950, that this was a new dawn which would see the railway achieving profitability. Whether anyone actually believed this rhetoric is hard to say, but the reality of the balance sheet was that as costs continued to rise and as traffic fell, the Board lost money from the start of its operations. The average losses between 1953 and 1958 were in the region of £1 million per annum. Had the GNR Board had the support which CIÉ enjoyed in these years from broadly sympathetic political masters, had its stakeholders allowed it the resources to modernise and invest in more railcars and diesel locomotives as CIÉ was, then these losses would surely have been a lot less. The problem for the GNR Board and its staff was that the Northern government had little interest and no faith in railways, something it could be argued which was apparent as far back as the 1930s with the formation of the NIRTB. The Stormont government was also following that yellow brick road which was supposed to lead to public transport making a profit, and the deficits of the UTA were put down solely to the losses incurred by the railways, even though its predecessor, the NIRTB, had been making losses in the 1930s in much more favourable conditions. The Northern government made it clear in 1955 that it wanted to close all the cross-border lines, with the exception of the main Dublin–Belfast line. As these routes involved the Dublin government and required some sort of process of consultation and negotiation, to warm up for the big game, the UTA ended the remaining goods services on the former NCC lines serving places such as Magherafelt, Cookstown and Limavady in mid-Ulster. Further closures forced on the GNR Board were of their lines in County Down to Newcastle, Banbridge and Scarva in 1955/56, along with the final section of the erstwhile Newry & Armagh line, from Goraghwood to Markethill.

The GNR lines earmarked for closure by the Northern government were all within their jurisdiction: those from Portadown to Armagh and Tynan, from Omagh to Enniskillen and on to the border at Newtownbutler, and most of the Bundoran branch from Bundoran Junction to Beleek. The effect of these proposals was to render the parts of these lines which lay within the Republic, the rump of the former Irish North from Clones to Dundalk, the section of the old UR main line from Clones to the border and the final 8 miles of the Bundoran branch in the Republic, virtually useless, as their connections to the rest of the country were severed. However, there was an alternative to the Stormont government's butchery, if the Dublin government chose to exercise it. Under the terms of the legislation which had established the GNR Board, the Dublin government had the right to insist that these lines remained open, provided they picked up the bill for all their losses. In 1937 a new Constitution for the Irish Free State promoted by the then Taoiseach, Eamon de Valera, claimed jurisdiction over the six counties which constituted Northern Ireland, so these lines could be viewed, in terms of that Constitution, as much a part of the state's responsibility as those in any of the other twenty-six counties. However, political rhetoric is cheap, as are unenforceable but provocative constitutional claims. Saving the Irish North would have cost money. Rather than seizing the opportunity to have some tangible influence on life in Northern Ireland, maintaining an important part of the economic infrastructure west of the Bann, an area increasingly marginalised as development was focused in the east of the province and perhaps reassuring the nationalist community there that they had not been forgotten by the state they aspired to join, the bean counters in Dublin did nothing and the heart was ripped out of Ulster's railway network as a consequence. The Northern government and the UTA are rightly to be blamed for their anti-railway attitude and for initiating the closures, but the complicity of their southern counterparts who could have stopped them in their desire to rip up these tracks is often overlooked. A further casualty of this carnage was the SLNCR which, despite decades of penury, had survived as a vital link carrying mostly livestock from the north-west to the east coast ports. With the closure of the GNR line through Enniskillen, there was no outlet for its traffic and it was forced to close on that day of infamy which saw the demise of a quarter of the GNR system, 30 September 1957. While CIÉ maintained some goods and parcel services from Dundalk to Clones and Cavan for a couple of years until road services could be improved, these closures left a huge gap in the railway map of Ireland and undermined the concept of a network serving the whole island which had taken so long to set in place. Today, if you head due south from Derry, you will not encounter a railway with a passenger service until you reach Mullingar, a distance of around 200 miles.

As the demolition trains were being prepared in the North, in the Republic yet another report had been commissioned. The brief from the government to Dr James Beddy, a distinguished economist who headed a learned team, was to inquire into the state of internal transport in the Republic and the role which public transport should play in the overall transport needs of the state. Inevitably much of the focus of the deliberations was on the future of the railways. CIÉ's submission to the committee was based on maintaining the status quo and imposing restrictions on private transport to force traffic back on to the railways. Even in the mid-1950s this must have seemed completely unrealistic. However, the company also made the point that if the state wanted the railways to continue, their losses would have to be supported by the public purse. The analysis of the Beddy committee was fairly predictable. It raised the possibility of abandoning the railways altogether or at least making drastic UTA-style cuts to the network. As things turned out over the next thirty years, Beddy's proposal for a core network was very similar to that which exists today, though some lines which he would have cut, such as those from Ballybrophy to Limerick, Portarlington to Athlone and the Limerick to Athenry route which is (at the time of writing in 2008) in the process of being reopened, would also have been closed. The aim of the proposed closures was again to stem the losses. The concept of what became known in Britain in the 1970s as 'the social railway' had not yet been grasped. Economists and politicians were still looking for the holy grail which in terms of the railways came in the form of an end to subsidies. We all berate the inadequacies of politicians from time to time, as I have done in the previous paragraph, in relation to the closure of the GNR lines in 1957, but fudge can be a tasty sweetmeat, and had the government of the Republic accepted the Beddy report and instigated the mass closures it proposed, much would have been lost for ever which is still retrievable as the transport needs of the country change. So, as with countless learned reports before, the Beddy report was largely ignored by those who had commissioned it.

What followed in its wake was yet another Transport Act, passed in 1958. This moved the fundamental debate about the finances of public transport in the Irish Republic on a little from the previous fantasy of making CIÉ profitable. The Act proposed to control the amount of subsidy CIÉ would get from the state to just over £1 million per year for the next five years, by which time its revenues and expenditure were supposed to be in balance. The politicians could not yet accept that this was as likely to happen as pigs taking to the skies! By this time the GNR Board was in the process of being dissolved, its assets being divided equally between the two governments. This meant that CIÉ, which had been making much progress in converting its services from steam to diesel traction, was landed with an additional eighty-three steam locomotives, albeit very fine Great Northern ones. It was also saddled with the losses which the remaining GNR lines in the Republic were generating. With the demise of the GNR Board and the SLNCR, for the first time since the formation of the Free State all the railways in the twenty-six counties were brought under one management. However, if CIÉ was to adhere to the terms of the Transport Act and not exceed the level of subsidy which it provided and aspire to the budgetary fantasy enacted in 1958, there was only one course which it could follow and that was to close lines.

To oversee this brave new world, the government appointed a new CIÉ chairman, Dr C. S. (Todd) Andrews, who had been previously the managing director of Bord na Móna and who was to gain the reputation as being an Irish precursor of the infamous Dr Beeching who, across the Irish Sea in the 1960s, was responsible for massive closures across the British Railways network. He had scarcely been in the job when the first closure under his stewardship was announced, the goods only branch from Sallins to Tullow, which had once been served by slip coaches from Kingsbridge. However, the next victim of Sweeney Todd, the railway butcher, was much more controversial, the line from Harcourt Street in Dublin to Bray. In the context of that era, there was a case to close the line. Though it had been dieselised, it was claimed that only about a thousand passengers a day were using its trains and there was the other route between Dublin and Bray along the coast through Dun Laoghaire. Passenger numbers on that line were also in decline at this time when car ownership in the affluent suburbs, which both routes served, was rising. In the depressed economic conditions of the late 1950s, no one could have foreseen the growth of housing in places like Foxrock and Stillorgan which was to occur from the mid-1960s onwards. The fate of this line was debated for years afterwards and it is one of those railway closures which would have had few defenders. Fortunately, after the Harcourt Street line closed on the last day of 1958, and the track had been lifted, the formation was largely preserved and much of it was put to good use when reopened as part of the Luas tramway network in the new millennium.

Andrews was the chairman of CIÉ until 1966. In that time he presided over a major contraction of the railway network in the Irish Republic. During his tenure not far short of 1,000 route miles were closed. These included the entire network serving west Cork, the last of CIÉ's narrow gauge lines, the West Clare and Cavan & Leitrim sections, the much-loved but perennially loss-making Hill of Howth Tramway, the Waterford and Tramore line, and the line from Waterford to Macmine Junction. Passenger services between Limerick and Sligo ended; the scenic branches off the Mallow to Tralee route to Valentia and Kenmare and many other branch lines around the country also lost their services. It is too depressing and would take too long to list all the lines which succumbed in these years. The closures continued after Andrews had left office. In 1967 the Mallow to Waterford route and the direct line to Clonmel from Thurles were closed, bringing the cull to an end pro tem! Some of the lines closed had been open for goods traffic only for a number of years, but even these closures brought more lorries on to a road system that was woefully inadequate to cope with the additional traffic which the rail closures provoked. Politicians north and south were always quick to promise road improvements in the same breath as they announced the closure of the local railway line, but more often than not these never materialised. In 1964 a further Transport Act was passed which increased the state subvention to the CIÉ to £2 million per annum for a period of five years. Interestingly, by this time the political climate had changed and the minister responsible for transport, Erskine Childers, acknowledged that a core railway system would be retained and that subsidies towards the cost of this were reasonable as railways in the rest of Europe were also subsidised by the state. As evidence of this, and with increasing levels of road traffic in the city already noticeable, the continuance of the loss-making Dublin suburban service was never seriously questioned.

While those of us with a passion for railways always regret the loss of any line, looking back at the position in which Andrews and CIÉ found themselves in the early 1960s with the financial imperative of the legislators on their backs, it is hard to make a strong case for the retention of many of the lines which closed in these years, the Mallow to Waterford line possibly being an exception, though it did take a roundabout route to connect Cork and Waterford, and the demise of the Harcourt Street line was soon universally recognised as a mistake. I think it is also important to make a distinction between the policies being pursued on either side of the border. While the Irish government sanctioned cuts to the network, these were not as brutal as those in Northern Ireland. With the exception of west Cork and the south-west of County Kerry, the only significant parts of the territory of the Republic which did not have some sort of railway still in place in the 1970s were Donegal and the two Ulster counties, Cavan and Monaghan, which had lost their railways through the cuts initiated by the Northern government in 1957. While the UTA started ripping up the tracks of closed lines at the first possible opportunity, in the Republic abandoned railways were often left in place for decades, allowing for the possibility of reopenings if conditions ever changed. The campaign in recent years in the west, which has had some success in reopening part of the Limerick to Sligo corridor, would have been a lost cause if the tracks had been removed after the lines closed and the trackbed was buried under road schemes, housing and industrial development. This is what happened frequently in Northern Ireland in places which were once major railway centres such as Strabane and Omagh. In the case of the latter, a new road bypassing the town follows exactly the route of the erstwhile GNR Derry Road, making any thoughts of reviving the railway completely impractical.

The early 1960s also saw the final elimination of steam traction from the railways of CIÉ, one of the first railway systems in Europe to achieve this. In order to do this, more diesel locomotives were required and this time they were not built in Britain but in the USA. The first of these was a batch of fifteen single cab 950 hp locos built by General Motors at La Grange in Illinois in 1960, which were turned out in a short-lived if distinctive grey and yellow livery. The last survivors of this class were still in service in 2008 displaying a longevity normally associated with steam locomotives rather than diesels. These were followed in 1962 by thirty-seven similar locomotives, though this time with a cab at each end, which later became the 141 class. Another twelve virtually identical machines were delivered in 1966. The arrival of the GM diesels allowed CIÉ to eliminate steam traction completely in practical terms in 1963, though a few steam engines remained on the books until 1965. To modernise the passenger fleet, between 1963 and 1967 fifty-two new carriages were built by the Sheffield firm, Cravens. These fine vehicles, some of which remained in service until 2006, were the last built to the full width of the Irish loading gauge (this was largely determined by the width and height of bridges and tunnels) which was more generous that that across the Irish Sea.

North of the border, inevitably, the future for the province's railways was a lot darker. The Northern government had made it clear from the time when the closures of 1957 were being enacted, that it saw no long-term future for the former GNR line from Portadown to Derry. Compared to the investment in new rolling stock in the Republic, the best the UTA could manage was eight new railcars delivered between 1966 and 1968. With the UTA's intention to close more lines, it followed that there was no need for new rolling stock. This meant that steam survived much longer in Northern Ireland. In 1963, to keep services going until the closures could be implemented, the UTA bought four ex-GNR steam locos from CIÉ. With the dissolution of the GNR Board, the UTA had renumbered its share of the GNR steam fleet and painted the locomotives black. CIÉ had retained GNR numbers and liveries and the four engines which came north in 1963 were all in the blue livery which allowed something of the spirit of the old company to survive for a while longer in Ulster. In order to legitimise what it had long planned to do, in 1962 the UTA commissioned a London accountant, Henry Benson, to report on the future of its railways. He told his masters what they knew already—and was no doubt paid handsomely for doing so. Benson's report, delivered in 1963, confirmed that the railways were losing money, that traffic levels were falling and that without further cuts the deficit on rail operations would continue to rise. The report offered no positives and no suggestions to improve the position through additional investment, just more cuts. Benson recommended the closure of the former GNR line from Portadown to Derry and truncated remains of the branch off this line from Dungannon to Cookstown, which was open for goods only as far as Coalisland. The report also called for the ending of rail freight services in Northern Ireland, the closure of the branch from Goraghwood to Newry and Warrenpoint, and the singling of the GNR main line between Portadown and the border. Apart from this final folly, the cuts advocated in the Benson report were fully implemented. Indeed the UTA managed to add another line to Benson's already comprehensive list. He had advocated the retention of the Belfast Central line and the rerouting of some Bangor line trains to the much more central ex-GNR Great Victoria Street station in Belfast, but the UTA closed this link in 1965, isolating the Bangor line from the rest of the Irish railway network.

Perhaps the one thing which the UTA had not bargained for was Benson's criticism of the way the authority was constituted. Basically, he found it not fit for purpose, but sadly he did not make a connection between its administrative and structural failings and the way in which it had been mismanaging the railways of Northern Ireland for many years. This led the government ultimately to abolish the UTA in 1968. Its strategic role, if that is not a solecism in this context, passed to the Northern Ireland Transport Holding Company, while the day to day management of its railway and bus services were given to two new bodies, Northern Ireland Railways and Ulsterbus. The Benson closures were implemented in 1965, as was the ending of railway goods traffic within Northern Ireland. Henceforth the only freight traffic carried on the railways of the province originated from CIÉ. The doomed lines were closed in the face of much local opposition. Tyrone County Council took the UTA to court to seek a review of the process but to no avail. At this time the old volcanoes of nationalism and sectarianism were beginning to rumble after being largely dormant for several decades in the run-up to the 50th anniversary of the Easter Rising which had led to the partition of Ireland. To mark the anniversary in 1966, fifteen of the principal railway stations in the Republic were named after leaders of the rising. The three principal stations in Dublin, Amiens Street, Westland Row and Kingsbridge, became known as Connolly, Pearse and Heuston from this time onwards. In Northern Ireland there were allegations that there was a political motive behind the 1965 line closures which served largely nationalist areas of the province. The railway closures were viewed in some quarters as part of a policy to concentrate development and economic activity east of the River Bann. The closures were cited along with other decisions made at the time, such as that which awarded Northern Ireland's second university, not to the city of Derry but to Coleraine, as part of this alleged covert political programme. There is no documentary evidence which I have ever seen to support these allegations; indeed the closures of 1965 had been flagged as long ago as the mid-1950s and there had been a consistent if irrational bias against the province's railways in government circles for many years. This final triumph of the busmen who ran the UTA reduced the railway system of Northern Ireland to the lines from Belfast to the border, Bangor, Larne, Portrush and Londonderry, though it was a Pyrrhic victory in the sense that the Benson report also led to the demise of this unloved body which had done so much damage to the Irish railway network in its twenty year existence.

The closures of 1965 in the North and the final line closures of the Andrews regime in the south in 1967 marked the nadir of the fortunes of the Irish railway network. CIÉ's route mileage had been reduced in less than a decade by over 800 miles. The size of the network in the Republic at the start of the 1970s was about 1,300 miles. In 1967 Northern Ireland Railways took over less than 200 route miles of track. The next decade saw a few more closures in the Republic including the goods only lines to Ardee and Castleisland and the so-called 'Burma Road' from Claremorris to Collooney, and the North Kerry line from Limerick to Tralee. One of the last rural branch lines in the country, that from Attymon Junction to Loughrea in County Galway, also closed losing its goods and passenger services in 1975. The end of the 1960s also marked the start of the troubles in Northern Ireland, a period of civil unrest, political terrorism and sectarian violence which was to blight all of Ireland for much of the next thirty years. Terrorist attacks on the railways in Northern Ireland, especially on the Dublin to Belfast line where it crossed the border, were regular occurrences, continuing a long and ignoble tradition which had begun in the 1920s. In fairness to NIR, after years of neglect at the hands of the UTA, the new management tried to make the best of what it had inherited. The company also became the last railway operator in the British Isles to use steam locomotives. A handful of the WT class 2-6-4 tanks were retained into the early 1970s for use on a contract to haul trains of spoil from a quarry at Magheramorne, on the Larne line, to the shore of Belfast Lough outside York Road station to reclaim from the sea the land on which the M2 motorway was subsequently built. In the summer of 1970 NIR introduced new rolling stock on the *Enterprise* services. Three diesel locomotives were built to haul the coaches, which were of the latest British Rail Mark 2 design and were constructed at the British Rail works in Derby. The locos were named *Eagle*, *Merlin* and *Falcon*, recalling the GNR V class locomotives built for the Belfast to Dublin line in the 1930s, three of which had carried these names. One other slightly surprising event, given that the UTA had ended goods services in Northern Ireland in 1965, was the opening of a new goods depot at Adelaide at the site of the GNR's former engine shed in Belfast in 1972. This was used by CIÉ goods trains from the south and at its peak it handled bulk loads of fertiliser, cement and beer as well as container traffic.

The most significant development of the 1970s in Northern Ireland was the reopening of the Belfast Central line and the building of Belfast Central station on the site of the old GNR cattle depot at Maysfields. It will be recalled that a central station for the city was part of the plans of the original Belfast Central Railway Company when it had been promoted a century earlier. The revived Belfast Central line enabled the Bangor branch to be reconnected to the rest of the network and the closure of the old BCDR terminus at Queen's Quay. Many trains from Bangor now

ran through to Lisburn or Portadown, providing a cross-city
service for the first time ever. Unfortunately Great Victoria Street
station, five minutes' walk from the City Hall and the heart of
Belfast, was also closed when the new station opened. Belfast
Central, located beside the River Lagan, was often a cold and
windswept place and was always a bus ride or taxi fare from
anywhere remotely central. The new station which opened at
Botanic Avenue on the Belfast Central line, close to Queen's
University and Shaftesbury Square, was a good deal more central
for most passengers than the drafty edifice by the Lagan. One
further consequence of these developments was the diversion of
Londonderry trains from York Road to Belfast Central via the
former GNR branch from Antrim to Lisburn, which had lost its
passenger service in 1960 but was still intact. While this enabled
passengers from the north-west to make connections at Belfast
Central into trains to Bangor and Dublin, it made the journey by
rail from Derry longer and slower, and passengers exchanged one
station some distance from the city centre at York Road for
another equally inconvenient outpost in the form of Belfast
Central. York Road, looking increasingly tired and neglected,
continued to be used by Larne trains. In terms of motive power,
NIR added some new railcars to its fleet with the BR-built 80 class
based on the BR Mark 2 body shell. Like the English Electric-built
railcars which the UTA had ordered in the 1960s and were now
known as the 70 class, each of the new two or three coach sets had
a power car, which contained the diesel engines, with the rest of
the vehicles being unpowered trailers. The 80 class railcars were
an immediate success and a second batch was delivered in 1977.
With their comfortable seats and large windows, I have always
thought the 80 class were a cut above most other railcars in which
I have ever travelled, especially if sitting in the trailers which are
very quiet and do not have the engine noise often associated with
this type of vehicle. Their engines make a most distinctive 'phut
phut' sound, especially when starting off from stations. Some of
them are still in service in 2008, and a few units which are
undergoing refurbishment should be around for another few
years.

At the end of the 1960s CIÉ's main operating problem was the increasing unreliability of the Crossley engines of the A and C class diesel locomotives. The availability figures of these machines contrasted very unfavourably with those of the General Motors diesels. With so many branch and secondary lines now closed, there was also little work for the low-powered C class with their 550 hp engines and the decision was taken to equip the entire fleet with GM engines. This was done in stages, with most of the locomotives being re-engined by 1972. This prolonged the life of these locomotives by many years. The final survivors of the A class remained in service until the mid-1990s. The C class diesels received 1,100 hp GM power units and many of them were deployed to haul sets of de-engined CIÉ and ex-GNR railcars on suburban services on the Howth to Bray corridor. The governments of the period, while not over-generous, did allow CIÉ some funds to invest in the railways in various ways. In 1977 a new and more powerful type of General Motors diesel locomotive entered service. Looking like an enlarged version of the earlier twin cab 141 and 181 classes, the eighteen locos of the 071 class took over the principal expresses on the Cork and Belfast lines on their arrival. Equally important was the first major step to modernise signalling on the CIÉ system with the introduction of the first phase of a new signalling system known as Centralised Traffic Control (CTC) in 1975. This replaced traditional mechanical signal boxes and semaphore signalling with modern colour light signals controlled remotely from a new signalling centre which was built at Connolly station in Dublin. The first line to benefit from CTC was the Cork line between Dublin and Ballybrophy. The system was soon extended to the Cherryville Junction to Athy section of the Waterford line and part of the Portarlington to Athlone route over which Dublin to Galway trains were being redirected. Gradually CTC was to be extended across the whole network over the next thirty years and by 2007 there were only a few locations where the old-style mechanical signalling was still being used.

CIÉ's rail freight business was also modernised in the 1970s. The traditional steam age goods train across the whole of the British Isles consisted mainly of four-wheeled wagons without continuous brakes. It was controlled by the skill of the locomotive driver and the guard in his brakevan at the rear. Sometimes at the top of a steep downward incline, the guard had to pin down the handbrakes on some of the wagons to make sure the train did not run away out of control on the descent. These trains pottered along at slow speeds, often stopping to attach and detach wagons at intermediate stations and were made up of a variety of wagons containing different types of goods and sometimes livestock, the latter for over a century a staple traffic of the Irish railway system until it was abandoned in the 1970s. One would not need to be an economist to see that this method of operation was long past its sell-by date by the second half of the twentieth century. On both sides of the Irish Sea, a new generation of wagons with continuous brakes controlled from the locomotive were introduced. CIÉ embarked on a major programme of rationalising its goods services. Dozens of small stations lost their goods facilities with freight trains now serving only the major centres from whence goods were distributed by road vehicles. Block trains consisting of a fixed number of wagons were introduced to cut down on shunting. Special wagons were built for bulk traffic flows such as cement, mineral ores, fuel oil and fertiliser. Containers were now carried by rail and special cranes were built at the remaining goods depots to handle these. While some unbraked wagons remained in service into the 1980s to handle the seasonal sugar beet traffic, CIÉ's freight services were transformed from relics of the steam age to modern standards in a decade. Despite this, they still lost money and indeed the deficits run up by the railways grew steadily throughout these years to a figure approaching IR£40 million by the early 1980s, but by now the argument had been accepted that the country needed its railways for good social and economic reasons, and reports from the McKinsey business consultancy organisation commissioned to look at CIÉ at the start of both the 1970s and 80s did not propose the abandonment of the network or further major closures, but rather explored ways of making the remaining network more efficient.

CIÉ was not without its problems in this era and indeed the

company had its worst ever railway accident in August 1980 when eighteen people died in a high-speed derailment at Buttevant station in County Cork. This was the result of careless operating practices associated with permanent way work in the area, which meant that a set of points on the main line were being controlled manually and not from the signal box. Even though there was work going on around Buttevant, there was no speed restriction in force on the main line, and a series of misunderstandings allowed a Dublin to Cork express to pass over those points at full speed when they were set for a siding, derailing it violently and immediately. Most of the dead and injured were in older wooden-bodied coaches which were badly damaged, and while the more modern steel-bodied carriages in the train were also derailed, they and their passengers survived the derailment relatively unscathed. CIÉ had been gradually modernising its carriage fleet as funds permitted throughout the 1970s, but the Buttevant crash prompted an effort to withdraw the remaining wooden-bodied stock as soon as possible. This was reinforced by another serious accident in August 1983 which occurred near Cherryville Junction in County Kildare, where the line to Kilkenny and Waterford diverges from the Dublin to Cork line. The accident happened when the locomotive of a train from Tralee to Dublin ran out of fuel and came to a stop. A following Galway to Dublin train passed a danger signal and collided with the rear of the stationary Tralee service causing the death of seven passengers. Again older wooden-bodied stock was mangled in the crash, reinforcing the lessons of Buttevant. From 1984 onwards, the first of a new fleet of over a hundred modern carriages based on the BR Mark 3 design began to emerge from Inchicore works, which allowed the remaining wooden-bodied stock to be withdrawn from service. Commendable as this was, the use of older carriages in these two incidents did highlight the constant problem of under-investment in the railways. CIÉ had to make do the best it could without having the resources it needed. To some extent this was evidence of trying to run a railway system on the cheap, and it was to continue into the 1990s when another accident, fortunately a relatively minor one without fatalities, would bring this sharply into focus and have far-reaching consequences.

The most significant railway development of the 1980s in the Republic was undoubtedly the modernisation and electrification of the Howth to Bray line, which not only revolutionised commuter traffic along that corridor but introduced a new word to the vocabulary of Dubliners, the DART. There could be no denying that this part of the network was long overdue for a major overhaul. As traffic levels in the city and the resulting congestion increased, the only suburban railway service in Dublin was in the hands of the re-engined C class diesels hauling sets of former CIÉ and GNR railcars. Both components of the service dated back to the 1950s. Breakdowns were not infrequent, the old railcars were a disgrace in terms of passenger comfort, and apart from the rolling stock the infrastructure and signalling on the route limited the number of trains which could be run. Despite this, passenger numbers had been increasing from about 14,000 per day at the start of the 1970s to nearly 30,000 by the end of the decade. CIÉ had been pressing for the funds to electrify the Howth to Bray line for a number of years, but governments had prevaricated. Then in May 1979, in the middle of the election campaign for members of the European parliament, the government gave its approval for the IR£46 million project. The whole route, including its track, signalling and stations, was renewed and a new era began on 23 July 1984 when the first electric service left Pearse station for Howth. Branded DART (Dublin Area Rapid Transit), the attractive green liveried German-built electric multiple units began to attract large numbers of passengers and showed just what a contribution the railway could make to the life of the city and the country, provided there was the will on the part of all stakeholders to make it happen. Those familiar with the way politics works in the Republic will not be too surprised to learn that the green light for the electrification was given during an election or that the later decision to extend the wires from Bray to Greystones was announced during a by-election campaign in the Wicklow constituency in May 1995.

While, fortunately, Ireland was spared the worst excesses of the 'greed is good' culture of the 1980s and the far right politics of those advocates of unbridled free market economics on either side of the Atlantic, Regan and Thatcher, and the ultimate lunacy of railway privatisation which did so much damage to the railways of Britain was never seriously considered in Ireland, there had been a feeling for some time in government circles that CIÉ was too big and monolithic. While we have concentrated on CIÉ's role as a railway operator, it should not be forgotten that it also ran the country's bus services, it had extensive road freight interests and had managed a small chain of top hotels, and the country's canals as well. The second McKinsey report of 1980 had taken the view that the company should be divided into smaller operating units to manage specific areas of transport, and this view was in time accepted by the government. The structure favoured, the creation of three operating companies, Bus Éireann, Dublin Bus and Iarnród Éireann, working independently under the umbrella of CIÉ, now a holding company rather than an operator, was proposed in the Transport (Reorganisation of CIÉ) Bill which was debated in the Dáil in November 1986. The legislation was duly passed with broad cross-party support and on 2 February 1987, Iarnród Éireann and the two bus companies came into being. Of the three companies, Iarnród Éireann had the most onerous task, made more difficult by a government that was determined to reduce the subsidy to the railways. This decision meant that despite the success of the DART, funds for investment were cut in real terms by perhaps as much as 25 per cent at a time when demand for passenger services and additional suburban capacity around Dublin was starting to take off. Nothing really had been learned from past investment deficits which had allowed, for example, old passenger carriages to remain in service for too long with the fatal consequences seen at Buttevant and Cherryville Junction. The consequences of this were hidden for some years but sprang up with a vengeance over a decade later.

North of the border, Northern Ireland Railways struggled manfully through the 1980s coping with sporadic terrorist attacks on its trains and infrastructure. In 1979 the company had acquired two new locomotives from General Motors identical to CIÉ's 071 class (a third followed in 1984), and these were used to haul refurbished second-hand ex-BR Mark 2 coaches on the *Enterprise* service. Nine additional three-coach railcar sets, the 450 or Castle class, went to work in 1985. I hesitate to use the word 'new' in relation to these vehicles, which used reconditioned engines and traction motors from withdrawn 70 class railcars. NIR managers, having to make do and mend with this sort of equipment, must have looked with some envy at the investment which CIÉ was being given by its political masters, even though this was far from adequate. With the opening of the Belfast Central line in the 1970s, two of the railways into Belfast had been linked and NIR was keen to complete the process. York Road station was remote from the city centre and NIR began to lobby for funds for the Cross Harbour link, as it was called, to bring trains from Larne through to Belfast Central. In 1989 the British government agreed to fund the work which entailed the building of a line less than 2 miles long but mostly on embankments or viaducts. The first part of the scheme involved the building of a new station called Yorkgate, which in October 1992 replaced York Road as the terminus for trains from Larne. This was south of and on a higher level than the old York Road station which became the site of a new maintenance depot for NIR. The extension of this line from Yorkgate to Lagan Junction, where it joined the Belfast Central line just outside Central station, opened to passengers in November 1994 and was officially opened in March 1995 by Queen · Elizabeth II, the royal train being a 450 class railcar. I bet she was impressed with that! The 626 ft long bridge over the River Lagan was called the Dargan Bridge, an appropriate acknowledgment to the great nineteenth-century entrepreneur who made not only a major contribution to the building of Ireland's railways but to the development of the city of Belfast.

The next part of this railway renaissance in Northern Ireland came about in September 1995 when the name of Great Victoria Street station was once again restored to the timetables. We have discussed the remoteness of Belfast Central before and the folly of closing the original GNR station when the Belfast Central line reopened in the 1970s. The new Great Victoria Street station was linked to the Belfast Central route by a double track line making an east-facing junction allowing trains to head for Bangor or Larne. A triangular junction was created here when the tracks from the site of the old Central Junction to Great Victoria Street station were restored. While the new station, in terms of both its size and its architectural appeal is but a shadow of the old GNR terminus, at least thousands of passengers every day can enjoy the convenience of its close proximity to the city centre. The final part of this modest revival in the fortunes of Northern Ireland's remaining railways came in 2001 when the original BNCR line to Londonderry, from Bleach Green Junction at Whiteabbey to Antrim, was reopened. This enabled Derry trains to resume their traditional route to the city and avoid the detour over the former GNR Antrim branch, which unfortunately then lost its remaining local passenger services in 2003. However, the reopening of the direct line did reduce journey times from the north-west and many trains from both the Larne and Londonderry lines now run through to Great Victoria Street.

In the 1990s in Northern Ireland, another change in the structures which delivered public transport was instigated. NIR, the provincial bus operator Ulsterbus and Citybus which had taken over Belfast Corporation's Transport Department in the 1970s to run the city's bus services, were all operating subsidiaries of the Northern Ireland Transport Holding Company. In January 1995 the government announced comprehensive changes in the provision of public transport whose principal objective was to encourage a transfer from private car usage to public transport and undertake the co-ordination of bus and rail services by offering co-ordinated timetables, through ticketing, feeder buses to railway stations and the development of joint bus and rail facilities. Under the umbrella of the NITHC, Translink was established to integrate the activities of the three operators, Citybus (later renamed Metro), NIR and Ulsterbus, which retained their separate legal status. For many with a historical interest in transport, this looked alarmingly like a case of back to the future, a revival of the UTA and the domination of public transport provision by bus interests. Perhaps I am paranoid, but on a recent visit to the combined bus and rail station at Coleraine, I could not help noticing the lack of any mention of rail services on the electronic departure boards which were filled with buses heading to exotic destinations such as Limavady and Garvagh!

In the mid-1990s, long overdue improvements were made to the Belfast to Dublin line, but 85 per cent of the IR£123 million cost was provided by funding from the European Community (EC). In 1996 IE and NIR took delivery of new rolling stock for the *Enterprise*, a name which had by now become a brand for the whole cross-border service. However, the lack of investment within Northern Ireland again raised the spectre of the abandonment of yet more of the network with talk of the lines from Ballymena to Londonderry and Portrush, and the Larne line beyond Whitehead being closed. The continuance of direct rule from Westminster due to the inability of local politicians to agree to a system of devolved government meant there was no effective local control over such areas as public transport. In 2001 a campaign was launched, backed by Translink, called 'Save Our Railways' to highlight the problems of the railways which were due solely to a lack of investment. There was no sign of any strategic vision. Funds were released in a seemingly piecemeal fashion to rebuild the Bangor line and then some more was found to revamp part of the Larne line, but this seemed to happen at the eleventh hour, just before services were curtailed or slowed down by speed restrictions caused by the state of the track. At the time of writing (autumn 2007), the line to Londonderry north of Ballymena is peppered with speed restrictions which add to journey times and make the railway uncompetitive against road transport, and again Translink has the begging bowl out looking for funding with the threat of closure always in the background if this fails to materialise. This is no way to run a railway system in the twenty-first century when almost every sentient being knows that railways are the only viable green alternative if car culture is ever to be controlled.

The formation of IE had been heralded by an increase in passenger numbers between 1985 and 1987 of some 40 per cent, though much of this was due to the spectacular success of the

DART. By this time the first purrs were also being heard from the 'Celtic Tiger', yet when the Irish economy began to take off in the 1990s, IE was woefully ill-equipped for the increases in traffic which this was about to generate. Increasing traffic congestion in and around Dublin led to commuter services being introduced on the routes to Kildare and Maynooth. The latter had started sporadically as long ago as 1981, the result of another election promise, but by the early 1990s four new stations had been opened between Connolly and Maynooth and regular commuter services were in operation. In 1994 IE took delivery of a fleet of new Japanese-built railcars which carried the Arrow branding, the first new railcars acquired for service in the Republic since 1952. These allowed IE to begin a commuter service between Heuston and Kildare. Then in 1994/95 thirty-two new locomotives of the 201 class were bought from General Motors, with two additional identical machines in the same number sequence being acquired by NIR at the same time for use on the *Enterprise* service. The new locomotives were used initially to haul expresses on the Cork and Belfast lines, but gradually began to appear all over the network. More railcars followed and improving public finances and funding from the European Union (EU) added to increased levels of investment in IE. 1998 saw a record number of 32 million passengers using IE services, an increase of some 8 per cent on the previous year. However, the economic leap forward, increased passenger numbers and longer commuter journeys from places like Drogheda and Longford, in part a response to rocketing house prices in Dublin, was stretching the capacity of the railways almost to breaking point because of the legacy of the cuts in investment levels which dated back to the 1980s. A relatively minor derailment in 1997 set off a reaction which could have had disastrous consequences for the railways of the Republic of Ireland but which, with the benefit of hindsight, was to be the catalyst for a complete change for the good in the attitude of the Irish state towards its railways.

On 8 November 1997, the 8.25 am train from Heuston to Westport was derailed at Curry level crossing between Knockcroghery and Roscommon. Locomotive No. 211 stayed on the track, but all seven Mark 111 coaches in the train were derailed. There were fortunately no serious injuries to passengers or staff and the line was reopened by 10 November. However, the resultant inquiry into the causes of the accident revealed the true condition of the network. Knockcroghery finally brought into the public domain what railway staff had been aware of for a long time: that years of under-investment combined with increasing passenger numbers and services had reduced much of the network to a condition that brought it close to collapse. Between 1987 and 1993, public funding had met the railway's operational deficit but had not made any provision for investment to replace and renew stock and infrastructure, let alone expand capacity. This had to rely on EU sources such as the IR£39 million provided in 1992/3. The Little report, commissioned by IE following the Knockcroghery derailment and released in May 1998, had some stark findings. It concluded that 40–50 per cent of the older jointed track had reached a critical state and would require major work in the next five years if speeds were to be maintained at their present levels. Further to this, safety audits conducted by International Risk Management Services (IRMS), also in the wake of Knockcroghery, showed just how poor the condition of much of the network was. In relation to best practice, signalling on IE was found to be deficient by 34 per cent and its permanent way by 52 per cent. Some worst cases investigated showed an 80 per cent shortfall from best practice. These reports presented the country and its politicians with a brutal choice: invest in the system or close much of it down. This was the stark question which politicians and CIÉ had tried to avoid confronting, arguably for most of the previous fifty years. The railway had reached the bank of the Rubicon. Fortunately good sense prevailed and the government began to authorise investment levels not seen before. Driven by the twin imperatives of ensuring a safe system and one which was able to meet the needs of a growing population and a buoyant economy, investment began to flow into track, signalling and rolling stock programmes. IÉ's own development plan for passenger services covering the years 2003 to 2012 calls for investment of 3.881 billion euro. Whether this very ambitious target is achieved remains to be seen, but IÉ is at last getting the high levels of investment it needs. In response, passenger numbers are rising at an exponential rate. According to figures released by Union Internationale de Chemins de Fer (UIC) in 2005, the average growth in passenger numbers across Europe was 2.5 per cent, but in Ireland it was 9 per cent, with 37.65 million passengers using IÉ trains in that year compared with 34.55 million the previous year.

In the space of less than a decade, huge changes have taken place. The railways of the Republic after years of decline or at least stasis are moving forward again. Hundreds of new railcars have been delivered allowing older rolling stock to be withdrawn. The first new city centre station to be built in Dublin for over a hundred years opened at Spencer Dock in 2007. The old MGWR line to Maynooth has been doubled and there are plans to expand the DART. New and long-closed stations have been opened and the virtually abandoned line from Cork to Midleton is being rebuilt. Passenger services are being restored to the Limerick to Galway line and at least part of the former MGWR line from Clonsilla towards Navan will be restored. Many miles of track have been replaced, as has most of the old mechanical signalling system as CTC has spread across the country. The one downside to all of this is the catastrophic decline in IE's freight traffic. Partly this is due to the loss of some traditional freight flows as the industries they served, such as the production of sugar from sugar beet and the native fertiliser industry, have simply closed down. But much else has been lost to the roads as hauliers have undercut the railways. Politicians now seem quite happy to provide subsidies and investment for passenger services but do not appear able to extend this logic to encouraging rail freight to survive, let alone grow. As processions of heavy lorries belching out diesel fumes continue to congest and pollute towns and cities throughout Ireland, surely there must be a concerted drive to re-establish the rail freight business, if only to rescue the environment from this unhealthy chaos. In the Republic the issue of the future of the railways has at last been resolved. In Northern Ireland the position of what remains of the network is still subject to some ambiguity, though a fleet of new Spanish-built railcars was delivered in 2003/04 and Translink is campaigning for funding to rebuild the Derry line and for additional rolling stock to cope with increasing passenger numbers.

The year 2009 will see the 175th anniversary of the real beginning of the railway age in Ireland, the opening of the Dublin & Kingstown Railway. From modest beginnings the network expanded throughout the nineteenth century to reach into every part of the island. Changing economic and political circumstances in the last century led the railways into a period of gradual decline and uncertainty which lasted from the 1920s through to the 1980s. In the bleakest parts of that era, some questioned whether railways had any long-term future at all in the country. At the start of the new millennium, these questions are no longer being asked (at least south of the border) and the future for the railways now looks brighter than it has done for at least fifty years. Rather than being witnesses to decline, those interested in Ireland's railways are now excited at the prospect of lines and stations being reopened, new rolling stock and faster and more frequent services. The railway, the most efficient and environmentally friendly form of land transport, is in keeping with the spirit of an age which has concerns for the future of the planet. This alone should do much to secure its long-term future. I doubt if there is a politician in the land today who would wish to be associated with a policy which advocated the closure of the network. It is fair to say that something of the romance of the traditional railway has been lost with the replacement of semaphores by remotely operated colour light signals and with the reassuring clickety clack of the old jointed track being replaced by the smoothness and quietness of modern continuously welded rails. However, there is still a great wealth of goodwill towards the railways and, more importantly, a greater willingness to use them, so that after the many vicissitudes which this brief history of the railway age in Ireland has recorded, it is fair to say that the railways are moving forward once again to, and will hopefully play a growing role in addressing, the transport needs of the country in the new century.

INDEX

(Note: italicised page references preceded by the letter p refer to picture number and caption)